ENGLISH FOR THE REJECTED

By the same author

POETRY

Imaginings	Putnam, 1961
Against the Cruel Frost	Putnam, 1963
Object Relations	Methuen, 1967

FICTION

Lights in the Sky Country	Putnam, 1962
Flesh Wounds	Methuen, 1966

CRITICISM

Llareggub Revisited	Bowes and Bowes, 1962
The Quest for Love	Methuen, 1965

EDUCATION

English for the Rejected	Cambridge, 1964
The Secret Places	Methuen, 1964
The Exploring Word	Cambridge, 1967
Children's Writing	Cambridge, 1967

COMPILATIONS

Children's Games	Gordon Fraser, 1957
Iron, Honey, Gold	Cambridge, 1961
People and Diamonds	Cambridge, 1962–6
Thieves and Angels	Cambridge, 1962
Visions of Life	Cambridge, 1964
The Broadstream Books	Cambridge, 1965

Shortened editions of novels for school use:

> *Oliver Twist*, by Charles Dickens
> *Childhood*, by Maxim Gorki
> *Roughing It*, by Mark Twain
> *Pudd'nhead Wilson*, by Mark Twain

I've Got to Use Words	Cambridge, 1966
The Cambridge Hymnal with Elizabeth Poston	Cambridge, 1967
Mr Weston's Good Wine, by T. F. Powys with an Introduction	Heinemann, 1966
Plucking the Rushes Chinese poems in translation	Heinemann, 1967

ENGLISH

FOR THE

REJECTED

TRAINING LITERACY IN THE
LOWER STREAMS OF THE
SECONDARY SCHOOL

BY

DAVID HOLBROOK, M.A.

Sometime Fellow of King's College, Cambridge

CAMBRIDGE
AT THE UNIVERSITY PRESS
1968

PUBLISHED BY

THE SYNDICS OF THE CAMBRIDGE UNIVERSITY PRESS

Bentley House, 200 Euston Road, London, N.W.1
American Branch: 32 East 57th Street, New York N.Y. 10022

© CAMBRIDGE UNIVERSITY PRESS 1964

Standard Book Numbers:
521 05287 4 clothbound
521 09215 9 paperback

First published 1964

Reprinted 1965, 1968

First printed in Great Britain by Spottiswoode, Ballantyne & Co. Ltd., London and Colchester
Reprinted by photolithography in Great Britain by Bookprint Limited, Crawley, Sussex

*For King's College and
those who made this book possible*

. . . a raid on the inarticulate
With shabby equipment always deteriorating
In the general mess of imprecision of feeling,
Undisciplined squads of emotion.

T. S. ELIOT, from East Coker

CONTENTS

PLATES

between pp. 152 and 153

PART I
ANOTHER DIMENSION

What was wrong was the sense of finality. Condemned to death and no hope of a reprieve. All the pupils and a fair number of the staff wanted to be elsewhere—anywhere else . . .

The streams were not called 'A', 'B', and 'C', but Red, White and Blue. As one of my kids said (and he might have been speaking of the whole disastrous system) 'We're Blue, sir. Blue. We ain't never gonna be White.'

An Oxford graduate, BRIAN WINSTON, *writing in* The Isis *of his first experience of secondary school teaching.*

INTRODUCTION

THE PREDICAMENT OF THE UNEXAMINABLE

In a society which values reasoning power and the intellect more highly than the creative and imaginative functions of the mind, perhaps inevitably we substitute in our minds the theory or abstract account of a process for the more complex living experience of the process itself, such as we might seek to capture in a poem or story. We favour the abstracting rather than the poetic function. Something of this kind happens in education: the article we read or write, the Ministry pamphlet, the book, or even the conversation in the staff room are taken to be 'what we are doing'. Meanwhile what we do in the classroom is something quite different. It will probably be more human and warm-hearted; more sporadic, disorganised and haphazard than we dare allow. It will contain hidden elements, important and even crucial elements, which neither we nor any of the printed or oral discussions of 'education' will yet have apprehended or made vocal. Yet these hidden elements may be the most important ones.

The present book is written with the conviction that with the 'backward' child the 'unseen' elements of sympathetic respect for the creature, and the imaginative-creative element in teaching, are the most important and efficient means to develop the child's capacities. In fact, I suppose, I have tried to insist once again that teaching is an art, and to suggest how this art may be made more efficient with the most unacademic, unexaminable children—those whom our society rejects because they yield no 'results'. The unseen creative elements in education are as yet insufficiently recognised, given authority, or made more effective by adequate conditions, except perhaps in the infant school.

When they are recognised throughout they may help us to solve many pressing problems—chiefly that of finding direction and aim in the new education which our society demands.

Education, at the time of my childhood, was thought of by parents such as mine as something valuable to a 'bright' child which could help him to 'make the best use of his gifts'—to become, perhaps, a

3

professional worker in the service of the community. Working-class mothers and fathers thought at best not in terms of their children, if they happened to be 'brainy', finding the means to 'climb into a higher class', but of being respected in their value to the community as clergymen, doctors, chemists, engineers—as professional men. I am generalising from my own experience, but I feel sure that the personal 'sacrifice' parents made to give their children a 'good education' then was mostly based on a humanitarian idealism, and not only on a mere greedy impulse to have their children live a 'white-collared' life. Of course there were impulses towards security—the security working people often miserably did not have. But the aim in seizing the 'scholarship' opportunity represented a genuinely democratic ambition—to give to good brains at large the chance to contribute to common life. It also reflected something of an understanding of the value of 'learning' to human life.

After the war, as a logical extension of the 'scholarship boy' idealism, came the demand for 'secondary education for all': and this began to become after 1944 an organisational fact. Unfortunately there seemed to be a false element in the idealism here—in the attempt to turn every child into a 'scholarship child' fit for academic education. Since most of them were not 'brainy' in that kind of way, there seemed—and still seems in many secondary schools—too little for the new schools to aim for, except a thinner, 'watered down' grammar school education, as I tried to point out in *English for Maturity*. In the absence of any fundamental reconsideration of the content of education teachers inevitably worked on the assumption that education should be the kind of thing they themselves experienced at the grammar school. Thus they followed both the bad and the good in the grammar school tradition, but with children for whom neither was suitable. This process of continuing a mode and pattern, of course, is largely unconscious—as is the way we all repeat with our own children the mistakes of our own parents. If the children in the 'modern' school look as clean and orderly, if they have coloured blazers and Latin mottoes, if they take G.C.E. in *some* subjects, if they learn one language, if they have as much homework as their grammar school friends (or enemies), if they are quietly working away at text-book exercises, if they have sports days and speech days, then 'parity of esteem' has been achieved. There has, of course, been much brave experiment here and there: but the very conservatism of the grammar schools with their lower streams, in sticking to the 'O' level grind, has caused a clamour in the secondary modern schools for a different kind of 'parity'—that of the 'certificate', the examination pass, at the expense of a truly liberal education of the whole being, by more free imaginative and active practical methods suited to the unacademic child.

So, many secondary modern schools imitate grammar schools, hiding behind their respectable façade a concealed inadequacy. Or if they do not mimic grammar schools, at least they claim parity of certification, often with the commendable motive of securing an equal chance for their pupils in competition for good employment. The inadequacy lies in the reality, that the children, having been separated because they are not 'brainy', are being given a form of education largely derived from that given to the brainy ones. Their education is to be examinable, as the grammar school child's is examinable. Yet the secondary modern child cannot benefit from this kind of training because it is too abstract, formal, and too much based on memorising information. The resulting frustration is enormous and pervades the whole educational system. The secondary modern schools are now to have a new certificate of examination, to complete the false face of the new secondary education for two-thirds of the population. The motives behind these developments are pathetically *not* such as would seek to give the average child the best possible liberal, rounded, whole education. They are often irrelevant social motives, sometimes attributed to the demands of 'employers' or 'parents', but sometimes probably preserved by the more insecure and uncreative teachers and headmasters. At bottom they are an index of the failure of our civilisation to know what civilised living might be.

'A' and 'B' stream children can cope to some extent, even if unhappily, with the consequent frustration and tedium. But in the 'C' and 'D' streams it must become apparent that to mimic grammar school education for the less able children, to give them a simplified formal education based on ways of imparting abstract information, is inefficient, and often irrelevant to their needs. Sometimes it seems as though the sheer incapacity of 'low' stream children to cope with the information-acquiring, abstract, memorising kind of work threatens to expose the whole pretence of a secondary modern school to be a grammar-type school. If anyone were to reveal that the children in the C's and D's are sitting there day after day simply being 'kept quiet', the whole respectable façade of routine in the school might fall in question. So the threat is hidden and suppressed, sometimes cruelly. The futility goes on, and the actual limits of these children's abilities are often simply not recognised and accepted. (See Appendix 2.)

The inevitable result is frustration in the teacher, and resentment in the pupil—even the creation of unhappy and disturbed men and women and delinquents. The idealism of 'secondary education for all' is running sour in many places, and has become derided in subfusc ways in many staff-rooms. Those who talk about raising the school-leaving age should come and spend a morning with 4C! Yet among those giving a tacit shrug of acquiescence to cynicism will be some who know that of the 40 members of 4C there are at least 20 who have been redeemed for life—by the unseen elements of warm-hearted care and imagination, even in the futile routine of 'practical' exercises, lists of dates and industrial products, or even the periods of time passed merely in 'keeping them quiet'. To send them out into the world at 12 or 13, uneducated, would be to betray such fundamental values as we may still claim for our democratic society, and would create an underprivileged caste in the meritocracy. Teachers know this, even when they are outwardly speaking bitterly or disparagingly of their 'low stream' work.

How can we relieve the agonies of futility among the 'bottom' secondary school population and their teachers? There must be a solution, based not on an idealism which distorts the facts, but rather one which embraces them. Here I am concerned with the 'bottom' half of the three-quarters—the 'lowest' three-eighths of the whole secondary school population. We call these children 'dim'—but by this we imply a standard of brightness. In fact we merely mean brightness in the kind of intelligence demanded by a technical, urban, industrial society. These children are different: but in what ways? Perhaps we can try to distinguish between kinds of capacity: the educational system tends to measure and sift by only *some* of our human capacities. If we remember this we may bear to breathe a little more freely, and look at what we are doing.

If you want to have a bright discussion on the merits of the latest process of automation you will not be able to have it with James or Rose of 4C. But suppose you want a second-hand door, or to find someone who will sit in a copse and wait patiently to destroy every pigeon that comes there in a day—then James is your boy. Or if you were hurt on a mountain in the snow, and one of the party had to be left with you, to keep you comfortable and awake, and fed with hot fluids, wouldn't you find that Rose would take to you, like, say, a mother animal? Unbright, limited, dumb—all these, but yet these children sometimes manage a home from 4 p.m. until the widowed father comes home at 8 p.m. Or can be and are trusted all day mucking out pigs with a tractor: or as a lorry-driver's mate on Saturday handling animals. They suffer as keenly as 'bright' children: they love, certainly, as fully. Some are obviously going to be more successful as lovers, husbands and parents than some dons. For affection, loyalty, kindness, warmth of feeling, these children may sometimes be found to be unequalled. Are they 'lesser beings'? This question I hope will be in the reader's mind throughout this book—*because our society and its system of education at the moment imply inevitably and often mercilessly that children who do badly in intelligence tests* are *inferior creatures*. Such mere organisational changes as the comprehensive school do not amend this fundamental wrong. Below I reveal the capacities for fineness and vivid perception of an average class of such children. They are not capable of certain intellectual uses of the intelligence. But they *have* intelligence and they are human.

We need to be reminded of other qualities in human beings which are by no means dim, even in those we call the dim. We need to bring ourselves to value these creatures as creatures, as equal in terms of their wider needs, to develop what potentialities they have. Once we stop despising them because they cannot perform 'brainy' tasks, we can then see how monstrous it is to give them worse equipment, worse accommodation, overcrowded classes, and a lesser education than their fellows. We can see that it is inhuman that the teachers who choose to work with 'C's and D's' are exploited, discouraged, not given real responsibilities, refused sufficient free time for preparation and thought about their work, refused money for books—and even driven out of the work they love. Yet this is what is happening, here and there, as my quotations from some 50 teachers in Appendix 2 show. Touches of such blight pervade all 'low stream' education, because our society implies that to be a 'dreg' is to be a failure, against a scale of mere acquisitive 'success'. Our brightly painted 'teenage secondary modern' girls with bouffant hair styles, frilly petticoats, and a libidinous flair to their manner are *quite justifiably* flaunting their vitality against these implications given them by the school. The sad fact is that their demonstration is so empty of true culture, and is only acquisitive itself.

7

Perhaps we can begin to develop an education based on *a real acceptance of the nature of these children and their needs*, and do away with the present hidden frustration in the 'low streams' of many of our schools. If we can, we can begin a positive revolution against under-privilege in secondary education, towards a truly democratic recognition of the needs of each creature in our community to become civilised and to realise his potentialities. From this revolution in attitudes and content, changes in prestige, then in organisation, then perhaps in social life may come—even perhaps demands for sound popular culture established in the school experience. Three-eighths of our population is a large proportion—some 20,000,000 by the time they all grow up, the 'dregs'. Their lives could be enriched by their school experience much more than they are at the moment—if we study their needs and try to meet them.

This book is about ways of helping to make these children literate. It is based on some limited experience, of a poet and writer who chose for a time to become part-time teacher with a few less able children. If I learnt nothing else, I did learn that for these children there is no point in thinking in terms of 'subjects'—apart from games, art, crafts, dancing and music, everything else virtually became English. Their most successful mathematics was related to stories about hire purchase or car rallies. The only sense of history they could gain was that given by imaginative accounts of, say, a medieval peasant's life. In geography they responded to what was really anthropology, much mixed with imaginative fantasy about modes of life in other lands. And all these subjects by the time they were interpreted to 3 C became, virtually, English, and *mostly imaginative English, in the context of a close personal relationship with the teacher*—closer than that in other kinds of teaching except perhaps in the infant classes of the primary school.

This central subject is for them the main means towards self-expression, self-knowledge, imaginative order, understanding of the world, the possession of values, and a guide to conduct. One must, with these children, stop thinking in terms of 'teaching a subject', and think rather of educating the child, giving each creature what he may be given of civilised powers and refinement, and effective release of his potentialities. This is even more evident in the less able child than it is in the brighter child whom I was considering in *English for Maturity*. This is why in this book I discuss the work of 19 children in detail: I try to

8

show why at the centre of English as a central subject there must be imaginative work, serving each child's inward needs. And I try to show that this can best be done in the context of a sympathetic relationship with the teacher that can only be called a form of love, so deep do these children's emotional needs enter one's soul.

Any revolution in the education of backward children, then, centres round English—largely imaginative English in the context of affectionate sympathy, in the context of teaching-as-an-art, and in conditions in which one may come close to and work with the individual animula, the child spirit. But the work cannot be begun until conditions are created in which it is possible. To bring such a change, we must reduce the size of classes to make it possible for the teacher to do this work in free and favourable conditions. Twenty to twenty-five is the maximum size for a class of slower difficult children. We may also throw away the text-books, give up much futile formal and 'practical' work, and find authority for—*toleration* for—all kinds of imaginative informal experiments, sometimes noisy, uncertain, untidy and even risky. We must seek to get books written and published for these children to use, which are based on both their emotional and psychic needs, and on a realistic acceptance of their limited capacities. But these must not be books which make the impertinent assumption that their needs and sensibilities are coarse, clownish and incapable of fine and deep feelings.

First of all, of course, we must know what we are doing, so again it is necessary here—as in *English for Maturity*—to cover in detail some of the elementary points about teaching English. Unless this is done this book will not provide the complete argument which I seek to put in the hands of the teacher of 'low stream' children to strengthen his authority. Nothing makes one feel more lost to the world, more sunk in an obscure limbo of human waste than labouring with a trying, unstable and restless backward form, in a bad school, without sufficient aims in view, among those who are implicitly despised by society. The teachers of these children are doing a very important task, helping hundreds of thousands of young creatures yearly to grow up and take their place in society with confidence, self-respect and developed potentialities. There is no cause for them to feel inferior because they do not have the parades of certificate holders at Speech Day and all the varied vicarious satisfactions that teachers of grammar school children may have. The harder task is socially and humanly the higher calling. Not all teachers are gifted. Not all are capable of what I have called love—or even of easy sympathy. But there are many who, given a chance, less exploitation, better conditions, and more freedom, could begin to work, as artist-teachers, and find a sense of satisfaction and service in work with the 'C's and D's'. Alas, many who are made to feel the task is degrading and degraded—damaging to one's career, even—sink into frustration and bitterness. Many fear that, absorbed by work with the C's and D's they will virtually become 'lost'—and they often do seem to disappear, because of the emotional strain. (See discussed below the depressive effect of the work of these children, p. 21 ff.)

Additional strains are sometimes caused by the school exploiting a willing teacher of backward children. Meanwhile, we are, virtually, over 100,000 teachers short: this whole situation, with the overworking of teachers, has grave social dangers, which should become apparent to the reader as he progresses. But we can do much by preventing the discouragement of young teachers, and by offering them this kind of work, free and informal, but satisfying to their altruistic impulses, as a challenge. If we present the task realistically, show what real gains and satisfactions may be obtained from it, and make experiment possible, then many more young adults may be attracted to the work.

All very well to say such things: they are unlikely to have attention paid them unless they are backed by good reasons. Thus I have sought to give authority and prestige to the work of the teacher of the less-than-average child. This is why I have written this book, and this is why, I believe, King's College made me a Fellow to help me write it, with the assistance of Cambridge University Press. I want to put into the hands of the teacher of the child of less-than-average ability a book which, even if he disagrees with parts of it, at least establishes as of the gravest import work which seems often irrelevant to the march of the industrial world and 'external' civilisation. That is, the nourishing of imaginative power, and psychic vitality, by sympathy and creative work, in all children, not excepting those who are least endowed with intellectual capacities.

In this book I shall use the term 'the poetic function'. By this I mean the capacity to explore and perceive, to come to terms with, speak of, and deal with experience *by the exercise of the whole mind and all kinds of apprehensions, not only intellectual ones*. This poetic function, I consider, is neglected too much in all education and not least in the education of children deficient in intellect. I want to try to establish in this book that nourishing what I call the poetic function is certainly the most important work with less able children, and that the most efficient work a teacher of backward children *can* do *is* the free, informal, imaginative and often pleasurable and rewarding work of creative English, towards literacy and insight into personal and external reality. This is the best way even if one conceives of the work as merely 'training operatives for the lower echelons of industry' as some depressing person once expressed the function of the secondary modern school in *The Guardian*. (To conceive of one's work in such terms seems to me not only inhuman but inefficient, as will appear.)

I also wanted to imply that what I say here about 'backward' teaching is true of all education. I hope the implications will be taken by the grammar schools, the universities and certainly the training colleges. The most entertaining and satisfying work—creative work —in school is the most efficient means to fluency and literacy. This would be a happy fact if only circumstances allowed teachers to do the real work. The text-book mill of exercises, boring and inefficient, is preserved by poor material and administrative conditions: the revolution in secondary education requires changes not only of content but of political and administrative attitudes and practice. I hope this book will help bring about further changes: our society shows by its luxury spending that it could afford them. But exciting changes may come by a new relaxation. We should not be so anxious because some children are less able than others. What we do need is a more honest and real acceptance of the 'less-than-average' child as a fine and valuable, if mentally limited, creature, by humane rather than mercenary or academic standards. He needs to be happily accepted for the capacities and needs he does have, as an *equal*, or what Lawrence would presumably call a 'disqual' creature, in terms of his living needs. Such a change of attitude alone might relieve much unhappiness, boredom, frustration and worse. That these exist may be seen from what must lie behind the accounts of their work by the teachers of backward children quoted in Appendix 2.

I think there is no child who is not capable of fine feelings, of sorrow, of sympathy, love and delight. There are some who are coarse, limited, obtuse, maddening—and some in whose company one would not choose to spend more of one's time than one was forced to. But all—except for some very sick or disturbed, subnormal or damaged children—all 'bottom stream' secondary school children are capable of much finer things than are usually put before them, or expected of them. Because they are so often denied the best things, some come to hate the school which does not understand them. Some of these children stay away from school—and little is done to bring in the 'unattractive' ones: truancy is highest in the lower streams. A boy was even found dead recently in a cave, who had run away from school because he hated it so much. Childhood unhappiness of the most terrible kind did not end with Dickens. There are many who are unhappy and cannot run away. They could find fulfilment at school, but are often suppressed or crushed or bored—and still suffer. A revolution of approach—in terms even of recognising children as equal in the sight of God—or, as I would put it, in terms of psychic need, or needs of the sensibility—could relieve much of the suffering which comes to be expressed in various forms of hostility to school and the adult world among the less able, or emotionally disturbed or unhappy young. Of course these psychic needs and unhappinesses are not confined to 'C' and 'D' streams, but are found in gifted and academic children, too. The same problems are found in other forms in technical, university and higher education. The urgency of our needs for imaginative nourishment, for insight and understanding, unites us all from childhood to old age: this is the clue to what a liberal education should be. The teacher can open the door to these—even to many of our own capacities to learn from life itself. Thus our concepts of what can and should be given a child at school both mark the quality of our civilisation, and form it.

There remain only two things to say in this introduction. First that this book cannot be made simple and easy to apply, if it is to establish sound foundations for the use of free imaginative methods in the education of the less able child. While I have tried to make it clear, I have not tried to write down to the teacher of backward children, or to make his complicated task sound at all simple. If I cast any light on the nature of these children, or teaching methods which seem to me to be more efficient than formal ones, I hope the reader will be able to make use of this book indirectly in the classroom, in his own way, as a teacher-artist. Those who want direct 'practical' aids won't find them given in simple easily digested form in this book. The practical suggestions given here won't be much use to anyone unless they are willing to study the principles behind the suggestions in the last section and the nature of 'backward' children as discussed in my analysis of their writing. There is no point in deceiving people into supposing that short cuts are possible in this work—they are not. I can only hope that the teacher's own capacities to invent methods opportunistically in his own way of teaching may be enhanced by the book. I do not believe it is possible to make a text-book for 'backward' children, because with them one has to work so opportunistically, from an arsenal of all varieties of powder and shot. They cannot really follow 'schemes' because they cannot concentrate for very long, or see long-term connections easily. But I have tried to produce some stimulating material in a group of course books to accompany this volume, providing 'exercises' which may be used at random, flexibly and informally (in preparation, and provisionally called *I've Got to Use Words*).

Finally, another spur to the writing of this book has been the disastrous move (following the Beloe Report) to extend external examinations to the secondary modern school. I have done what I can to attack this development in the press. It seems to me a betrayal of these children by default. The essential problem was to revise the syllabus in the secondary modern school, creatively and imaginatively, free from the narrow demands for certificate-grading in a meritocracy, and inspired with positive liberal humane aims. To substitute an examination seems to me an abrogation—a deadening move that evades the exigencies. The pressure surely comes from those who fear the demands made on the profession, towards making education real and effective, a true liberal discipline, painful and rare? One can only hope that in the end the examination won't be too bad—and that we shall still be able to educate in spite of it. Alas, in the grammar school it is obvious that education 'in spite of' G.C.E. is becoming more and more difficult. (Representative is the chemistry master quoted in *Education and the Working Class** who claims he can get any boy through 'A' level in two terms—'leaving the educational thing aside, of course'. Too much grammar school education now consists of 'leaving the educational thing aside'.)

Certainly the effect of yet another futile examination to stand in the way of true education will be greater hardship for 'C' and 'D' stream children, the unexaminable ones. They are likely to be even more rejected and despised, neglected at school, only too sadly aware that they are not in the running. After school they will be the uncertificated unemployables, fit only to take any ungraded task. Who shall blame them for becoming a resentful group expressing their contempt for a society which treated them as 'dim dregs', by taking to forms of

* Brian Jackson and Dennis Marsden, Routledge and Kegan Paul, 1961.

delinquency and violence, or by other forms of unsocial behaviour? Yet, when one knows these children, one knows what suffering is involved, for a child to feel itself a 'D' streamer from eight to fifteen. There is no doubt that much of their trouble is related to their sense of failure. They may sink into deeper suffering as a young thief, or prostitute, or the slatternly parent with all self-respect gone in the violent, disorganised home, or as the confirmed youthful criminal; or they may simply vegetate as they did in school.

But, thank heaven, there are doubts even in heaven, and perhaps I may end my introduction by quoting the then Minister of Education, (Sir David Eccles) at the Conservative Party Conference, in 1960.

. . . It isn't much good keeping children in school if we cannot hold their interest. We don't yet know enough about what to teach at the top of the Secondary Moderns. I am very anxious about this, and therefore, building on some first-class pioneering that has already been done, I'm going to have a thorough study made of what to teach at the top of Secondary Moderns. This study should be as valuable as the Crowther Report was from the Grammar Schools.

For we ought now to insist and insist strenuously that children of less than average academic ability are as worth while as children above the average.

And this care for the lower half of the school population is so necessary because as our methods improve of selecting children for Grammar Schools and for Grammar streams inside Comprehensive Schools, and as more children pass the G.C.E. or some other exam, the danger will grow that we depreciate and devalue all those children who are not selected and who cannot pass exams; the danger will grow that we divide the whole of the next generation into successes and failures according to their academic record.

Such a division would be unjust and unkind to millions of children and it would spread bitterness and jealousy in our society. It must not happen. But I must tell you that it will happen unless parents, teachers and employers look for, respect and encourage other good qualities in the young than simply the capacity to pass exams.

How strange that even with such sentiments Sir David Eccles was unable to resist the proposals for external examinations in Secondary Modern Schools! But this is another spur to the expression of strong views about the aims and purpose of education—to encourage authorities to be informed and inspired enough to keep ahead of the pressure-groups impelled by those with shallow, back-sliding and short-sighted motives. I hope this book will seem as clear and considered to the reader as I know it to be written with strong feelings.

I

A PRETTY WIDE SEPARATION

'Oh, but really? Do tell me. Are they, though?' she said.

'Are they what? And are who what?' said Steerforth.

'That sort of people. Are they really animals and clods, and beings of another order? I want to know so much.'

'Why, there's a pretty wide separation between them and us,' said Steerforth, with indifference. 'They are not to be expected to be as sensitive as we are. Their delicacy is not to be shocked, or hurt very easily. They are wonderfully virtuous, I dare say. Some people contend for that, at least; and I am sure I don't want to contradict them. But they have not very fine natures, and they may be thankful that, like their coarse rough skins, they are not easily wounded.'

'Really!' said Miss Dartle. 'Well, I don't know, now, when I have been better pleased to hear that. It's so consoling! It's such a delight to know that, when they suffer, they don't feel! Sometimes I have been quite uneasy for that sort of people; but now I shall just dismiss the whole idea of them altogether. Live and learn. I had my doubts, I confess, but now they're cleared up. I didn't know, and now I do know, and that shows the advantage of asking—don't it?'   (Charles Dickens, *David Copperfield*)

I said I had had some good work from 4 C that morning. 'Yes, but they're so uncouth,' said a colleague, 'I can't stand 'em.' He was being honest. More often teachers make rationalisations. At a meeting of teachers recently I was asked whether I didn't really think it was a great mistake keeping 'the C's and D's at school until fifteen'. And one is asked privately time and time again, 'Isn't it a bloody waste of time for most of them?' At the same time one knows that much work with children in low streams *is* truly a waste of time, because the level is made too difficult for them, or the work is too formal and abstract, or too remote from their interests. They can't do it. They make no progress, they get no satisfaction, they feel despised, the teacher becomes frustrated and then turns hostile. Yet the school mill must go on turning, or perhaps the teacher is too hard-pressed to find time to revise the whole content of his work to suit the needs of his more 'backward' charges.

He feels he hasn't the ability, or wouldn't have the cheek, to revise the whole approach to English or History or Geography to suit 3 C or 4 C. He might be flinching from his duty to 'educate' them if he simplified the work to their level. He feels that education, to be sound, must be the abstract process he himself experienced: he resents work which is reduced to a 'low' dimension which he feels is 'baby minding' or 'messing about', and which makes him spend his day in infantile modes instead of the sophisticated ones of grammar school subjects.

One difficulty seems to be that of accepting the level and dimension of work with the 'backward' child for what it is. As we shall see the 'C' and 'D' stream child is still at an infant mental age and responds best to the freer Infant methods. I feel sure that many teachers try to teach above the heads of their less able pupils. The reasons for this are unconscious, and perhaps not unconnected with such fears as we all have of mental illness and other disabilities—fears which express themselves in unconscious hostility or falsification, to seek to allay our own anxiety. It is possibly a rationalisation of his fear of 'backward' pupils that makes the teacher cling to his 'subject' at a 'higher level'—we all know that the strain of teaching backward children is relieved if we have mixed with it some work with 'A' stream children. A teacher will say, 'It's my "A" stream work that stops me going mad.' We often fear to relax our hold on our 'subject' at the level at which it helps us feel the self-respect of an educated person: for some reason to scale our subject down to the level of less able people sometimes makes us feel humiliated or insecure. Because of our own uncertainties of how mature we are ourselves, we fear to enter the world of the low stream child's immaturity. Any teacher of backward children finds himself under the strain of his own insecurities and instabilities as soon as he begins this arduous work.

Besides such disturbances that dealing with the rejected, 'backward' children generate in us, we also feel the effects of having to deal with emotionally disturbed children, a proportion of whom are actually mentally ill. I will be dealing with this point throughout this book, and have been fortunate to secure the help of a woman doctor who has paediatric and psycho-analytical experience, who will comment on some of the pupils and their work. But the depressive effect of this disturbed element in any backward class is more difficult to overcome than most educational books admit. The problem is recognised by books of educational psychology: but to overcome the difficulties is not achieved, alas, by reading books of educational psychology: they may leave us simply like Miss Dartle—knowing, but dismissing the whole idea of these people from our minds. It is true that we need to study the facts of mental disturbance, and that this will help. But the deepest problem is to bring ourselves to a capacity for compassionate understanding of human nature. We cannot come to understand human nature from mere information or even from what science tells us about it. Of course we should check ourselves by devising meticulous routines for dealing with suspected mental illness. But we still have to learn to deal with all manner of difficulties of human nature in children. Understanding human nature means a considerable adjustment of our whole make-up, and this can only come by the development of insights.

These insights can come by two main conscious disciplines other than by the experience of life and from our normal development of understanding—which of course everyone has to some degree. One is the use of the power of intelligence in collaboration with the effect of sympathetic understanding (the form of 'love' which develops in the transference situation) through psycho-analysis. This is an expensive, rare, and exacting process which is not only in short supply, but properly reserved for those who are mentally ill, or those who are seeking to be trained as psychiatrists and psycho-analysts to relieve further suffering caused by mental illness. Very few teachers will ever be lucky enough to have a course of psycho-analysis behind them, though it must be of very great benefit to those who have.

Deep insights can also come by the disciplines of imagination—by the true response to art which allows the bowels of compassion to be moved. Of course, by 'art' I mean all the arts, not simply painting. And I mean creating as well as responding. True creativity is exacting and often painful. True art disturbs our awareness, and the reward is that it fosters our sympathy. Through it we may grow to understand others, and understand both the common elements in human experience, and the uniqueness of each human experience of life. We may, through art, grow more reverent, more full of awe at the mystery of human life, more aware of its reality, including the reality of human nature—and thus more tolerant and compassionate. We may become more able to be positive and creative in our attitudes to our own living and in our actions and choices—less afraid of the exceptional, the challenging, the mysterious. The arts may bring us through these stages, not only by informing us about these aspects of human life, but by affecting our spirits, by stirring our deepest nature, and changing it, enlarging perceptions and potentialities. Many of our potentialities from childhood to maturity depend upon our souls being nourished from imaginative sources by the creative processes of metaphor. Our unconscious phantasy, which art nourishes and helps towards order, is the source and basis of many of our capacities, including our intellectual ones. The nourishment and exercise of the imagination is the root of true literacy in all, from low stream children to the genius.

Because they are dealing with minds, and with tender minds at that, in a creative process, an art, teachers need more sustenance from imaginative sources than others. The teacher certainly depends upon his understanding of human nature (which may grow through many forms of experience, of course, as well as art) for help in dealing with his more unfortunate, less endowed, or unhappy pupils.

Here the capacity for art and other creative experiences to release sympathy and deeper understanding has a direct relevance to the classroom situation—to the need to be warm-hearted, positive and humane, and to stimulate the imaginations of children. Among children with a history of 'failure' behind them the need to be creative and understanding is even greater. There are blockages and disturbances in the emotional make-up of all of us which will throw up defences, and continue to undermine our self-possession beneath them, whatever preparations we have had for our work. There are children so disturbed that they are driven unconsciously to search out our weaknesses and test them—whereupon we may possibly lose control, and become hostile to them, or at least anxious in their presence. There are situations of this kind for which the only answer may be psychiatric treatment for us, or for the child. But a healthy and sympathetic relationship between adult and child depends, I am sure, for nourishment much on what one must call the whole culture of the teacher, taking into account, of course, his intuitive 'nous', his own emotional maturity and his experience of life. A man's culture develops not only through the pure arts, in poetry, painting, drama, dance, the novel, but may be found in many other pursuits, such as sports, travel, mountaineering, natural sciences, the study of history, social work, crafts, work contact with others, the application of his energy and potentialities in a love relationship, or in creating a home and cherishing a family. I know that I became a better teacher by experiencing the exactions of give and take in family life, by the exactions of married love, and by having to help deal with a succession of babies, growing up to young persons. Love itself is an exacting discipline by which the soul grows. We learn by experience, from inherited 'learning', through imaginative expression, and through all that we call civilisation. But the sap will flow more in us the more we open ourselves to finer minds and sensibilities, through poetry, imaginative fiction, painting, liberal studies, drama, music, the 'numinous' in the environment where it may be found, as in great architecture, and the spatial arts. We may find more significance and meaning in our lives through art, as through study, religious contemplation, and scientific pursuits. Many teachers obviously understand the value of creative activity in their lives, and gain great sustenance from these activities—as, for instance, at the remarkable Studio Workshop, run by the Institute of Education in Cambridge, as part of its regular provision for teacher refreshment. The experience of imaginative art seems to me an important need for the profession, and not least for the teachers who have to deal with backward children. Experience of the arts and creative activities are obviously primary for teachers in training.* Teachers urgently need to gain insight into human nature, into inner reality, and gain thereby the understanding they urgently need both to protect themselves in the daily tasks to maintain their balance and élan, and to come to terms with their more unstable charges. The crucial problems of educating today's 'average' and 'backward' children demand an approach based on an understanding and experience of human nature through imagination and art rather than merely on knowledge of psychology or educational information or theory. Creative art equips us to practise our own art—and, of course, illuminates what we take in from theory and scientific sources, too.

The implication of this aspect of work with backward children I have tried to use to govern the preparation of this book. I would urge it on those who train and refresh teachers, the need for the art of teaching to be nourished by creativity. I have read many books on backwardness in education but I find that much of the writing hardly helps me at all. Certainly the psychographs of measurement of ability, even data on learning processes, and the accounts of the nature of various disabilities, seem to help very little. They may help one to avoid wasting one's

* Fortunately the need for imaginative nourishment is beginning to be accepted by the Training Colleges. Students are painting, dancing and miming, and undertaking creative writing. Colleges are also commissioning music and buying paintings and sculpture, and upholding a creative syllabus against attempts to make the syllabus more 'academic' in order to achieve 'university status'.

time, by speeding up one's diagnosis of difficulties in need of attention. But they do not help teaching as an art as much as one might suppose they would—not even Burt's considerable works. They provide useful knowledge: they do not nourish the sensibility and the powers to employ one's potentialities creatively in the classroom. As so often, the mere knowledge about a subject, mere information, does not flow easily into one's work—in the bewilderment of a noisy lesson in school one strains one's mind in vain to remember what so-and-so said in his book on backwardness—one needs aid which flows naturally into action and insight. And I found that the most useful passages in Burt, for instance, were those in which an actual child was discussed, and its work quoted. Yet even here the content of the child's writing—the most interesting aspect of the whole case—was often passed by without comment, of the literary-critical, analytical kind, on the imaginative content and its meaning. The technical quantities of the expression were accounted for, but not the meaning of the elusive voices of the animula. Much more useful to the teacher are such books as *Coming Into Their Own*, an analysis of the creative work of primary school children, by Marjorie Hourd and Gertrude Cooper (Heinemann, 1959), or Sybil Marshall's *An Experiment in Education* (Cambridge, 1963), where the accounts of teaching are themselves creative and warm-hearted. Too many conferences and published discourses on the teaching of less able children are sterile because they lack humane creative spark.

What I think can help us greatly is to penetrate into the mind of the child—to penetrate into his imaginative, phantasy world, and share his view of life. This we may do with comparative ease, even through the painting and writing of 'backward' children. We may gain much from sensitive portrayals in art of the child's mind and view of life (as in *Huckleberry Finn*). If we have read William Blake, Christopher Smart, Kafka, Joyce, John Clare, Emily Dickinson, and Lewis Carroll we shall not find it embarrassing or irrelevant to respond to and study the strange, mystical and obscure expression of our 'backward' pupils. If we are able to respond to the most exciting moments in these writers, then we shall become able to see how the writings of our pupils express the turmoils and sorrows in their souls. By this means we may rapidly gain insight into their natures. In finding that in fact they are very much like ourselves, and trying to make sense of life *in exactly the same bewildered way as we are*, inwardly, then we will be changed.

We will not only know 'about' difficult children—we shall enter their very natures, and find, perhaps, how sad, how brave, how beautiful their inward creature can be. And see how, cowering perhaps, or shivering behind an external sophistication, it is very like the animula that lurks behind our own eyes, bewildered and afraid—if only at times when our confidence and self-possession desert us. We may recognise in some of them that the collapse of self-possession we most fear is their continual state of existence, as they feel 'failed' from the age of eight or nine. They may be more or less continually in the 'depressive attitudes' we experience only at our worst times, unconscious attitudes to experience by which we suppose we are victims of a hostile universe, and have no resources to deal with it.

Thus the problem of discussing the teaching of backward children becomes at once one which cannot be solved by imparting information or by outlining methods and techniques. To become an efficient teacher of backward children we have to go through a kind of initiation —along with the harrowing experience of actually teaching these children when one first begins. We have to develop capacities for understanding creatures who are at once very different from, and at the same time very similar to, us. They are different because they are not endowed as we are with high intelligence. Some have actually damaged brains; some have lame minds because of psychic damage or deficiencies caused at crucial moments of development; some are unhappy because of grief or fear. But they are similar, too, because they are suffering, sometimes in gross forms, from psychic weaknesses which we all have, and which we unconsciously fear, particularly when we are faced with them in active and obvious forms, as they tend to be in the low stream class. They are rejected: and this is something we all deeply fear. The anxious little child in 3 C whom one finds oneself fearing and hating matches exactly the weakling part of one's own nature—the area of one's being about which one is least assured, where something immature cowers, too, in the darkness. We may find ourselves urged to punish the child, because we wish to punish the same thing inside us. If we know of this danger we may try to avoid it. But a deeper approach is to be prepared to open ourselves to a deeper awareness of the human weakness in ourselves—which we can do by, say, reading George Eliot, going to see *King Lear*, or looking at the work of the great painters, Delacroix, Degas, Picasso or Bruegel. And then to open ourselves to an understanding of the child's inward life by studying his imaginative expression in the same spirit. Of course, this has parallels with the child psycho-analyst's approach to the difficult child, as set forth in Melanie Klein's *Narrative of a Child Analysis*, where she analyses the symbolic meaning of little Richard's paintings and verbal expression. But, in the creative act itself, the child, in expressing his inward unconscious conflict as art, finds 'relief' as Melanie Klein confirms. And we have the privilege of being able to gain from this expression, without the need to interpret as a child psycho-analyst does, a deeper understanding of the individual child, of childhood—and even of ourselves. I have learnt from my backward pupils a great deal in recent years about myself, and also about art. It is the mysterious and primal value of art to the distressed and questing psyche with which we as teachers are concerned. Such psychology as I consider here is chosen because of its relevance to the child's imaginative needs and the poetic function.

I shall leave the teacher to find his own way about books on psychology, though I make suggestions in a book list (p. 278). I am mainly interested in two aspects of child psychology, neither of which really belongs to the psychometric kind which seems still to dominate, without very much justification or success, much of educational development, research and planning. I became especially interested in the processes of unconscious phantasy in relation to imagination and art, and particularly in the writings of Melanie Klein. The other field to which one's attention is drawn by teaching 'low stream' children is the whole problem of child psychiatry. As David Stafford Clark says in *Psychiatry Today*:

> 'it is probably true that unhappiness, anxiety or boredom and frustration are more frequent causes of apparent dullness or backwardness at school than is sheer lack of intelligence'.*

And from one's experience with backward children one soon comes to see that probably something like 4 out of every 20 'backward' children in 'C' and 'D' streams are actually mentally ill. There may be many thousands of mentally ill children in such classes in secondary schools alone. They are different from the others because they are incapable of responding to normal educative processes. The teacher cannot, with them, make the progress he can with others, despite all his care, his idealism, his sympathy and understanding. He cannot

* Penguin Books, 1951, p. 61.

function as a teacher because these children are debarred by actual mental sickness from profiting from his efforts. It seems to me a major social problem, the question of what we, as a nation, ought to do for these children. Perhaps only a full course of psycho-analysis could cure some of the worst: this they cannot, by the nature of things, have. Many could benefit from psychiatric aid—the emotionally disturbed, if not mentally ill ones. But they can have more care and treatment than they receive at the moment, and this would relieve their distress, and the teacher's difficulties. Without more care for them we shall always have a stream of disgruntled and confirmed delinquents entering our social life, marked out by having been 'dregs', confirmed in their sickness by being marked down—'watched' by headmasters and others—as 'uncouth' and 'liable to make trouble'. This I discuss later, in dealing with some of my more disturbed pupils (see pp. 106, 137 and 180). From this group come men like James Hanratty, a young man of limited mentality who committed murder and rape on the A 6 in 1961, a mentally ill homicide who had been 'backward' at school: the community could, it seems, do nothing to cure him, from school to prison, and he was hanged.

It is the presence of such sick children among the other insecure and restless ones that makes the teaching of 'backward' classes so exhausting. I shall deal with ways of alleviating this later. Here it is enough to say that I found teaching one backward class of 19 children, for the whole of one weekday only, apart from other odd periods, sufficient of an emotional drain to reduce considerably my capacities for other forms of work during the rest of the week. At the end of the day, as many do, I had to sit quietly for an hour by myself to recover. And, in general, I found my sensibility coarsened, my élan depressed, my capacity to cope with irritation and emotional demands from my own children much lowered, and my mind generally confined to a much more limited scope of awareness and enquiry. These would seem to be some of the occupational hazards of teaching backward children, and this explains why, having taken on these children, a teacher so often goes into a kind of retreat from the world—one sees less of him, he seems less articulate. He has, in a way, 'gone under', and is often unable to explain what he has been doing, or even to discuss his work easily with others. At worst he is, in addition, discouraged by administrators and headmasters—and leaves the profession.

One reason for the exhaustion is that the teacher of backward children must give out much of himself in terms of affection—as a kind of 'love' for his pupils. It is true that one does grow very fond of one's pupils, not least the 'worst' of them. And this is reciprocated. For instance, two little boys in a 'B' stream, both of whom would clench their fists under the desks when I walked by in class, turned up at my farewell party with my 'C' stream—because they also wanted to be loved, as desperately as they hated me at times. One cannot resist such appeals from small creatures, and it draws sustenance out of one. But it seems also likely that there is another drain on one's energy, which is that employed to help restore order in one's own soul where disturbances are caused by the neurotic needs of the pupils. This representative passage from an American treatise on child psychology confirms the disturbing process that makes work with 'C' and 'D' streams so exhausting:

Teachers, parents and others who play a major role in child training do not possess any natural ability which will enable them to distinguish between the dangerous trends in children from the more benign ones. The ability to make such discriminations must be learned. To clear the way for this certain other prejudices must be overcome.

In the first place an individual may be extremely intolerant of deviations in others: there are certain weaknesses that he simply cannot endure; their presence makes him furious and, without the least evidence of mercy, he wants to punish or isolate the person showing them. Now the teacher cannot deal sanely with her pupils unless she rids herself of this attitude of intolerance; and the nature of intolerance will indicate why this is so. To rid herself of this trait, the teacher must understand its causes within herself. If she has a weakness which she has had a hard time overcoming, it means that she has had to be on her guard lest that weakness should come to the surface and cause an undesirable act. If a slip does occur, she is filled with chagrin and remorse because of her failure. Such a struggle leads to intolerance with herself. Now, suppose another person exhibits the weakness against which she has been struggling—the tendency in herself of which she is so intolerant. Her attitude will be projected toward his activity and she will have the same reaction toward his conduct that she would have toward that conduct in herself. Furthermore her feeling would probably be intensified, for the reason that the other person may perform the objectionable act with no feeling of remorse; and she will feel angry that he can do, with no apparent evidence of conflict, what causes her the deepest chagrin. Hence, she will want to heap upon this individual all possible punishment, because of her attitude of projected intolerance and because of the anger that she feels when he coolly does what she continually schools herself not to do. How can she deal with her pupil unless she realizes the reasons for her attitude towards his conduct?

In the second place, her attitude may be coloured by an entirely different condition. She may have had an undesirable trait which she has overcome with great difficulty and which she has tried by every conceivable means to forget. As a result, all the evidences of it are ignored. This leads to a condition which is the opposite of intolerance—that of a failing to see similar peculiarities in others . . .*

This passage explains perhaps why the work with 'low stream' children makes such heavy demands on one's emotional resources. Intolerance takes the form of strong emotions, of the origins of which the teacher is unconscious: the conflict between the impulse to punish and the prevailing code in school complicates them. The struggle between the impulse to make a scapegoat of a child or 'isolate' it, one's idealism, and the contest with unconscious hatreds—these drain a teacher's nervous energy. The teacher must strive to overcome prejudices—but this takes the more energy the more they are evoked by neurotic children. Then one may be defending a hidden weakness in oneself, and find oneself full of strange feelings of remorse if one finds the weakness indulged in without conscience by the children. I have overheard my children discuss sexual relationships with their sisters, masturbation, seeing adults (they were teachers, too) half-naked in sexual acts, besides other matters of cruelty, and petty sin such as drinking and smoking. These children talk 'to' one obliquely, under cover of apparently talking to one another and it is difficult to know how to respond. No one exposed to 'backward' children can escape something of an anxious undercurrent of unbalanced behaviour, and news of strange forms of violence or sex often done (apparently) without conscience. The adult inevitably reacts strongly—just as adults react to public symbols of the remorseless indulgence in 'forbidden things'. Compare, for example, the reaction of people in a public house to such an event as a hanging, or to an attempted suicide by a film-star.

All such conflict of emotion, which becomes inevitable in handling 'backward' children, uses energy, largely at the unconscious level, and makes for very great exhaustion. No one escapes this drain on his resources. This is the very good reason for giving teachers of these

* *The Psychology of the Unadjusted School Child.* John J. B. Morgan, Ph.D. (Macmillan, 1948 edition), p. 2.

children better conditions of work—special responsibility allowances (and *proper* responsibility), the best possible classroom environment and equipment, a good deal of free time, sympathetic encouragement, and the relief of periods with more stable and more intelligent children. Teachers of these children require a special, and an especially creative training. Teachers of backward children also deserve sabbatical periods of a term to a year, from time to time, to help them recover their nervous stamina, and opportunities to refresh themselves at Institute training courses. It is not possible to educate these children efficiently at all under prevalent conditions of work, with teachers too hard pressed, classes too big, and equipment inadequate.

The second part of the above most relevant quotation, however, reveals why it is that so much of the reality of work with backward children becomes disguised and remains hidden. I seek to reject, of course, the attitude of those who assume with Steerforth and Miss Dartle in the quotation at the head of this chapter that 'backward' children, being often mere common children, are 'clods and animals' —capable of responding only to coarse material (see the note on books— Appendix 3). A much deeper problem is a tendency to ignore weaknesses, the strange way in which the actual disabilities of these children are often passed over—and nothing is done about them. 'I don't like to say this, but he's the sort who'll do somebody in one day. I'm glad he's gone.' The headmaster who said this was a good headmaster, who treated his children with kindness and respect, and who would do everything in his power to help them. But his tone expresses the prejudice which every one of us feels, by which we refuse to accept fully the terrible possible consequences of weaknesses in children which we ought never to allow to go untreated. The tendency (as Appendix 2 shows) is for 'C' and 'D' streams to become dumping grounds for all kinds of deficiencies, weaknesses and unattractive qualities. Of course, when a headmaster says 'I give my children a year to make good —*after that the weakest must go to the wall*' (p. 268) he is disqualifying himself from the right to be trusted with children at all. How can we expect such a man to help to civilise the young people of modern society?

In one class of children which I taught was a girl who was supposed to be deaf. She worked well at handicraft, but in any writing subject she simply wrote page after page of material remembered from the television screen, *Reader's Digest*, or advertisements. In fact, she hardly understood one word of this material, and when I worked carefully with her

I discovered that she did not know the meaning of such words as 'on', 'by', 'under', neither did she know the words 'hedge' or 'window', and other such simple terms. Yet her report books were full of encouraging remarks such as 'Pat★ works well', 'Pat is trying hard'. The girl was occupied in school only in making some kind of defensive ploy to protect her disabilities from being discovered. Yet she was not really functioning normally at all. At a glance her books looked 'filled'. She bravely did try. But she took in no meaning from anything the teacher said or wrote; the diagrams and text in books meant nothing to her; her writing down from memory of random passages, remarkable as it was, meant nothing to her either. Yet nowhere in her report book was the fact of her disability recorded! No one ever wrote 'Pat does not understand words as well as a child of three'—which was the truth. Why not? The case is discussed in detail below (p. 167).

My point is that *because of the teacher's unconscious fear of the weaknesses embodied in such a child*, the tendency may be to ignore the urgent needs of what was here really a psychic problem. To overcome such difficulties teachers need to be trained both in questioning their attitudes to unusual or difficult children, and to put schemes of diagnosis and treatment into operation. Of course, these can only be put into operation where they exist. In some authorities nowadays a valuable cross-checking system of diagnosis is used so that problem children are not 'overlooked', for unconscious or other motives. In the case quoted a conference early in the child's school life, between staff, lip-reading teachers, child psychiatrist and parents might have brought new approaches that might have helped restore the girl to normal relationships in society. Instead, the problem was concealed by a process not unrelated to burning witches and chaining lunatics.† No qualified diagnosis was ever made, even in an enlightened education authority, even in an enlightened city. I reported several children for psychiatric treatment, but I think none received any examination. The only child I knew to be receiving psychotherapy had attempted to murder a sibling.

Pat was an obvious case of disability and need. How much more do schools tend to gloss over the weaknesses which only show themselves in occasional psychic aberrations? And how much does intolerance go

★ All the children's identities have been disguised by fictitious names throughout, as also have the identities of places, etc.

† See Dr. David Stafford Clark's two disturbing chapters, *One Way of Beginning* and *Psychiatry Yesterday* on attitudes to psychic disorders in the past. *Op. cit.* pp. 8–57.

with an outraged idealism that really wilfully and defensively disguises the turning of a blind eye to pathetic needs? 'I've done my best for that boy, but it's useless. You can't do anything with him.' This feeling is prevalent when we are dealing with 'backward' children—often because it is true that, with some, 'kindness' and ideals, discipline and imaginative teaching, religious devotion, all possible normal care, still can do nothing. This is true only of a minority, but with them the obvious answer is to leave nothing undone which can in any way help them to find effective medical treatment. They suffer from psychic disturbances which only the very special skills of psychotherapy can begin to touch. Accounts below from teachers seem to suggest many hidden neglected disabilities in 'low' streams. It is not that any individual is to blame: the need is for a system of qualified examination of every child with double checks, and systems of therapy.* Besides concealed psychic or other disabilities there are still children with physical deficiencies 'kept quiet' at school routines which mean nothing to them, and these disorders are also often neglected. The teacher of backward children must be prepared to link his work with psychotherapy and therapeutic approaches to school work, and seek every aid he can in this way.

I hope I do not here have to deal with the prejudice against psychiatry 'as a substitute for discipline'. I shall deal later with discipline, encouragement and marking in classroom practice. Disturbed children, more than normal ones, need to find a strong authority, and welcome discipline: it may help them find security. But there is point in discipline only if it is effective, and one knows that sometimes, with a neurotic child, it is not. At the end of my teaching experience Jack O'Malley was very restless and antipathetic. His work was poor and slovenly, and he wrote only verbal attacks on teachers and the school. In the playground he formed gangs to bully other smaller boys. He was caned, twice, but would say, 'Take me to the old man if you like. I don't care. He can cane me. And he can cane me again. It don't hurt.' He meant that it didn't hurt as much as his inward turmoil, and yet one didn't know what this turmoil was about. Then one morning he said, 'Did you read in the paper about that woman what got raped at Melton? Police come and took a statement off my bruvver.' That was it! I discuss this pupil's work in detail below. The woman doctor who has advised me on the psychopathology of these children suggests

* I have since heard of such very thorough systems in Bradford schools.

28

that I am too hopeful about this boy, and that indeed very little could be done to 'civilise' him by normal teaching methods without psychiatric aid (see p. 106).

While 'backward' children require the adult to *be* an adult in establishing authority, demanding that they do work, and that they keep their place as children in a school, where the adult word is law and order—there will come times when discipline to the neurotic child becomes ineffective. However much discipline is applied, the work in hand, because interest in it is exhausted, cannot be adequately or efficiently done. Or a boy may have a disturbance which makes punishment irrelevant, as the law recognises it to be to a maniac—there is no point in hanging a man who is so mentally ill that he does not realise what he has done, or what is being done to him. Some children are in a parallel state, in which they seem to be unable to benefit from adult firmness or punishment. Thus we may distinguish in life between three kinds of individuals who are 'bad characters'—those who will benefit from punishment, even welcome it as something against which to make firm their own inward character; those whom we wish to punish as scapegoats for our own weaknesses—which is unfair, since we deserve the punishment rather than they—and thirdly those to whom punishment is meaningless.

It may help the teacher perhaps to practise distinguishing between these kinds of characters by reading fiction—it is always a problem for the author to know whether to 'account' for the weaknesses of his villains, and thus excuse them, or treat them as embodiments of bad aspects in human nature. In some, as in Dickens's Bill Sikes, who is presented as irredeemable, an author can be seen punishing cruel impulses in himself: the same author with Uriah Heep and Littimer in prison sees them as embodiments of aspects of human nature totally incapable of reform. Dickens's attitude to 'fallen' women such as Little Em'ly is most suspect, since he himself kept a mistress—yet his Sissy Jupe is unadulterated goodness.* Actually only very ill people in real life are incapable of change for the better: only a grave psychotic will be beyond any reform bar lengthy psychiatric aid, or actual restraint or incarceration. And while one aspect of reality we must take in, from poetry, the novel, psychology and history, and not least from

---

* A fascinating study of Dickens's attitude to crime and to the capacity of human nature to respond to reform is made by Philip Collins in *Dickens and Crime* (Macmillan, 35s.). See the same author's *Dickens and Education*.

experience of life itself, is that a large part of human nature is capable of terrible evil and destruction: one must cling to the hope that more is good, and mysteriously capable of great altruism, even if much is bad. What is perhaps too often lost sight of is that the quest for good by man is an undeniable fact, and that this is the greatest reality of human existence. Some students of the new truths of human nature, even Freud himself, have tended perhaps to undervalue this positive impulse in human nature, though they themselves may have been evidence of its truth in their own dedicated lives. But the fact of the human inclination to strive for good requires that law and punishment shall embody a realistic recognition of discrimination between good and bad—to help that altruism which is a main feature of our evolution, in its contest with the destructive and malicious.

With children it is urgent to see the bad child—while maintaining strict discipline—as unhappy, sick, or deranged, and in need of help, rather than as 'a bad 'un' to be punished. These are aspects of the teacher's plight in his work with 'backward' children.

But rather than discuss general aspects of his predicament I would prefer to look more closely at the 'C and D stream' children themselves. I will, below, present to the reader pieces of work from each of my pupils, with a brief discussion of the child and his work; by this means perhaps we can get to know them, their difficulties and of what they are capable.

Of course a great deal of one's work with 'average' or 'less than average' children is dull and tedious, and at worst saddening and depressing. But one of the things I seek to do in this book, if I do nothing else, is to disprove the following statement which is made in a recent book about teaching backward children:

Imaginative written compositions or essays cannot be expected of a really dull child, and they will see little purpose in them, but they can be taught to write simple, straightforward paragraphs on things they have learnt or seen or heard.*

I shall set out to demonstrate if I can that the primary and urgent need of the less able child, not least the 'really dull child' is for the exploration of inward phantasy, and the expression of it in many forms, but chiefly in words, by imaginative compositions of all kinds. This should

*Josephine Stopa, chapter on 'Reading and English' in *Teaching the Slow Learner in the Secondary School*, ed. M. F. Cleugh, Methuen, 1961.

be the basis of all their work, not only in English: but in English it is the root of literacy. Without a great deal of such work they can neither begin to bring their own souls and personalities into order, nor begin to become effectively articulate for normal social life, and literate. I have proved, I think, that there was no child among those I taught, with I.Q.s from 70 (say) to 100, who could not produce an imaginative piece, *understanding what he was doing and what good it did him.* Moreover, if we look at their work in the right spirit, it may be taken with an interest parallel to our interest in a work of literature—because it was doing for the human mind that produced it, what Shakespeare's *Sonnets* did for his very great mind at a very different level. To share imaginative work with children and to see them benefit from it can bring us to see all children as equal in terms of the needs of the sensibility, with that consequent liberation I have discussed above, of positive attitudes to our work. But let us first look a little more closely at what these children are like, and later see them as revealed in their writing.

2

BEINGS OF ANOTHER ORDER?

In every human soul there is a ray of celestial beauty (Plotinus admits that), and a spark of genius (nobody admits that) . . .
(Charles Ives, the American composer)

I have tried to suggest in the last chapter that a first problem with backward children is for us to overcome our own difficulties, in approaching them, and in seeking to determine what we are doing with them. As I go on I shall ask the uncomfortable question, 'What are we doing to these children when we are teaching them?' and attempt some answers. But even before we get so far, we need to struggle with ourselves, in order to reach an acceptance of these children as they are.

It is possible that if we were still a merely agricultural people, or a food-gathering or hunting community, then many of the 'lower stream' individuals would be more highly honoured than those who are rewarded for being 'bright' in our society. Certainly some of my 'backward' pupils were willing to stick patiently at a task such as cleaning out pigs, singling sugar-beet, or slaughtering animals, to a degree far beyond the capacities of an intellectually brighter child who would soon become bored in such tasks. As a patient hunter, contributing significantly to the tribe's food supply, Gerald Goodchild, the butcher's son, might well have been a top person in a different kind of structure of merit, in a primitive society.

Yet it would hardly help us in our teaching to deny that the children who are placed by this society in 'low' streams are different from those whom we select for 'A' streams, even if it seems wrong that they should all be weeded out and bundled together by themselves as 'rejected' pupils. Maybe the very sense of having 'failed' makes them even more different: but they certainly are different, not only because they have been rejected. The atmosphere of the low stream classroom is quite different from anything we have ever experienced in the course of our own education: Edward Blishen has called the atmosphere 'rather like that of a four-ale bar'. And this atmosphere contains all those strange emanations which come from a proportion of emotionally disturbed children and mentally sick children, together with an environment coloured by the attitudes to experience of limited, dull, and restless individuals.

Any effective attempt to bring about changed and improved attitudes to these children, so that we may help make them feel valued, rather than undervalued; any proposal to revise the organisation of education, or the curriculum, or methods of teaching, so that they may be brought towards better use of their potentialities—these can only start from an acceptance of these young creatures as they truly are.

Because they are full of social idealism some teachers deny publicly that these children are really different. In reply to a broadcast of mine, for instance, on 'The Dregs' (reprinted in *The Listener*) a teacher wrote:

I have yet to meet 'C' children who (in Holbrook's words) 'have less mental equipment'. Barring the 2 or 3 per cent who are seriously handicapped what has struck me in 'C' class after 'C' class is the 'ordinaryness' of the children; the obvious signs that these are average citizens who, had they been given a fair chance, could have done anything any other ordinary citizen can do, including the not really so formidable G.C.E.

This teacher commendably attacks the way in which the 'C' stream children are 'already rejected' at six years of age, and the way this is confirmed by their parents' 'ill-concealed disappointment', and by the neglect of these children in school because preferential treatment is given to the 'A's'. He goes on, 'by the time they reach eleven-plus there is almost an excuse for imagining we have two different kinds of children'. But the social idealism revealed by his enthusiastic use of the emotive word 'citizens' blinds him to some of the truth. What is more, he assumes too easily that it is desirable—and a proof of their 'ordinaryness'—that they could do G.C.E.!

To this letter, a former Primary School Headmaster now a training college lecturer, replied, also in *The Listener*:

I cannot imagine how a serious and experienced teacher can assert . . . that there is not a considerable group of children who 'have less mental equipment' than the rest. Of all the children I have taught, about 50 per cent have in fact been endowed with less than average ability—even though I have not always been sure (nor cared) to which group any particular child belonged.

He goes on to point out that it can be harmful to expect more from a child than he is capable of, and that there are some hard-working children who, given the best teachers and the best conditions, still wouldn't reach 'O' level in the G.C.E. 'Why should they?' He goes on to say that he thinks many teachers become frustrated because they have an exaggerated respect for intellectual and academic ability. As long as teachers generally think more highly of their clever than their less clever children the less able will not do as well as they should, and will become frustrated, hostile, indifferent, or destructive—but it is no help to them to pretend that their 'mental equipment' is not inferior. Neither will it matter whether they are in streamed or unstreamed schools.

I would endorse this reply. It is to deceive oneself to pretend that 'backwardness' somehow marks *only* the effect of social underprivilege. There may be a correlation between social class and academic ability of a kind. The grammar schools almost certainly underestimate and fail to foster some of the best strengths of the working-class community, in favour of aspects of middle-class gentility of speech and manner. The inferior treatment of backward children certainly reflects underprivilege, and is a social evil with grave consequences, sometimes giving rise to the creation of a delinquent, resentful, debased group in the population. But the incapacity to learn in certain ways which our society values highly may be observed in half the school population as a fact. The 'C's and D's' cannot perform abstract functions, cannot easily memorise, cannot concentrate, are poor at absorbing information, and learn technical functions such as reading and writing only with great effort and at a very slow pace. The trouble is not that these children are normal in their faculties and only limited by being rejected: what is wrong is that our society punishes and rejects them for lacking certain special capacities—and fails to commend them for those they do eminently have. These children do have other potentialities, which should be more highly regarded by society, such as warmness of heart, generosity, reliability, kindness, fine character, courage in the face of life's conditions. The fault is in our education, which deals so little with these and does not foster and cherish them sufficiently. They may have gaiety, green fingers, astonishing capacities with animals, capacities for craft skills, the power to love, a fascinated interest in and sense of harmony with the natural world. But the school does not recognise these gifts or develop or reward them.

None of my 'C' stream pupils, however much time and care I spent on them, could ever pass one subject at 'O' level. For them to try—or feel it was important to try, in order to 'make the grade'—would only make for unhappiness. I would see no point in putting them in for an external examination, though I am miserable about the fact that when the new examination comes such children will get even less attention, will be left behind throughout their lives without certificates, and thus without passports to certain jobs, some of which may be more highly paid than the ones in which they will be landed. Ours has become a society which values people less for what they are than for what skills they can acquire in certain limited'ways, and for certain industrial-commercial ends—to 'get on', and become 'successful' (and this does not mean successful at living). Neither is service to the community as highly honoured as is service to one's own interests. The attitudes of headmasters quoted below in Appendix 2 about 'results', have terrible implications about 'success' as our world sees it. And so Rose Jameson's children may have clothes and a diet inferior to those of the 'A' stream children, possibly, and Robert Shire's never be able to tour Europe; Pat will never be able to buy a sports car, or own a pony. But 'brighter' children are more likely to be rewarded, because they had a set of determining genes which gave them intelligence of the kind our world finds useful. It is terribly unfair, but yet it is not helpful to deny the differences—they are conditions of our children's existence. Disease, accidental death, pain, and chance personal gifts such as beauty or physical strength are no more fairly distributed than intelligence. One may detect sometimes in refusals to accept the nature of 'backward' children an underlying refusal to accept the inescapable conditions of human life, a fear of the actual, and a fear even of 'disquality', as Lawrence called the essential and mysterious difference between human beings. Social idealism too often contains an element of the more misleading kind of *idealising*, in the sense in which the psychiatrist uses the word—a process of disguising aspects of reality which we find too painful to accept, by demanding of reality an impossible degree of ideal perfection. The improvement of society will never remove backwardness. It may improve the treatment of backward children, and make them happier, because they feel more respected. It may make the benefits of material living more evenly distributed. But there will always be children with small mental endowments. Improvement in social conditions, even the establishing of almost universally happy families (supposing this were possible, which it is not: nor is it a matter of material comfort)—even this would not eradicate emotional disturbances and mental sickness. It would do much: but there are still many mental disorders in which there is no established connection between social or family cause and personal effect, and even in the most loving home a child will be born dull or grow with grave psychic disturbances. Babies are even born with a psychic incapacity to take the breast, to turn to the mother and begin the process of drawing on sustaining love—just as there are children with cancer. Some children have birth traumas for no apparent reason—shocks which remain with them. These aspects of life are terrifying and painful to accept—as terrifying as the fact that 'in the midst of life we are in death'. We may come to accept them through contemplation, or prayer or poetry and the arts, or by psycho-analysis, or by the rigours of scientific discipline —all of which bring us towards the acceptance of truth and reality. But it does not help to deny the sad, terrible, and disturbing fact that human beings are not equally endowed, not equally lucky or beautiful, not equally able to respond to all the beauty and richness of human experience and the natural life which surrounds us.

The most important task with 'backward' children is to bring them to a condition of awareness of their potentialities so that they cease to feel that there are certain satisfactions and achievements they can never know: but are happily sure they may attain many others—and more easily, so long as they can be brought to value themselves highly, for other capacities, from being good and loving parents, to giving service to the community. In fact those potentialities they have—for, say, love, or physical prowess, to find satisfaction in work (if possible!) —these are more marvellous than the potentialities of other living creatures, because of consciousness, memory, self-awareness and intelligence. Each child has his human uniqueness.

In some such terms the sense of valuing oneself may be given to less able pupils without hypocrisy. A chief way to this is by imaginative creativity. To be able to bring these children towards such a state requires, of course, that we ourselves can come to accept them as creatures as valuable as any other human beings. Teachers find this especially difficult, because, being professionally concerned with improvement of mind and intellectual powers, they often become frustrated and unhappy when they are brought to deal with children who are not very capable of substantial efforts of mind and intellect. (This problem I discuss at length in more general philosophical and psychological terms, in *The Secret Places*.) It will help us to make 'backward' children able to see themselves as valuable creatures if we see in their predicament a prejudice of our civilisation against certain human attributes and powers that it values too little—the intuitive, the creative, the creatureness—the simply *being* and living, and relishing that. 'Being' brings no 'results', of the kind our society expects. We have to make a radical reassessment of our attitudes, and so the argument must be as thorough and watertight as we can make it. In general terms it means we must everywhere seek to restore a primary concern with what I have called the poetic function to education and culture. And restore, too, the poetic way of looking at people—as D. H. Lawrence sought to look at them—as mysterious creatures, emanations from the mantle of life which clothes the earth. A 'backward' girl cannot do algebra: but she can create and foster an infant. Her capacities as wife and mother should be her basis for pride and sense of fulfilment as a civilised creature. Yet many women teachers face 'low stream' girls who have much more maturity than they, because the girls have known greater suffering than their teachers. Who, then, is 'low' or 'backward' in what? Of course some children inherit, alas, all the coarseness and ugliness of their parents: but our work can be more efficient if we are able to seek gains and fulfil needs in them, rather than dismiss them as capable of nothing but the crude and coarse.

To help adjust our attitudes to less able children, I propose to give, in a 'section of evidence' that follows, examples of the best work of the nineteen children I taught recently in a 'C' stream. I will try to draw the reader's attention to their limitations, but also to show how and where they transcended them, not so much in techniques of writing—though this they do sometimes—but in apprehensions, perceptions, inventions, creative expressions—surprisingly beyond, at times, the child's average capacity. I hope the reader will at times be moved as I have been, by the best these children can write, and see how terrible it is that we should endorse an educational system that rejects them and denies them the civilising influence of a good education. Because I am often asked at conferences, 'Aren't you just telling us your success stories?', I discuss in my section of evidence the work of *all* pupils in one 'C' stream class. I shall describe later how we set about some of our creative work, stage by stage. Some of the tricks I developed will seem naïve and simple, as will some of my satisfactions. It may seem pathetic that one has to develop a simple trick such as refusing to make anything but positive comments to these children on their work—'Well done, Rose!', 'Good, Gerald', 'Here's a good bit by Joan'—never to pick holes, or to say 'That won't do', or 'This is poor stuff', in the sardonic grammar school manner. But such small changes in approach represent a necessary change in attitudes to children's work at school. Of course I was angry with lazy or slovenly children, but I tried to be always positive. All teachers could perhaps gain by ceasing to regard children as naturally wicked and only to be encouraged by chastisement.

This positive approach has, I think, vindication in such work on children's psychic growth as that of the late Melanie Klein. The child has to strive for a positive attachment to 'the good object'—the good side of Mummy and itself. This positive good-seeking goes with all his development, of powers of literacy, of capacities to love, of capacities to learn, of maturity. These depend upon his early development of the capacity to attach hopeful feelings to the good object, starting first with the mother. This is a much more real and effective attitude to the child than the old-fashioned one which is based on the assumed need to chastise the 'young viper'! Some of us still work by the ancient traditions of the classroom, by which it is supposed that admonition, punishment, shame are the means to self-improvement and self-respect.

The old-fashioned attitudes perhaps had their origin in attempts to explain the inescapable suffering we experience in childhood. Children do suffer, and their suffering is partly the accident of the great processes of life. But they are also inevitable consequences of the mysterious growth of the human consciousness. We have to accept also, in relation to this, the disturbing fact that all our life is a struggle against imperfections and limitations. The rich and awesome truth is that children, beautiful, life-seeking manifestations of the continuity of life are forever coming into being, and that they, like us, make this creative contest as we do. Their occasional miseries are but happenstances in the mystery of their own creation and growth to maturity, with all the great powers of human potentiality. Of course, there is guilt in childhood, because part of children's growth to consciousness is the experience of terrible unconscious phantasies, in which they suppose themselves persecuted and defend themselves by projection or aggressive phantasy. When tormented by these phantasies, they feel that retribution may come upon them. Thus, inevitably, guilt becomes part of the child's growth to consciousness.

Against these psychic torments which lead to guilt and envy the child exerts its creative capacities and its sense of goodness which it mostly develops in its relationship with the mother. The infant is aware that he is not only being gratified by her, but is also being kept alive. Hunger, on the other hand, is a threat of deprivation and death, and so love and gratification are ranged on the creative side, and death and deprivation on the other. All through his growth to maturity the infant seeks to maintain an identification with the good and life-giving object —the good aspects of Mother which he has taken into himself—made part of himself, in his unconscious mind. Superficially, later this identification may manifest itself in terms of coveting the prestige, wealth and power of others, but its actual aim is creativeness. Thus, in children's phantasy, being princesses, or heroes, and overcoming odds are creative manifestations making for life. This is a rough summary of Melanie Klein's attempts to explain our inward conflicts between love and hate, envy and gratitude (I discuss her theories at length in *The Secret Places*).

'But the capacity to give and to preserve life is felt as the greatest gift, and therefore creativeness becomes the deepest cause for envy,' says Melanie Klein. So, our unconscious destructive impulses as infants take the form of directing destructive wishes towards the mother. These attacks on the good creative object, in the child's mind, result in hostility, criticism and envy being supposed to return as retribution from the mother—and this persecutory hostility may be internalised as what Freud called the 'super ego'—though it seems sometimes dangerous and misleading to divide the mind into such separate elements. Certainly the result of such unconscious envy and destructiveness directed at the creative mother may be the growth in the individual of an unconscious censoriousness which 'interferes with thought processes and with every productive activity, ultimately with creativeness,' as Melanie Klein says. Thus in a world such as ours, where the nervous, distractive and uneasy life of society interferes with the natural development of relationships between parents and child, and the growth of love, there are not only too few creative people—but there are many who, because of their inward censoriousness, are actively hostile to creativity.

This antipathy to creativity not only reveals itself in antipathy to art-creation, of course, but also to sexual creativity, creative attitudes, and positive attitudes of life. Melanie Klein quotes the description Spenser gives of Envy as a ravening wolf, a predatory sickness:

> He hated all good workes and vertuous deeds . . .
> And eke the verse of famous Poets witt
> He does backbite, and spightfull poison spues,
> From leprous mouth on all that ever writt.

Here we may find a clue to many ineffective attitudes to children's work, and especially to their creative writing and its place in education. 'Constructive criticism', says Melanie Klein, 'has different sources; it aims at helping the other person and furthering his work. Sometimes it derives from a strong identification with the person whose work is under discussion. Maternal or fatherly attitudes may also enter, and often a confidence in one's own creativeness counteracts envy.' Long before I read this sentence of Melanie Klein's, I was aware (as many other teachers are: see letters in Appendix 2) that it was because I was a father that I could feel fatherly towards my backward pupils so that I could encourage their creativity: because I identified myself with some, remembering my own bewilderments at times at school: and because I had some confidence in my own creativity as teacher and writer. Most teachers have natural intuitive gifts which enable them to give this creative encouragement to their pupils: but there is no doubt that these capacities can be greatly enhanced, in all education, by training the capacities of teachers through the creative imagination. Interestingly enough, some of the best teachers I have known have been painters, or have written songs, essays, books or poetry, or have had their own crafts, from fabric printing to small-holding or cabinet-making. These are not for them mere 'hobbies' but directly related to the constant need to replenish one's positive source of creative energy, and one's capacities for delight in the creative progress in children towards the 'good object', and a 'good' attitude to life.

In the same relevant passage of Melanie Klein's we may find a clue to the value of creative work in helping restore the damage done to a child by its being put in a 'low' stream. The situation is created in which the child cannot but be envious—especially if it is reinforced by discrimination against rejected children. Of course, antipathy, indifference and the attitudes of 'not wanting to get on' are but corollaries to the bitterness of the envy that 'backward' children feel. Being already disturbed children, some of them, the 'backward' pupils find their persecutory feelings reinforced by rejection and the failure of some teachers to foster their creativity. Their personalities decline more and more into disbalance and lack of inward order. Here we have the clue to the link between dullness and emotional disturbance, which we know from classroom experience to go hand in hand. Society despises and rejects these children, because it values intellectual capacity, and not essential creativeness of being. Thus despair, envy, and feelings of persecution in a million children are deeply reinforced, and damage their psychic capacities. They cannot muster sufficient of that creative power we all need to exert, to find life 'good' and exert and fulfil ourselves.

They are often virtually made spiritually ill and disabled by a society which cruelly forces them into a situation in which they cannot but be overcome by envy, and find their creative capacities wither.

But on the other hand the fostering of creativity—in imaginative work, art, dancing, drama, crafts, even in animal and garden husbandry —can alleviate this suffering. In all children, as I try to show in this book, at least above the I.Q. of 70, there is creative verbal capacity. There is probably creative capacity of one kind or another in less intelligent children. All children have remarkable creative capacities in paint, play, mime, even modelling and experiments with their material environments. But in this creative expression there is no quantitative distinction to be made between achievements. The idea, apparently being put forward in America, of measuring C.Q., or a creative quotient, is ludicrous, because creativity is essentially immeasurable—in quality, and in quantity. All impulses to measure creativity should be regarded with contempt as misguided and bogus. A child in a 'D' stream can produce a poem which, taking say the Oedipus theme, (see 'One day a man killed me' in *The Secret Places*) is a complete expression of a profound human myth—and there is no more to say about it, except that it is complete, beautiful, valuable and makes a pattern of an inward experience of life. It can in no way be measured by any external scale.

In terms of such considerations the 'backward' child can be made to feel his 'equality in disquality' with every other living creature. And in being praised for creative expression one is helping a child to find happiness in seeking the positive 'good object', and may actually be contributing directly to his balance and sanity. Creativity, Melanie Klein says, 'is the basis of inner resources and resilience which can be observed in people who, even after great adversity and mental pain, regain their peace of mind'. This relief obtained from creative exertion is experienced by all of us, in greater or less degree, from time to time.

The reader who studies the work of Rose (p. 117) will be able to see how both the creative work itself, and the encouragement of the creativity can enable a child to make courageous struggles against 'mental pain'. I would ask the reader to keep in mind whether this creative aspect of education is to be found in grammar school education, in

further education, at the university and elsewhere? There are signs
that it is not, and that education is becoming an aridly uncreative—even
anti-creative—force in our society.

No wonder, in the secondary modern school, that imaginative teaching methods are often attacked and resisted by some rationalisation
(such as that they are 'too untidy', 'too fancy', or 'too noisy'). Our
education tends to be governed by people trained by an uncreative
education. But because our teachers have been educated uncreatively,
and are sometimes envious of and hostile to creativity, pupils like Rose
may be unconsciously disliked even for their very potential creativity
both as persons and in their self-expression. A secondary modern
school girl's dress and attitudes may express great capacities for the
creativity—not least sexual creativity—by which she may overcome
her personal difficulties and find fulfilment. Yet it may be these very
things which bring down on her opprobrium, suspicion, punishment
and further rejection.

What is certain is that carefully cultivated habits of encouragement
and creative attitude work like charms with 'backward' children, and
I shall describe below several such approaches in practice and the reasons
why I suppose they work (see below, p. 204 ff.). But I make the general
points here to bring my reader to study these children's efforts with the
following observations in mind. First, there is no child of my random-
chosen 'C'-stream form who is not represented in the collection of
pieces of work. All the children produced interesting pieces of imaginative composition (except the deaf girl who was a different kind of
problem). *And they all saw the point of what they were doing.* Secondly, I
used no techniques which cannot be employed by a teacher who is
willing to make this approach to English teaching and is convinced
of the importance of it as a central discipline. I had some advantage, I
suppose, because I am a poet and writer and thus naturally consider writing
valuable. But the attitude can be conveyed just as well by a teacher who
loves books and writing himself, and who understands the human
mind's need for expression and contemplation through symbolism and
metaphor, through language and the other idioms of art and science.
Many teachers know what to do about creativity in children intuitively:
others, one hopes, will be sufficiently convinced by arguments in this
book, and others like it, to see that they must undertake this important
central work of imaginative training if they are to be *efficient* teachers.
And I hope those who train teachers will come to see that teachers need

to experience themselves the true creative disciplines before they can teach. But teachers practise their art in their own ways and what I say here about teaching English is, I hope, just as relevant to those who tackle the problem of the development of less able children through their own other methods. Teachers will, I hope, find most encouragement in my insistence that it is all an *art*, and only successful in that it is so. And that this art needs more respect, training, encouragement—and dare we say money?—than it sometimes gets from society or governments, even if we think of it in terms of creating an efficient society.

3

SPARKS FROM A DIFFERENT ELEMENT

A WARNING

In this section I discuss the development towards literacy of nineteen children in one 'C' stream class in a secondary modern school, child by child. This section is intended to convince readers of four main contentions. First, that so-called 'backward' children are not inferior beings, but are in fact sensitive, perceptive, and full of deep feelings, ambitions and capacities for making contributions to human life and culture.

Second, that the best way to make them literate, in the fullest sense, is by imaginative work; that this is well within the capacities of any teacher.

Third, that half the trouble with 'backward' children is that they feel rejected and despised by teachers, the school and society—and that the fact is, unhappily, that they are so despised.

Finally, that an important part of our work with them must be devoted to curing them of the effects of feelings of failure.

Before I embark on this section, I must, however, give a warning to the teacher reader.

For the purposes of this book, in order to establish my argument, and to convince readers of the above points, I make interpretations of pupils' pieces of writing. These are usually no more than the kind of interpretation one trains onself to make in literary criticism, but in some instances I go beyond the bounds of literary interpretation and make interpretations which are 'psychological'. In making these analyses I have no qualification, and do not wish to claim any truth for them. I make such interpretations only to try to indicate that 'something deep is here being expressed', though I have also consulted a child psychoanalyst about my interpretations. (The 'Psychiatrist's Notes' below are hers.)

There is a sense in which the psycho-analyst, like the poet and critic, works by intuition and a kind of art criticism, by the examination of metaphor, in the interpretation of dreams—and there can be many interpretations of the same dream. What matters is the unconscious art, the creative power, of the dream. What matters is the remarkable order some dreams have, the organising power of the human consciousness, and the beauty of its processes. We should regard children's revelations, then, with delight and gratitude, rather than in morbid fascination with the psychopathological states they may reveal. And we should recognise the power of their phantasy to give relief, to nourish, to give harmony, to gain a sense of significance and insight, and to be constructive.

Yet here and there I have sought to show the courage of the child's use of phantasy, in making its quest for psychic truth, seeking a deeper apprehension of the truth of the world. I have therefore had to say at times what kind of inward troubles I think it is symbolising, and so have had to do some interpretation of the psychic meaning. Such interpretations should be regarded by the reader with reserve, but as a clue to possible psychic myth-material he will find in his pupils' work.

The teacher needs to do something of this kind for himself—certainly to recognise that a child may well be symbolising some inward unconscious perplexity. And he may even find it illuminating to consider what kind of perplexity it may be. He must certainly realise that the phantasy is as important as psychic myth to the child.

But it would be very dangerous ever to base an action on such an interpretation, other than encouraging or praising a child for the beauty and skill of its work. *To interpret phantasy material to a child referring in direct terms to his family situation and inner impulses, as in psycho-analysis, could be dangerous and cruel in the hands of the untrained.*

I cannot speak too strongly against anything of the kind and would be much disturbed to think I had encouraged any such practice by this book. What we think we perceive of the inward life of a child must be as sacrosanct as what a priest learns in confession or a doctor in diagnosis, and our unqualified interpretations must be withheld from the child itself. That he would possibly be able to resist us is beside the point. To tinker with the mind is the greatest impertinence, and destructive of trust and of the context for the poetic function.

The reasons are not difficult to understand. The child works in phantasy directly from the unconscious to the conscious mind, but, of course, its deeper disturbances emerge under a heavy disguise—because to consider them directly would be too painful and even cataclysmic. The soul could not bear the truth unmasked without pain and distress. The disturbing apprehensions might have to be thurst away so forcibly from the mental pain they would cause that they could be 'split off' and thus cause serious disintegrations in the personality.

The child, in an atmosphere of trust, encouragement and sympathy, can bring out inward torments in symbolic form—the best instance in which to study this is that of Rose below. In school he may obtain relief, satisfaction—and literacy. His poetry will bring him joy and insight. In a clinical psycho-analytical situation such dreams, symbolic acts, pieces of play with toys, drawings and phantasy stories are deliberately interpreted back to the child—to uncover and remove barriers to the patient's self-fulfilment and full use of his potentialities. *But the immediate effect is one of deep anxiety, and disturbed behaviour:* unskilled interference could be disastrous. One only needs to read a case history or two to realise that such anxieties can only be dealt with by a highly skilled doctor, sometimes only with nursing, surgical aid or drugs. A doctor will only interpret in circumstances in which he can be reasonably sure that he will be able to 'follow through', with all the facilities of medical care at his disposal.

Of course, the expression in symbols and metaphor in the normal way can only do good, because of the organising cultural effect of art and imaginative expression, bringing relief and escape from isolation. The turmoil is expressed 'out there'—and the expected retribution or doom has not fallen! This alone brings peace. (My psychiatrist consultant confirms that the children found great relief in finding that all other children had their guilty secrets too.) There is no harm in discussing the content of children's art in terms of the phantasy, or even of real life. What I mean is, one can say, 'Where has your witch put her broomstick?' or, 'Surely if they found an old witch in a tower dead they'd tell somebody?' But what one must *never* say is, 'You see the witch is your Mummy and you're frightened she'll eat you, aren't you?' This is to tinker with work which even those fully qualified approach with awe, reverence and a deep regard for the mystery of the human mind. To be superficial in such matters would be a betrayal of our professional trust.

From the educational point of view, too, such impertinence would destroy the whole value of our work. Even if children protected themselves against it they would at once lose trust in us, in the context of our work and even in expression. We might deprive them of the regenerating poetic function itself. They might dry up entirely, and find themselves unable to use brush or pen for seeking insight and understanding. The complex of art by which children may gain self-possession in a world that often seems hostile or without succour might be broken. There could be no more relevant application for the maxim about 'a little knowledge'. We should stick to the art of teaching and the arts of expression within the limits of poetic function. There is plenty of scope there, without entering the realm of other disciplines we cannot fully understand.

Throughout this section of evidence I italicise odd, exciting, strange or stirring phrases where I find them among these children's pieces of work. These seem to me the places where, looked at as 'literature', their writing comes to life, and shows a progress towards literacy.

1. NIGEL THRUSH

(I.Q., as given in his primary school record, 77.)

Nigel Thrush was a rustic little boy, with a broad country accent. He was personally somewhat slow and sluggish but also cheerful, and not a disturbed child. He would produce mostly dull and repetitive work, pathetic in its lack of élan, as in this, for example, on *My Family*:

I have four in my Family Dad Mum and siter. My Dad works at Melton. My siter go to Tonbury. My Mum goes out some times. I go to Bridgebrook i go out some times on Tuesday night i go to Youth clob. On thursday nights I go bell ringing on Saturdays I go down to the farm. on sundays I go to church. I go to bed at 10 o clock I wakh TV at 5 o clock I live in a house. *The house is in the world.* I live at Boar Parva it is near Melton and Bridgebrook and Smallerden. The house is white it has stone up the frount it is the first from Bridgebrook and the sexeon from Smallerden. My Mum is at home She goes to the shop on fridays My Dad goes to work at Smallerden . . .

. . . and this is where I came in, the teacher will sigh. His life is that of the stagnant small village, and one may become oppressed with the sense of Nigel's being a stagnant small creature in it. The gay prospect of the Melton hills beyond the school windows was never more inviting than when one is ploughing through the vile hand-writing of one of Nigel's duller pages. But notice the sentence I have put in italics. Here, in Nigel's piece, is a clue to possible developments: *The house is in the world.* Even here there are metaphysical aspirations, and even a wry humour. Later these elements appear, in Nigel's more successful writing, more and more. But my italics draw attention to one aspect of this work—one has to train oneself to spot, and enjoy, the least small spunky spark as it evanescently appears in these children's work. And applaud.

Of course, with such a child, the influence of the mediocre tawdry fare of television becomes a dulling influence:

What I do when I get home from school.

On monday I sometimes go down the farm in the night I wach TV there is BBC and I.T.V. I like I.T.V. We call Anglia I.T.V. We have got Anglia like to wach cow Boys. On Tuesday I get off the bus and some times in the night I go to the Youth colbe.

I like to wach T.V. there is a lot of things on T.V. I wach it each night. . I thing tv is good but *people say it gives us squar iyes . . .*

Nigel's first attempts at creation therefore tend to be television-influenced:

The Murder Car.

1 night when it was dark about 12 oclock a man was nock down by a car. The body was found a 7 oclock in the morning. The name of the man who was kild was Jack Robbinson he has black hair brown eyes blue Jacket and blue Jeans. No one see the car. there had bean a lot of people nock down by a car so they cald it the murder car. The Police cam out to look for the car. The other cars were black so one of the other people said. The murder man has a black beard The next day one of the policemen were killd the next day they found the car over the Hill the was the man near it he was dead.

Then suddenly he produces a bright little lyric out of his adolescent romantic needs:

> I kissed a girl one night
> Here iyes were burning blue
> She said o do you love me
> Of course of course I do.

This was included in a class magazine and became very popular, giving rise to much teasing of Nigel whenever it was read—but not maliciously, because his classmates liked the sentiments. So did I. From this experience he went on to write with a little more excitement about one of his special interests, mentioned above, bell-ringing. Even in such a dull little village boy one finds aspects of the variety of human enterprise—and so when I pass Smallerden church at bell-ringing time I know that Nigel, with his bird-like smile, is in the belfry hanging on his sally:

Bell Ringing.

When you start Bell Ringing you haveto ring a bell be for you can do anything als. It takes a lot to ring a bell on the rope there is a sally. ON the bell there is a weel. the weel has the rope on it some sally are green and the other are red white and blue. When you can ring. You have to ring rouns that is when you go 123456 when you can don that. You rings like this. These are the names of them plain Hunt, Plain Bob, Grandsire Doubles. Grandsire Triples it takes a long time to ring them. I have been ringing a long time we go to Smallerden and Oakwell and Guildwell we will we going to Smallerden this Thursday I ring 1 2 and 3 but not 4 5 and 6 I like going bell ringing, some time the bell brakes And the rope goes up and if *you are not carfull you will go up with it,* we start at 7.30 and end at 9.0clock Me and my dad bike to Melton.

Nigel is at his best with his feet well on the ground—writing accounts of walks in the fields, or on how to look after pigs. One must not forget how much imagination is needed even to write of 'practical' subjects. But with his feet still on the ground Nigel can tell phantasy stories, too, though these, again, often draw on television or film material. Here, for instance, is the tale of some comic incident derived from a mass-medium source: yet he makes it his own:

THE SICK SOW OF THE ARMY COURT

One day Sergent S. M. Bullimore told Hut 29 to clean Cynthia pig sty out. When Hut 29 got there they had to go and get some gass marsks because the smell was to strong When S M Bullimore came to the pig sty the pig was laid out on the foor when they came back S. M. Bullimore said wat have you been doing to my sow we have not done anything we had to go and get some gass marsks because the smell was to strong that is only the soap wat I wosh it with prasp [perhaps] he et some soap *Flogger said shall I go and get the vet get back in the line be for I put you on charge Flogger said under is breath 'go and have a poney run' what did you say o nothing sir* go and get some wiskey okay sir put some soap in it Flogger said Oswald OK said Flogger Flogger went off a little while after he came with a large soape-wiskey he cave it to S. M. Bullimore Then he cave it to the pig A little while after the pig go up and there beside here were six little pigs S M Bullimore said that made here better that was not me that was the sope you are on charge wat did you give here I cave her some wiskey and sope you cave her that no I knver I sir you did thats one thing sir It has made her better.

Once the imagination begins to function in a dull little boy like Nigel Thrush it takes this mad, wry comic form. I realise now that I missed two opportunities here—one of reading Nigel's story aloud, and making more full use of its dramatic qualities, a development not found in his writing previously. The other opportunity was that of using this piece as an exercise for all of them to tackle, in the punctuation of direct speech. By these two exercises we could have worked as a class to revise Nigel's piece, making it more logical and orderly and so more effectively comic. The pride of seeing his work the subject of such collaboration would also have helped his writing to become more fluent. There is even an illustration to this *Comic Cuts*-style pig story—with a well-drawn pig's head with floppy ears, and a neat brick wall.

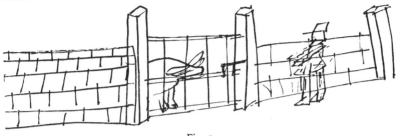

Fig. 1

A personal form and character is coming into Nigel's work. On the one hand he can write with more effective realism about the care of pigs.

Pigs
When young up to being kild for bacon

When they are young you have to wate 3 days then you can injeck them for pneumonia diseases you have mack shore they have drye straw when you clean them out you should not leave a falk in with them because the mother might nock it down and the little pigs might stab them souve we give the worme pouder that is when they get the worme this will stop them from going thin you should box a little place off so only the little pigs can get in it that is so they can ge out of the way of there mother some people put a light in with theme to geep them warm you have to make shore that mother has a lot of milk. If she as not got a nougth milk you will have to feed them on a bottle when they came eat a little bit you can get them some little nuts of fating they can eate some meal when they get a little biger we give them some fating food called Nomber 2 whe you wean that is take them from their mother you have got to see if they fight if there is any little wones fighting when they and bing (when they are big) you have to see about waying (weighing) when they have been waid and reddy to go away to be kild.

And on the other hand his phantasy is loosening up: there are mad little rhymes, too, here and there in his book.

Billy Bunter was to large
So they sent for Im in charge
Im in charge was to thin
So they sent fro Rin Tin Tin
Rin Tin Tin heart is poor
So they sent for Barbra Moore
Barbra Moore was having dinner

> So the sent for Yule Brinner
> Yule Brinner sang to high
> Then they went to space in the sky

His work becomes at once more childish, but also more interesting:

> My heart is full of sadness
> My heart is full of joy
> It might be my wife
> Or it might be Helen of Toy

The teacher of the average 'A' and 'B' stream child will perhaps feel that these efforts are pathetically below those of his ordinary pupils. But I suffer in discussing the work of these pupils from the eager need that every teacher of the backward child has—to find something even a little out of the ordinary, transcending the dull. And for dull little Nigel to write about 'Helen of Toy' makes one's heart glad, even for such a small mercy. But by now—in his third exercise book of the year—Nigel is writing reasonably fluently. He writes now a semi-imaginative piece about Motor-cycle Racing: here the violence and death are explored in phantasy in a lively way, as a small boy needs to explore them:

One Saturday I though I would go to the Races at London I went on my Royl Enfield they can go quite farst this was a Royl Enfield Consulatoin there were some Royl Enfield Racing there as well I saw a Royl Enfield come first it was like mine.

(This is an obvious process of identifying himself in phantasy with men, and with a man's potency, of which the motor-cycle is a symbol.)

there were the new Japannese Hondor they are very farst and geting quite popular in England I saw one man come off he was on a B.S.A. One man had to go in Hospital because he broke is lege a nouther man hearte is arm in a sidecar race I dont thing it was much I sow a side car turne right over the side care man was alrigh. but the motor bike Rider was thrown into the crowd I dont no what hapend to him he was heart quite bad.

Here the exploration of the fear of being hurt, and of death, such as there is in all of us, and the exploration of his inward aggression, produce a vivid piece of writing: notice the touches here in what follows—the hat being blown down the track, and the breaking away of the side-car from the motor-cycle. Here is a dull boy using English very well, graphically, and with economy. Though he can't spell or punctuate well, the reader may notice how many words he does take the trouble to get right, such as 'first', 'popular', 'because', 'quite', and other commonly troublesome spellings.

the sidecar broke off the moter bike and spund down the track for 7 yards then hit a man who was on the corner and killed him his hat was blowing down the track the moter bike caugh fire and blow up the petal went all over the track but they sone put it out by sand there was some oil got on the track as well it made it very slippery They were quite a few people there because it was a nice dry day The fianl race was on there were 2 Royl Enfield 3 Japanese Hondor 1 B.S.A. 3 Triumh they were on the starting line Bang there off one BSA is still on the starting line the rest are round the bend I can see one man off he is on a trumh I think a Japanese Hondor is in the lead I think he is go to lead his one [i.e. he's won] by 3 yards and a Royl Enfield 2 and a Hondor 3.

The End

Here the phantasy becomes so captivating that Nigel changes tense and is actually *there*—giving a wireless commentary on the race he is watching. This story has an illustration too: a Japanese Honda, the name Nigel is so proud of using.

The final reward from Nigel is a piece of writing about a country walk: on this kind of work, requiring the country boy's observation, he was excellent. These are merely a few phrases in the two and a half pages of foolscap writing which show that he has had his eyes opened by imaginative writing, and that with this goes an enhanced fluency, despite his occasional lapses into Mum's duller phrases—'*quite nice*' and such.

we went over the football field it was *quite wet and soon made my toes cold* . . . the grass was quite long now *it shon with the dew on it* . . . a field ploud next to it I think it was don yesterday . . . on the other side was an hedge it had a lot of thorns in it . . . *they hade cleand the river and made it very wide fore the ducks there were some potato in the water* . . . *there were some brussels men sitting in the parth way round a fire we had to go on to a ploud field to get round them this made my shoes hevey* . . . this was quite muddy some boys did not think much to it nor did I but we still went . . . *the dew on the brussels leaves made them look (like) pirls* . . . Mr. Holbrook went over the brook first some were boys going round but only one went after all the rest went over the tree Gerald nealy went in one foot toch the water then we went across the new pice of grass into school we went and cleand our shoes with paper then the bell went for brack . . .

Never much more than pedestrian, but at least a simple fluency in which there are very occasional 'pirls'.

2. JOAN STALL

(I.Q. 76. Accompanied on her primary school record with the phrase, 'Has no originality or imagination'.)

In answer to the phrase of condemnation let us quote from Joan's examination paper at the end of her first school year with me:

> *A poem*
> *A little yellow bird sat on my window sill*
> *He hop and poped about*
> *He wisheld he cherped.*
> *I trid to chach my little yellow brid*
> *but he flew in to the golden yellow sun,*
> *O how I wish that was my yellow brid.*

Do we not hear William Blake faintly in the background?

How inefficient of the primary school, to suppose that Joan has 'no imagination'! This is not the way the 'summer fruits' may come from that civilising process called education. And add to the cold comment from the primary school the fact that Joan is plain, wears glasses, is physically behind her sisters, and very timid, then you have a clue to the yearning for the little yellow bird that vanishes into the sun. Is it womanhood she yearns for? Joan's work is full of interminable dialogue by which she seeks to contemplate maturity in terms of adult difficulties, adult quarrels, adult attempts to find whether one is 'wanted' or not:

ANN   That's what you think
JOHN   That's what I no. (know)
JEAN   the longer you stay here talking we carn't get on with you here
DENNIS   Come on John I no when were not whanted
JEAN   Yes your not whated here
JOHN   Good by
ANN   I knew that would happen . . .

Joan became, as it were, the Ivy Compton-Burnett of the class: one follows endless impassioned exchanges in her writing, but only gradually could one build up a conception of what it was all about. It was about Joan's own uncertainties in dealing with other people, and her desire to grow up sufficiently to be able to deal with things in a grown-up way.

Her work gives a clue as to how it may be possible to break away from the usual dull level of 'composition' on 'subjects'. Her best work is prompted by her experience (with my colleague Geoffrey Hawkes) in free drama: this work enabled her to exercise her imagination often in quite remarkable ways for such a limited girl—and on matters which were profoundly valuable to her. Her 'plays' went on for pages. They were rambling, and episodic, without structure. But when I made tape recordings of them there were moments of real dramatic excitement which sprang from a child's fear of parental conflict, of more mature relationships, and of the need to deal with others when one could no longer rely, as a child, on parental backing.

At first Joan's compositions were unexciting. On apples, for instance, she wrote:

> Apple red and green start are bright★
> The apple trees are tall
> The leavs are small
> The apple fall in Aount [autumn] time

When yow get to the corres inside the corres are pips yow thorght the corres on the fire to brun then. the boys in our village go in the orcher and clim the trees and pinch then all then they run away with then. *then the eyewigs fall out in there pocket* the apple are sweet. the trees are fall of apple. some of then are cookers. *the apples are so gay haing on the trees. with the sun on then. no wonder the boys like pinch then*

Even this is not just pedestrian—the 'eyewigs' and 'the apples are so gay' suggest something penetrating even through Joan's thick pebble glasses. She has ambitions:

What I am going to do when I leave school
When I leave I whant to be a hair dreser in Melton or Tonbury. or I whant to work in a shop. I do not whont to get marryid till I am twentone. When I have children I am going to leave work and the husbon has got to like children and tack them out. I whant twins. and I whant four bridesmaids. I whont to live in a bungalow. for my holiday I would like to go to butlins, for a hunemoon I like to go to Scotland.

This was obviously discussed with her desk-neighbour Judith Ward—but has individuality. Joan, however, does not yield a reward for every stimulus. A piece of sculpture produces only this:

On our table there is a sculptor modal this was made by Mrs Chalmers This

★ 'Apples are red and green, stars are bright'?

is Just like a real think. this is a modal of a boy it is staning on a block wood This was malod in clay not a whole molad Just the Head.

A teacher without determination might take such a failure as evidence that 'free writing' does not work, or that he wasn't gifted enough to bring it off. The answer is but more persistence, more encouragement, and hope. Not very much later Joan wrote as follows about a reproduction of Stanley Spencer's painting *Swan Upping at Cookham*. Here the unconscious sexual symbolism of the swan (cf. the legend of Leda), the activity of the figures, the wrestling forms, and the beauty of the picture bring out some deeper and more interesting material: of course, when she first becomes excited in her expression her spelling becomes worse for a time:

Swan upping

When they do this kind of think they need comer [calmer] waters. they have to handle them very caresll [carefully] They use small Boats *peolpe think this is very corller [cruel] to cash [catch] them and put stamp on there wings*, in this picture there is a man carring on [one] out of the Boat *its Wing are tied so that it can not brick [break] the mans arms, the swan are dellitent think* [swans are delicate things]

Here is a moment when the teacher can feel a leap of gladness, for despite the pathetic spelling—which is, in general, probably due to emotional disturbances, worsened by the attitude of the primary school to Joan as 'unimaginative and unoriginal'—Joan here gives us delightful phrases. She is writing, unconsciously, about the cruelty, violence and delicacy she senses in human love—as part of the nature of creative life, as in birds—'they need calmer waters', 'they have to handle them very carefully', 'people think this is very cruel', 'its wings are tied so that it cannot break the man's arms', 'the swans are delicate things'. She tries to use 'difficult' words—'delicate', 'carefully'.

Later one gets further glimpses of her interest in this picture: she herself yearns for kindness because she says elsewhere: 'I think the children will be kind to the animal, the animal need kindness . . .'

A little later she reveals perhaps a lack of love and kindness at home, at times:

Pome

one day the sun was out and up the stairs I went.
My mother in a temper, I spent my day in bed.
for fear of my mother I darnt go near.
For fear I dident get to see the sun,

Thus Joan begins to enter into deep imaginative experiences, and can write thus of the dead child in John Crowe Ransom's *Bells For John Whiteside's Daughter:*

> There she lays
> So quitely there
> Waiting for the day
> People weeping waiting
> Sighing all the days
> There hearts are weeping
> Crying so
> *Hearts beting so raperly* [rapidly]

The freeing of emotion in a child with such an ungainly sensibility, together with the experience of free drama, can eventually yield a remarkable fluency—to a degree one would hardly believe when one started work with her.

Here are some moments from her dialogue stories:

LINDA   I not going out tonight with him, I don't want to see him again.
MARRY   Linda stop it and come out hear at once.
LINDA   You can't mack me.
JOHN   What wong. [What's wrong?]
MARRY   I told her that you were thaing [taking] me owt at half past 12 to night
JOHN   You what.
MARRY   Well I had to tell her
JOHN   *Yes I suppose you did well it not her falt. its my falt for traing* [trying] *to be a pig.*
MARRY   *mine too, still you got the job of ching* [choosing] *her or me,*
JOHN   *I think I had bet go home and think it out*
LINDA   *theres nothing to think out I am through with you for good.*
JOHN   *Linda wait*
LINDA   *What the good of waiting for you is it.*

Linda slander the door in his face.

Joan's quarrels always have a most convincing rhythm in the speech: even if she is only remembering family quarrels, this is surely what the novelist does, in half-memorising, half-realising, selected aspects of life's experiences? Here is one from another story. I hope the reader will take in the quality of *life* in the writing—despite the hopeless spelling, and the poor punctuation. Ignore these mere graphic aspects, and look at what Joan is doing—her mind is working quickly and vividly, holding in suspension a complex of human relationships, which she is putting into verbal form. Here is a different kind of memory at work from that required by examinable education. This accomplishment is a considerable one, as anyone knows who has tried to write a play or novel: Joan's dialogue has much more reality, rhythm of life, than that of many modern plays:

JOHN *hello Jean carnt we tallk it over and come to some disson (decision)*
JEAN *Talk about what for instead (instance)*
JOHN *Well make it up.*
JEAN *I am sorry John. theres nothing to make up.*
JOHN *What do you mean; There on one (no-one) eles us is there.*
JEAN *Well what if there us its got nothing to do with you*
JOHN *look I am only trining (trying) to be nice*
JEAN *Well, don't*
JOHN *all right them I won't be nice, it looks like I got to be rought with you*
JEAN *if you lay a hand on me I will scem (scream)*
JOHN *do you think that scards (scares) me*
JEAN *well I wornd (warned) yew didn't I*
JOHN *I don't care what yow said. yow just whant to hert me*
JEAN *no I don't you think you can hert me well yow rong*
JOHN *I don't want to think of it*
JEAN *Well perhaps yow better not see me eney more*
JOHN *Don't be silly I want to see yow to night*
JEAN *I don't no about that*
JOHN *I see yow at 6 o, clock*
JEAN *well all right then*
JOHN *Your a doll*
JEAN *I dont no about that*
JOHN *Well I do*
JEAN *goodby see you to night*

What seems to me remarkable about these pieces is that, although one sees in the writing elements from television and film drama, there are also echoes direct from parental rows, and Joan can thus here explore intuitively the strange compulsion there is in cruelty between partners, the habit-formed sexual cruelty that makes lovers want to 'make up' even though they have just been bitterly unpleasant to one another— so unpleasant that, were the sexual attraction not strong, they would separate for good. At Joan's level this fiction is a valuable piece of imaginative contemplation of emotional reality. She has caught something of the 'felt life' of lovers' conversation such as, say, George Eliot catches as between Grandcourt and Mrs. Glasher in *Daniel Deronda* (Chapter XXX).

The civilising value of imaginative writing for such a child is obviously great, because she is able to contemplate over and over again possible events in her adolescent emotional life—the roots of her contemplation being in an unconscious awareness of underlying psychic needs. Here is Joan's final examination paper, in which she chose to write on the subject *They Ran Away to Get Married*: her writing is neater than before, her spelling has improved, and her literacy is good. I am sure she would never have overcome her myopic nervous scrawl, her disturbed spelling, and her general illiteracy—no doubt deeply implanted by the attitude of her primary school that she had 'no originality or imagination'—had she not written several thousand words about such imaginary episodes:

charickter

There parents

David and Jill

It all started with a row with there parents,

JILL	*I am fed up with yow telling me how to go out with I am not a two year old I can make up my own mind without arsking you what to do*
PARENTS	*that will be enough from yow my girl or els your find your self in bed, I just had engouh of you my girl,*
JILL	Well I am going to pack my bag and move out.
PARENTS	If you move out your never come in this house again.
JILL	Well thats good engouh for me, I be out in an hour.
PARENTS	*When you get out you can stay out*
JILL	thats good.
	Jill ran up stairs to pack a case she came down, put on her coat and went out of the front door.
PARENTS	She not coming back in this house what ever happends.
	Jill went to her boyfrends house, she rang the door bell David opend the door.
DAVID	What are you doing hear? I was just coming round to your house to see if you could put me up for the night, I have had a row with my parents. They told me to get out.
JILL	Show has (so have) my parents.
DAVID	Lets go and get married, thats if you whont to married.
JILL	Of course I do.

59

DAVID   Well lets go and get married then we can get a flat or somethink
         Well they got married and got a house.
         They live happly ever after.

                              The End.

Beneath this is a 'letter':

                              5, Elmden Road
                              Nr Melton
                              21 November
Dear France,
         I thought I had better write to you telling yow what we do in
English with Mr. Holbrook, well we do a lot of writing such as story and
letter, so that it helps when we leave school. It helps speak properly when
we leave school.

                              Love Joan.

Joan has a few more months at school: her letter is as much as
anyone could ever hope for from such a limited child. Without the
bulk imaginative work she would not have been able to write such a
reasonably clear letter. Although she omits the name of her village in
the address, a bad fault, the whole is quite well set out, and conveys a
message reasonably clearly. And while her story at the explicit level is
improbable phantasy, it represents a valuable intuitive consideration of 'what life is like'. In her story Joan is exploring her needs,
which she is beginning to feel, to make her way towards independence
and marriage ('if you whont to married . . . Of course I do'), and
to leave home; leaving home has such fears for a child. And a child
needs to prepare itself in phantasy, before it becomes possible for the
adolescent to begin to cast away into the waters of independent
responsibility. Joan's arguments, over which she takes great creative
care, are her exploration of mature personal relationships. The imaginative content of her dialogues shows true literacy. Confidence in this
gradually improved her graphical literacy* a little, but the barriers to
this becoming fully developed were partly emotional, and partly
implanted by bad teaching in her primary school, and her disparagement there, just at the time when she was developing her sense of

---

* I shall use the phrase 'graphical literacy' to distinguish mere matters of setting words out on the
paper, punctuation, spelling, and indicating where sentences end and begin, from the deeper
aspects of literacy—the capacity to express experience in words. I suppose I could say typogra-
phical or calligraphical—what I mean is the mere mechanics of setting out words and punctuation
symbols on papers.

the shapes and patterns of words. It is worth looking, however, at the number of words she bravely attempts and spells correctly in the passages above.

✻   ✻   ✻

PSYCHIATRIST'S NOTE

Though it is clear that 'Joan Stall' benefits from the English work here described, I would be doubtful about ascribing her low I.Q. solely to neurotic disturbance. I think she does show a neurotic preoccupation with aggression and its consequences, because of her recurrent concern with quarrels and making them up. Because of this preoccupation her personality is perhaps intimidated—that is, she has not come to terms with her own aggression, included it in her potentialities. The primary school record might have spoken something rather nearer the truth had it said 'dare not have originality or imagination'.

AUTHOR'S NOTE. In some children the inhibition of learning seems to be associated with unconscious anxiety about the meaning of such activities as expression itself—it is 'forbidden' as a form of aggression. Such work as Joan's here in inventing quarrels, in a situation in which she is encouraged to feel this is 'alright', is thus a form of therapy, as well as teaching English.

3. GEORGE GREEN

My experience of George Green was one of my life's most remarkable and gratifying passages. His I.Q. is given in his primary school record as 77, but this, I am sure, only reveals the relative uselessness of intelligence tests. George was personally charming, agreeable, and placid. He came to school only when he pleased, and when he was not at school I sometimes met him walking on my afternoons off. On such occasions he would come up to my wife and myself and talk pleasantly in a friendly way. He had no need to be aggressive or overdependent, or to try to break up a lesson. He had brown, calm eyes, friendly and innocent, like a calf's, perhaps, and he had much of the frolicsome trustfulness of the young animal. He enjoyed *being friendly* most of all, and though he was as obviously sex-conscious as the other boys he had the least furtive itch and anxious obscenity about him. His tendency was always to be helpful, and to bring you information about the world that was exciting and new, like an infant.

Yet there was no doubt that George was by far the least intelligent child in the class, by any standard of measurement of intellectual ability. And he was the least literate. He could not read more than one or two words such as 'at' and 'the' when we began work, and could write hardly at all. There was no possibility of training George to write, say, an adequate letter before he left school, even if he came to school regularly, even if I spent most of my time with him alone.

But before my work with him was finished George had written three or four pieces which had become part of the class culture, as pieces in class magazines, used as reading books. And instead of telling me, as they did at the beginning, 'It's no use asking 'im, sir, 'e can't read, can ye' George?', they often asked, 'Can I read George's piece?' or 'Get George to read 'is bit, Sir'. If I had stayed with 4C I would have used one of George's pieces for choral work, with drums—had we had any drums—so effective is its rhythm and so lively its élan (see *The Sick Sow*, below).

But certainly from his experience of writing and reading with me George Green not only came to astonish himself by writing as much as a whole side of foolscap, and reading a whole paragraph of prose time and time again, but gained from this work a degree of relief and self-respect obtainable for him in few other ways. Certainly he came to be able to converse better, and even to give a talk, and act. He was the kind of boy for whom tape-recorder work is a great help.

Here we are at the minimum capacity of literate effort, and so I will in this note on George be able to quote virtually every word he wrote. We may also consider the psychic value of his work, by examining it, as we examine literature, for its qualities of rhythm, imagery, and texture.

I confess I was baffled by George at first. We began work on the story *The Blind Date*, a joint project of which I give an account below (p. 212 ff.). This is how George copied my initial synopsis from the board:

A stors
The BlinD Date
People

Rex harrison work at visor television factoy
Jean smith aiso wors at nsor
Audrey watston wonrs at the gnenhouen in Melton.

It was obvious from this that some words meant nothing at all to George, so that he merely copied the shape of the writing, more or less accurately, as with *greenhouse*, and even with *story* and *works*. It took three weeks to get George as far as writing this contribution to the story:

Jean said to Audrey has a sweet and Audrey said to Jean we are This Rex is is exited and Jean and Rex wetn two the house of He mouthr and Rex said to Jean is it my house and Jean sald to Rex it is a nis

This represents perhaps some four hours work. But it took its place in the composite story which I had duplicated—and George read his piece, aloud, when we came to it, with only a little prompting. (See p. 224.) He then wrote a story of his own. Even in his short strange pieces he manages to include a sense of danger and incidents of violence: yet George did not seem a deeply disturbed child. (He was helped here with spelling—he was encouraged, as they all were, to ask to have unfamiliar words written on the board.):

The sneking gang are dangerous and a tedeboy went in the shop and the sneking gang went two the shop wated for the tedeboy and the tedeboy kom out of the shop and hit a old man out sild of the shop and the sneking gang got the Tedeboy and three of sneaking gang the tedeboy . . .

But here inspiration gave out. George's rhythmical style derives from the fact that having put down a phrase, name, or title, he repeats it as often as possible. His ability to make the shape of a word is so limited that he organises his tales so that a well-established phrase repeats itself on nearly every line. This suggests a deep anxiety in relation to his writing, which he allays by stepping from known phrase to known phrase, taking comfort from the knowledge that at least one phrase can be properly written. The style also, I think, may derive from his long experience of work at the primary school and perhaps in remedial work in the secondary school on repetitive early readers. There would be no point, of course, in trying to break this habit, but to make it a literary advantage, by stressing it in reading as a rhythm. As will be seen in George's later efforts, this can be exciting, as part of the style.

George's most triumphant story was the culmination of a number of preparatory exercises. The special conditions of the school examination provided a discipline by which George was able to write a whole side of foolscap. It happened that I had a week in bed with influenza just afterwards, and so had time to decipher George's tale. In doing so I found that not only was it marvellously rhythmical, and well-organised as a piece of writing, but it seemed to have a deep meaning, in terms of unconscious phantasy. Here is the story:

The Sick Sow.

Won day The Sow was sick and the old frm went four the vethn and the old sow whdn't not hethy an fanit and the old frm sidn to vethn the old sow is on hethy so the vethn sidn to the frmh I will kumh and see. the lod sick sow sidn the vethn and the frmh went two see the lod sick sow and the vethn and the frmh see lod fat sick sow sidn the frmh and went at the frm and not the frmh ouht the big fat sick sow went and ladh down the frmh went two with the big fat sick sow and saw behism and the frmh. went in he house and he sat down and he bav he and sick sow went two ladh down and the vethn went and the vent see wat is ron wis and the sick sow went to seph and the vethn went two the frmh house and sick sow the vethn to the framh and the vethn sidn two the old big fat sick sow is a seph and the sick sow not the vethn and frmh run and run up sechrus and the sick sow went to the pigs house and ladh down and went seph and the frmh hot vethn and went bakh to Melton and frmh weth to see see sick sow and he ruth humit and sick old sow wok up and old sow is beth—the And

64

Here it is as translated:

The Sick Sow

One day the sow was sick, and the old farmer went for the vet. The old sow wasn't healthy and fainted. The old farmer said to the vet, 'The old sow is unhealthy'. So the vet said to the farmer, 'I'll come and see the old sick sow'.

The farmer went to see to the old sick sow, and the vet came to the farm. 'See the old fat sick sow', said the farmer. But she went for the farmer and knocked him out. Then the big fat sick sow went and lay down.

The farmer went with the big fat sick sow and then he saw he was bleeding.

He went into the house, sat down, and bathed himself. And the sick sow lay down.

The vet went to the sow to see what was wrong with her. The sick sow went to sleep.

The vet went to the farmhouse and the sick sow got up and followed him. The vet said, 'The old big fat sick sow is asleep.' But the sick sow knocked the vet over, and the farmer ran and ran upstairs. Then the sick sow went back to the pigs' house and lay down and went to sleep.

The farmer took the vet back to Melton. Then when he got back he went to see the sick sow and threw something. And the sick old sow woke up—and the old sow is better.

The end.

We may note where George makes his boldest efforts at spelling unfamiliar words—'not hethy', 'belhism', 'run up sechrus', 'ruth humit'. All his stories are about violence, and here the sow knocks the farmer over and wounds him, then later attacks the veterinary surgeon, while the farmer runs upstairs. The words George makes a special effort to tackle here are 'unhealthy', 'bleeding', 'run upstairs', 'threw something'; We have a glimpse of a family background rather like that of T. F. Powys's Mr. Tasker—where a sleeping sick animal would be woken up by 'throwing something'. A sow is a creature which gives birth, and I chose this subject with this in mind. The fat old sick sow is possibly George's mother, at the level of unconscious symbolism.* The violence may be that between mother and father of which the child is unconsciously aware (i.e. perhaps sexual relations conceived of as violence, sometimes confirmed, apparently, by actual violence in family quarrels). And the violence, too, which the infant George has at times unconsciously wanted to exert ferociously on his mother and father, and for which he fears retribution. Perhaps George identifies

---

* See possible evidence for this below, p. 72.

with the farmer who 'runs upstairs'—something a child is likely to do, rather than a farmer.

Some such unconscious material is here, and the underlying unconscious symbolism explains why the rest of the class find such violence as George's comic. The obsession with violence may be related to the way in which George's difficulties about spelling (*sidn* for *said*, *lod* for *old*, *ladh* for *laid*, *belhism* for *bleeding*, *ruth* for *thru* (i.e. *threw*), *ron wis* for *wrong with*) enact the back-wards to front-wardness of his attitudes to life, or a kind of camouflage over his perceptions. For while George seems not to be a disturbed child, his chief problem is that of amiably 'not being able to start'—his books are a sequence of half-begun, unfinished pieces. When I first taught him he did not consider himself able to do any of the things the others could do. Interestingly enough the strict formality of the examination room produces his freest and most fluent piece of work.

What I have said in the previous paragraph is not offered as psychoanalytical, but as a search, through literary analysis, for some unconscious psychic pressure under the surface. These aspects of his writing are worth taking note of, even if we admit that to interpret his phantasies to ourselves properly we would need to know a great deal more about George, and that there must be other possible interpretations. Yet we may accept that the phantasy is a symbolisation of something of this kind, and it helps us to help him if we are aware of it, as we can be from our own reading and analysis of poetry. And this is confirmed by other evidence. Later George told the Head, 'That old pig I wrote about, sir—she won't bother no one no more. She got out and got in front of a train. She's six foot down.' The humanisation confirms George's more than casual interest in the family sow, and the train story, which we were unable to confirm, may yet be a further symbolisation of destructive impulses. It is not just a funny story, but an important contest with strong unconscious feelings. It is as important to George as that—and as valuable in overcoming possible unconscious fears, by dramatised comedy.

This story was the culmination of a sequence of stories by George, in which there were always trouble-makers who want knives, to make trouble with. They seek to hit people, sometimes women, over the head, sometimes men 'in the house of love'. Young boys are murdered, and run away—authority is always clashing with the protagonists. Such material is familiar in all small boys' work, but here there is so little else, and we see with bare starkness the Oedipus material and unconscious conflicts within him which obsess George. Yet because he is encouraged to write about these disturbing things, *he does write*, and covers page after page with his scrawl—which is not altogether unreadable. In the end he is even able to write an almost passable letter, and this I feel sure is as far as anyone could ever get with George in the secondary school, given his writing ability when he left primary school. The free expression of unconscious material as fiction both helped George with the self-respect he needed at incipient adolescence, and also helped him to begin to write effectively. He could certainly in the end read a passage of his own into a tape recorder, read paragraphs of the class magazine, answer questions at an interview, and give a short talk on 'what I did on Saturday'—all, I am sure, accomplished to an extent that would never have been possible had he always been allowed to give in to the implications of the attitude, 'It's no use asking 'im, sir, 'e can't read nuffing, can ye' George?' or kept at formal work.

Perhaps the clearest confirmation of George's preoccupation with unconscious themes of an Oedipus kind came one day when the children were copying poems they liked from *The Poet's Tongue*. George laboured his way through the whole of this passage from the *Mumming Play*: the beheading:

> Good people all, I pray you now behold
> Our old Fool's bracelet is not made of gold
> But it is made of iron and good steel
> And unto death we'll make this old Fool yield.

FOOL: I pray, forbear, my children small
> For as I am lost as parent to you all,
> O let me live a while your sport for to advance
> That I may rise again and with you have a dance.

> *They sing*
> Now, old father, that you know our will
> That for your estate we do your body kill
> Soon after death the bell for your shall toll,
> And wish the Lord he may receive your soul

THEN the fool falls down, and the dancers with their swords in their hand, sings the following song.

> Good people all you see what we have don
> We have cut down ous father like ge evening son
> Ane here he lies all in his purple gore
> And we are afraid he never will dance more

I copied this from George's book, and it is perhaps interesting to see that he copies it with great care, even correcting the spelling of 'receive', but makes mistakes, indicatively, at the awful moment when the 'sons' confess what they have 'don'—'cut down ous father like ge evening son'. There is little doubt why George chose this passage, having spotted the words 'father', 'kill', I dare say, unconsciously.

Here are George's stories:

NOVEMBER 11 1960

The sneaking went to the Pub and a pint of brown and went out of the Pub and went round the corner to the shop and see Teddoy starte troefle [trouble] and the sneaking went the teddoy and the Teddoy running up and down the streets and the sneaking went rownd the corner to see the Teddoy on the . .

15 NOVEMBER 1960

The Redex*
Jack O'Malley: Boss George Green 2 Head John Young 2 head went two the pictyres and hit the maneger and he went down the stars and hit a women and he fainted We home. The end of the story.

15 NOVEMBER

THE POEM OF THE OLD women
My old man a he   Old women Hurbured she

29 NOVEMBER 1960

I am a man 6 ft tall he laded in the kitching ft in the hall
[i.e. a poem about his growth to manhood, an 'Alice' poem:

I am a man six foot tall,
I landed in the kitchen with my feet in the hall.]

The School.

The school in the meadoy a school the road a man the cornfield where daffodill do grow.

This sequence shows how patient the teacher of the low stream child has to be—allowing fragments of nonsense, glimpses of perception, false starts, failures, untidiness. Then comes a small spark, which becomes afterwards one piece in the class magazine which George reads

* George is always forming gangs with his friends to exert their strength against the world—here it is the 'Red X', probably something from Television.

again and again with pride—justly, for it has a stirring power derived
from its unconscious meaning:

The House of Love

The man is a policeman and he to the house of house love and he went in a
man crowsed the hed and the policeman went down on the floor and house
of love wos haunted and the police went to the haunted house of love and
police got the man in house of love the end

In the class magazine this became:

The House of Love

*The man was a policeman and he went to the house of love. A man hit him across
the head and the policeman went down on the floor. The house of love was haunted
and the police went to the haunted house of love. And the police got the man in the
house of love. The end.*

I think some of the boys thought George was writing about a house of
ill repute. I never discussed the meaning—accepting it merely that the
house of love *is* haunted—in our experience of love and the sexual we
receive time after time blows from the unseen regions of our unconscious anxieties and fears. The man who hits authority or the father-
policeman across the head is the same ghost that D. H. Lawrence's
Mellors feels with the 'grasping white hands in the air'—the ghost
of unexorcisable neurotic fears which inhabit all our houses of love.
George Green spoke here better than he knew.

In adolescent boys' work the disturbing feelings of sexual impulse,
aggressive needs to exert themselves as men, fears about potency, and
guilt, often take the form of phantasies about knife attacks, piercing
and cutting. George here explores the need to restrain these impulses,
which are 'teddyboy'—i.e. bad.

The teddyboys are a Big haded and Police wat to get a grip of the Taddyboys
and see a Bat (?about) the kniffe of the shap at the kiffe and two see the shop
keeper and to tell the shop keeper not two not to give the teddyboys kiffe.
They are two dangers and the murdered and we are try to stop.

—the passage in its rambling way says 'I am trying to control my more
troubling impulses'—it is more important that we should see this, in
George's writing as 'literature', than that we should feel the ground
opening under our professional feet because he makes such a hash
of spelling and punctuation. Of course, one puts before George

continually the right spelling and punctuation. Luckily his next piece was one for the class magazine, childish, but accomplished, a pattern:

Apple, Apple, on the tree
Can you come and please me?
If you can you will be
The sweetest apple on the tree.

Here is the positive gain which has been won by allowing George to explore his unconscious fear and guilt in the above fragments. Here the childish jingle moves towards the tree of life, and George is able to be glad in a feeling of joy and goodness.

A child seeks towards a positive sense of its own goodness, and a positive attitude to life. Thus George writes of the apple not as a symbol of guilt, but as something pleasing, and even of himself, really, as 'the sweetest apple on the tree'. This little poem, showing a capacity for a positive sense of goodness and pleasure in life, significantly outstanding among George's destructive themes, marks an important stage in his development.

Here is the bulk of George's later work (in all our time together—say, 180 hours with 3 C less the time George took off playing truant, say, 80 hours. Thus in 100 hours he wrote 1,924 words):

The stolen Goods

On Saturday Tom took a lorry up to London and the Police Star stopped Tom and a arrested Him and they took him to the Police Station and question Him and he went to prison for 7 years THE ANd

The MAN ded

On Monday a old man went to the old club and not man went see hm shot his self THE ANd

The ship

Tony went on the queen Mary on him met James and Phil and I went to see the Q liner

13 JANUARY

The hio (*story*) The Thieves

At Monday I went to the Car Park and see a man still a car and went to fetch the cops and the caps went to the Car Park and the man went out of the Car Park an the caps went to the cops station and I went London I see went up the pipe and went to the pipe and shook the pipe and the man kum down the cops come to the man and arrested The And

13 JANUARY

The shio of the Jap Case

On Monday I see Jap case taking bike and went to the shop and taking a bowl swet (a bowl of sweets) went on bike and the police wos waten for Jap Case and Jon case was arrested and the case on Friday and Jap Case was guilt of taking a bike and He (got) 7 (months) Jail
THE ANd

The down gang

Saturday the down gang went to the cafe and hit the old man and the cafe man went to ring the polic and the polic cam to the cafe and the down gang beat the polic and the down gang run for it a police car caught and the down gang got 7 years in jail and he wife wen to se She husband in Jail and warder in jail house wen to he husband and told she is tim you went said the warder and she went home and he did not coum home. The And. (For 'home' George at first wrote 'mouse' in both places—presumably 'house' with confusion over the 'h'.)

THE Murder hunt

In the day man and a girl went in two a cafe and man and girl never come out of the cafe and the old mae and girl went to a walk and the old man murder and he went home and mother father went two the police and the Pollce went in the cafe and the police said to the man at the counter ded you serve girl and lod man yes the man at the counter thank and the police went four walk and the pollce found the girl murbur murber hunt the found the mat died The And

25 JANUARY

The shio trmp [story of 2 tramps]

I went to work and I see a trmp Walking up the rod and I went to see the trmp and I said to the trmp wat do you woth I sald the old trmp

The rotter school teacher name is Mr. HoLBook he is a tramp he needs a wash and a haircut and a new shirt and he has a big head and beady eyey

I went up heath and I see a old man with a gun and I run down the hill and old man chase you and the is gaining my and I fellowed and I was on the side the road and sid to an Irish stop the man from shooting you and the Irish hit him knocked him out and went hom and sat down Bill sid to man do you want a fag and sid yes went out The And

In 19 January 29 a murder on the A 10 a young boy in the road coppers went along the road and see the young boy in road and *the coppers identify the boy he was John Easter the sergeant* [added verbally and written here by me, '*said "I will find the murderer if it takes me all my life!"* ']

71

30 MAY 1961

THE GiRL is lockEd in An Attic

The missing girl was found in a attic the Lady went down the rad got to manh
and she rung the police station and the fire brigade and *the fire manh smashed
a window and the giRl is safe* and the mand who might able to help them he
name is John Smith sandy hair and he is driving a stardnd tan XTV 212 If
anybody see it please ring Scotland Ysid Whitehall 1212

The And

Toms rotten house

*Tom Sullivans house sticks [stinks] and his chairs have holes in them his morther is
a fat pig his dad is tashie and Tom Sullivan wears baggy trousers like old somerset
people.*★

I give this complete sequence of George's work, to show a number of
things. First, that a teacher of English by the informal imaginative
method must have patience—these stories are George's output for
about four months. Many seem to be merely stock pattern television or
film play stuff. Yet under the surface a teacher concerned with literacy by
content rather than by superficial handling of the externals of language—
graphical literacy—will note occasional indications of George's
progress, in the order and sequence.

He is obsessed with guilt stories, and takes in material from newspaper sensationalism, and television violence. But he selects for his own
needs items of juvenile crime (stealing sweets, smoking, riding on a
crossbar—this last not quoted), material about 'tramps' and people of
unkempt appearance (in which he includes me, and Tom, his classmate
with whom he seemed to be having one of the unconscious homosexual
liaisons of adolescence), and about women being murdered, or confined,
or separated from their jailbird husbands, and so forth. I can see here at
times material which is probably symbolism of unconscious Oedipus
impulses and so forth—note, for instance, that George gives us a clue
to his Fat Old Sick Sow story here, by saying of someone else's mother
'his morther is a fat pig'. The incident where he 'shakes a pipe' to
bring a wicked man down for the police is outstanding enough to have
a particular symbolic significance, I daresay. But at these limits of
'psycho-analytical' interpretation I stop: yet these glimpses help me to
be patient, and hope for improved literacy, coming by some sudden
success. George has signally failed to learn to read and write at his

★ This piece of extravagance was taken up, and Roger Scott added to 'the mother is a fat pig'
'when her old man tickles her she grunts'.

primary school, so that he still confuses 'home', 'house' and 'mouse': there is little we can do about this except painfully and slowly in the secondary school in a remedial class.

But yet he is obviously asking me how to spell more words. He uses words like 'identify', 'baggy', 'Somerset'. He wants to begin to write with panache, and tells me the striking expiatory phrase he wants to write in one story, 'I will find the murderer if it takes me all my life'. But here and there he actually shows something of panache in his expression: he is obviously enjoying himself—'the rotten school teacher's name is Mr. Holbrook. He is a tramp, he needs a wash and a haircut and a new shirt and he has a big head and beady eyes'; 'Tom Sullivan's house stinks and his chairs have holes in them'. Of course, the flow comes out in strange ways—ways perhaps appropriate to a little boy of 8 rather than a boy nearly 15. But the enjoyment of even his slight and incoherent literacy becomes in the end the means to quite logical, ordered, and at times even beautiful pieces of writing by George. This, for instance, of a school walk:

I see a hare running down the fed and I see a fsh sticklebacks in the down in the water and a wild rose in the hedge and rook up in the hare (air) I see a waterrat it went in a hole in the bank. And I see a dead rook and we climbed over a willow tree and walk down the fed and walk back two the shool. Hare hare com to me or else I kick up a tree fish sticklebacks in the see I will sticklebacks out of the see or you can pull me in the see and I swam in the see. A rook has a long beak and a big head and long wings and big fet and the colour is black and in the sun is it blue.

The piece in the middle is sheer verbal enjoyment: George is remembering his apple piece, and its success:

> Hare Hare come to me
> Or I will kick you up a tree
> Fish sticklebacks in the sea
> I'll get sticklebacks out of the sea
> Or you can pull me in the sea
> And I'll swim in the sea.

This is perhaps how George meant it to go: the word 'sticklebacks' has its own onomatopoeic vitality for him, and the fish some deep symbolism of youthful vitality.* The last observation about the colour of the rook is beautiful.

---

* *Psychiatrist's comment:* this piece seems so astonishingly at variance with the other children's comments that 'George can't read' that again perhaps one may say, rather, that it was that he *dare* not read or write.

His strange stories of violence now take on a more orderly sequence:

The of old man

I come out of the old man house and run down the road two the telephone ring John and Paulkey [Porky] and James and I went up the road two the old man house and Paulkey and John and James and John has a gun and we threaten and the old man is bleeding John went to get a doctor and the went ring the hospital and the amblance come and the old man went tow hospital and the gang went two see the old man he is dieing and The boy went homse and the old man died

In the end George's literacy is no more than as in the two passages that follow—his answers to questions in an examination, with no one to help him with spelling. But this is as much as anyone in the secondary school could get from George, given that he had been so neglected in his earlier schooling and failed to learn the elements of reading and writing at the correct age in the primary school, where conditions permit attention to slow readers.*

A cat run two the boor [door] and sat on the mat a dog see the cat and cat see the dog and cat ran qu the molh [wall] and he the rhfn [roof] of a house and down cimbenr [chimney] and out of the fiar and old man jumth out of he sat and the cat ran ove the mat and dog run ou two the door the cat run up the wah [wall] two he house ran in the and and sat on the mat. the cat sat on the mat.

This has a marvellous rhythm, and is comic and exciting, but it cannot really be called literate. Nor can this.

A boy of 18 wens in the hrmehr [into the army] and denat lichr [didn't like] the hrmehn [army] and went on lefnr [leave] and he dednt not comr doch [back] and 14 day went bihr the cpn [captain] sedn to James Carr has not come doc [back] yeth go the he dus unz sun rod Londod [he has gone down the Sun road to London].

Yet there is something there—something that might well have been developed, had the primary school not assumed that George, like Joan, was incapable of imaginative work.

And, of course, things might have been very different had George

---

* For indications that the pressure to coach 'brighter' streams for the 11+ may draw attention in the primary school away from 'backward' readers who could otherwise be helped more, see p. 261. George would obviously have benefited greatly from the freer primary school methods usually used with infants, right up to the age of 11, as these give the child moral assurance by encouragement, about his anxiety over his aggressiveness. Effects of competition for the 11+ examination, or rejection, would have the opposite effect.

come to school every day—both at Primary and Secondary stages. Possibly he found he was despised and discouraged and thus took to truancy.

George's summit of literacy is shown in the letter he wrote, in reply to a critic of one of my newspaper articles, who had said that I was misleading George as to the nature of the world, and failing to train him to write practical English.* I think no one could have got George to the stage of being able to write such a letter by practical exercises only. After all the free training I gave him he could at least write a letter as competent as this:

The Gate house
Melton

Dear Mr. T.,

Mr holbrook is a better teacher than you thank and I tink your Idea is stupid and I do not like your ida

yourns sincerely George Green

This at least makes its point. What comes over from such literacy as George had now is character, amusing and friendly, with imaginative qualities. Here are his responses to some music—a march by Sousa, a piece of modern music, and a jazz band:

two clowns in a sercus ring playing a round with a old cat some drunk water hoses pooting it over each other the crowd laughing at them
A saw mill with cows in the back medow
A police car coming along the raod with its satren [siren] going and men hemmsering meny metet ot tin [hammering many metals or tins?]
A band playing in a dane hall and yung peope pncing to it
It sounds like anetes gnt killed [a nit's got killed?]

These imaginative capacities, with their potentiality for humour, and the strange ironic perceptions of the adult world as inhabited by tramps, fat old sow-women and tashies, will, I am sure, help protect George in the course of a life which is bound to present this limited but happy boy with grave difficulties and disparagements. He can just write and read enough to survive.† But the sense of pleasure in language I helped him develop in the last three or four terms of his school life could have been given him in his primary and early secondary years if he had not been

---

* For an account of the whole exercise see p. 184.

† Of 1,924 words written for me in just over a year, *The Sick Sow* is 245 words, his greatest effort. George now works as a plasterer and seems happy and sociable.

unconsciously and consciously rejected and derided by his classmates, and by some of his teachers. If his weird and striking imaginative powers could have been fostered and appreciated earlier, he might have come to school more regularly and overcome his graphical problems as he did overcome his difficulties of oral communication.

✻　　✻　　✻

PSYCHIATRIST'S NOTE

It could be that the 'amiable' non-starting quality of 'George Green' means that he has 'cut off' some half of himself—the aggressive part which comes out in the stories. He thus loses the energy and drive which would make him more effective, were he more integrated in his make-up. The diagnosis of his being 'amiably not able to start' is thus correct: if he were more 'un-amiable' he could start!

When George tells his story about the train running over the sow he may have meant symbolically that he had buried the bad-sow-George six feet deep inside himself. I think there are probably more disturbances in this pupil than the author permits himself to observe. These disturbances are defended against by not doing anything, just 'sitting tight' and by the back to front spelling, a kind of camouflage (as when he makes mistakes in copying out the killing of the father). No doubt the acceptance of his violent phantasies without moral condemnation must have contributed a good deal of relief, and encouraged him to bring out more.

AUTHOR'S NOTE

Some readers of my manuscript have suggested that my references to the Oedipus myth in the psyche of such a child may frighten unconvinced teachers away from my thesis. I can only suggest that any teacher who reads a good deal of free writing by small boys must inevitably be struck with the recurrence of this theme. See also the interesting first notes by Sigmund Freud in *The Interpretation of Dreams*, p. 260 ff., on *Oedipus Rex* and *Hamlet*.

4. JOHN YOUNG

John Young was a very pleasant, capable, co-operative boy, with an earnest face and a slight squint, amusing and trustworthy. Perhaps he was in a 'C' stream because illness had kept him behind in his work. I have no Intelligence Quotient for him. He has to exert himself as he is the youngest of a family of four children:

my family
They are 6 of us my dads the oldest my mums the second oldest. my oldest sister is 22 and marrede with 1 child of 3 month. my second sister is 18 and she worked for the mobile blood-transfusion centre she has a flat at Michems corner Tonbury my third sister is 16 and works at the milk coperney Tonbury and shares the flat with my other sister. I live at Elmden on a farm . . .
As I am the youngest peason in the family I get picted on for a lot of things here is a E.G. when we are all watching T.V. dad sais make a cup of tea mum. mum seis Doris you make a cup of tea. Doris sais peggy you make a cup of tea peggy sais sylver you make it. Sylver sais John you make it. So as I am the youngest and have now one younger to pick on so I have to make the tea.

People are a funny lot
some are nice, some are not
some will help you, some won't bother,
but there is one I like and thats my mother.

But in a class of restless and disturbed children John seemed to me one of the most stable. He explored violence in some of his stories, but not in an obsessed way—rather in a way appropriate to a normal adolescent boy:

macwillaims ran to a brick wall he began to climb it when he got to the top of the guard room then he heard the other guard coming he pull a knife out of his pocket witch he stole from the kichen he frow it at the guard it dug into his arm and he but he was still strong he pulled out his truncheon and hit macwillaims in the face he fell forword off the roof he fell to the ground head first he hit the ground with an almity thud he broke his head and diad

Maybe there was trouble at home sometimes:

The Jordan family were once a happy crowd. The family of six lifd in a counsel house Just out side Londen But something whenet wrong. Mother

77

and father were always shouting at each other the people across the street could hear them figthing the children would cry Tommy was the oldest he was 12 he was more groon up that than the others. Jane was 8 she was frightened of her mum and dad Jone was 5 and Alan 1½ years. He was to young to to understand he was ~~young~~ crying all the time never the less.

(Note the repeated 'young' crossed out, showing perhaps that John identifies himself with Alan here.)

The problem of being the youngest in a large family, in which a child like John is engaged in a contest for Mum's affection, is a common and normal one. John's spelling is poor and his work lacks proper punctuation. But he makes up for these by the vigour of his language and his forthrightness of expression, and in these we can help him engage with his living problems. It would be futile to add to such a child's difficulties by making him anxious about spelling and punctuation. John has been reduced to 'C'-stream status because he fails in the technical requirements of the graphical arrangements of words. His reading was not poor. And his expression is fluent and lively: it just doesn't look 'educated'.

In content, as with so many of these children, his writing shows a marvellous courage in the face of life. John's home difficulties, of being the youngest, of needing affection, of being troubled by his sisters' sexuality* and his parents' rows—these are no more than the conditions of the human child's mortal existence. He has come to terms with them. And often they mark the incredible insensitivity of the adult world— John's last 'five-minute' talk was about how he had his appendix out, at the age of fourteen—a talk which lasted a whole period. He was put in the men's ward at Tonbury Hospital, and told with obvious fear and shock how some old dying man had shouted all night, and how in the morning he had woken to find the body removed to the mortuary. Yet in hospital he was separated from his mother, and was facing an operation which he knew meant pain and even perhaps death for himself! The sensitiveness of his account moved me to tears. How often we forget in school that for children pain and death are present realities just as they are for us—yet they have not had time to become accustomed to suffering and the awareness of mortality! Hence their explorations of reality in story form are most valuable means of coming to terms—even with those experiences which they themselves have undergone:

* This is confirmed by conversations about mutual masturbation which I overheard but will not quote.

It happened to me

When I was 4 years old I very nearly diad. It was one sunday when my 3 older sisters and I were out for a walk I had my photo taken near a brook. I still have the photo. The brook was about 8 feet wide. The water was about 2 feet deep. But they was 6 feet off wet slimy mud I was the first to cross the bridge it broke and in I went. I slolly sank in the mud my 2 youngest sisters ran home but my oldest sister stoped and saved my life she held my head above water untill my sisters got home and told my parents. then they raced down to the brook dad have a hell of a Job pulling me out as the mud held me down eventually his got me out and carred me home. my clothes had to me distrod it took seven bath to get me clearn.

The mass media add to the child's problem of accepting the world as a good and beautiful place: John confesses to having being badly frightened by television:

Im am never alloud to sit up and watch programes not surtebull for children one night when dad was digging the garden mum had gone out, they was a film on TV unfitt for children I sat and watched it, it was all murder and killing, men were being hung and other were being shot or stabed. men had their heads cut in half . . .

John certainly is a boy for whom his good liberal education at his school has fostered much self-respect. And it has given him a determination to serve the community in his own way. There is little feeling of a sense of inferiority about John's last piece that he wrote for me. There are still mistakes: but his expression is not illiterate; indeed, how many of us could write so assuredly about our chosen function?

My work on a farm

I have live on a farm all off my life, I am not bosting but I think I know a fair bit about farming. I know most about cattle and only a little about machinery. Some people say farming is the lowest payed and hardest working imployment out. I agree with those people. but I would rather work for my living, than just sitting in a stufy old office adding up numbers all day or whatever they do. Give me the open air life. My father is a farm stockman and I hope to take on the same Job when I leave school. I am going to take my apprentiship course when I leave at easter. that means that I go to classis ones a week. I will learn a lot more about farming and if I pull through the course I will be a usfull chap about the farm. Will (while) I am taking my course I will be get 17 shilling less than the boy worker that is not taking the course. But when I am 17 and finished my Apprentiship I will get 10% more than the average pay off a boy my age. Many people asked me why I have choosen farming as my future carrer.

(1) I will be in the open air.
(2) I will be doing a diffrent Job every day
(3) I am not interested in enthing else.

For the last 2 or 3 years I am have been work on the farm in the holidays. And I can tell the men I have worked with have been good and give me a few tips. my dad has told quite a lot about farming which I know will help when I life school. So if anybody want an open air life, choose FARMING.*

* Written in an examination.

Here is a pupil, hampered in the primary school by illness, at the time of the normal formation of a sense of word-shape, and perhaps struggling against the difficulties of being the youngest of a large family, developing self-possession by this free informal imaginative work in bulk in English. And with the self-possession goes a literacy adequate for coping with the needs of the world. Here is what a letter from John looks like:

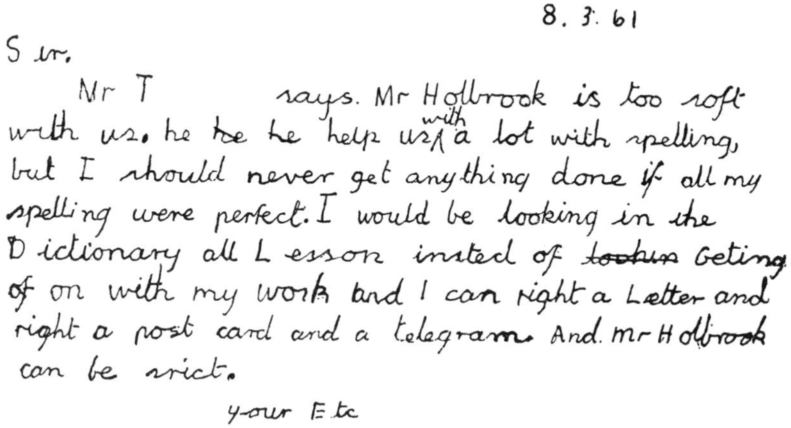

Fig. 2

5. ANN BARLEY

(I.Q. 77.)

On the extreme fringe of our catchment area there was a lonely piece of agricultural land, merging in character into fens. Here was the village of Deadley. The population is perhaps about a hundred, and the village consists of one short lane plunging down a bank from the main road from Tonbury to Bucket. The school is closed, except for its use, which I initiated, as a youth club centre once a week. The inhabitants bear all the marks of seclusion, the lack of vitality of the reduced rural community, isolation and inbreeding. Even six years after the opening of a new evening class centre from which we sent a bus twice weekly to Deadley in the evenings, the Deadley girls at their youth club meetings shrank shyly into corners, with the blank-eyed fear of the peasant such as one finds in remote parts of the earth.

Ann's family was one of the farm workers' families of Deadley, this tiny dull community where she had spent all her days. The many Barleys, as we knew them in school, were large, dull and good-natured —sometimes awkward, and often finding their satisfaction in competing, by disorder, for attention. They also suffered from fits of lassitude, in which their great limbs would sprawl over the desk and their whole being utter a grotesque and monstrous boredom.

Ann was most like her siblings in her capacity for boredom, and her lack of verve and horizon. But she made up for it by a pleasantly naïve childishness, and her plump good nature. She represents thus a common problem for the teacher of limited children—a child who is not greatly attractive at first, and who is dully repetitive—but in whom one can find the occasional satisfaction of naïve perception that transcends the nature of the material. Ann was quite fluent:

Dear Rose

I hope you are alright. I am writing to tell you about my English I have done with Mr David Hollbrook.

He is all ways making me write letters or stories. I know English will done me more good when I leave school. But some thime I get very bored. Mind you I'm not very good at English but I try.

Love and
Best Wishes
Ann

She sent me a postcard when I was ill:

Dear Mr Hollbrook,
I hope you will soon get better and come back to school and teach us Have you marked the Exams papers. I hope this letter will cheer you up. All the class were sorry to hear you had flu. Well soon get better
you
sincerely Joan Stall and
Ann Barley 3 C

These were, however, mere exercises by the way in Ann's considerable output of composition. She wrote just over 11,000 words as compared with George Green's 1,924 in the same fifteen months. But most of her writing was pedestrian, not only in the sameness of its theme— simple romantic stories culminating in marriage—but in the limits of her vocabulary, concepts, and perspectives. Her favourite word is 'nice': 'we only wonder if will have a nice afternoon so far we have had a nice afternoon it is now about 5.30'.

Another favourite phrase of Ann's is 'as the long days went by'—and gradually I entered with her imaginatively into the cruelly limited perspectives of the world of Deadley Street, in the winter months, with a large dull Mum, and a large coarse family, in which this plump little peasant girl was growing up. Against these surroundings some of her imaginative flights seem considerable efforts of mind: and I could accept more easily, too, the importance of her infantile little poems. She was still learning to walk, before she flew from the Deadley nest:

My family
They are eight in my family two boy and four girl a one mum and one dad I have one sister engaged she will not get married yet because she is only 17 years old she has a boy from Melton His name is Michael Coote and he is 19 My dad works on a farm and one of my brother works in a garage and the little one goes to the primary school Bridgebrook one of my sister come to the college and one at the primary. my biggest one works at the Handsome Half-hose my brother and sister which goes out to, work go at 7 in the morning and come home at 7 at night. My dad like a good meal when he comes on from the farm and so does my sister and brother like a good meal when the kids get home from school we have a cooked meal and then we watch children's hour

—it is all very homely, thriving, and dull, but yet horizons are being opened up, in the towns and by television. The trouble is that these horizons, things being what they are culturally, tend to limit the sensibility rather than awaken it. So Ann tends to be prosaic, and when she is first asked to write 'a story' she writes down her 'nice' ambitions:

My life when I leave school

When I leave school I would to work in a bookbinding at Tonbury where all nice boys. I should like to get married when I am 20 and have two children And a nice handsome husband with nice wavey hair and a nice big house *I would not like to have argument with my husband and always talk nice to him and he talk nice to me.* I should not like a fast boyfrend like some of the girls. *I would like one nice and steady.* When I have my children I would leave the book binding and look after the children. *I would marry a man who likes children not a man that hate children.* I should like twins two of each or one of each. *I should like to get married in a white gown and carry a prayerbook have two big bridesmaids and two little bridesmaids and one pageboy.*

I would like to dress my children in the same colur colhes

I should like a boyfriend with a car so that we cane go out for ride.

I like to go on holiday to the seaside and a honeymoon Touring all round the place. The End.

'The End' here seems to mark the limit of limited ambitions: but yet there are interesting elements here—the desire for a good relationship with the husband, and the desire that he should be a man who loves children. Ann can see, as a child, the importance of the security of love in the home, so that she may grow up to love. She is still a child, and the needs of the child colour her attitudes to love and marriage. It is perfectly appropriate, and a central refining activity in her education, and Ann *should* go on writing about romance and marriage.

Even with the sophistication that must have crept into her home from the nylon factory and television, Ann was never embarrassed at school, either in picking nursery rhymes like *London Bridge* out of anthologies to copy into her book, or at writing her own baby poems:

Poem 1

One, two, three, four,
As I am counting up the shore
Of course the shore is at the sea,
One, two, four, three . . .
Two large birds
Sat on a fence,
And they heard
They were dence

... 'some are dunses', Ann says about her classmates, and obviously she suffers a good deal from being at least intelligent enough to know she is 'average'. ('I got 88 for English ai.d spellings I got 88 and A . . . I like Exams because I like seeing where I came in the class I never come bottom'.) Thus perhaps her more important stories are those about protagonists winning large sums of money, or people having a wonderful time going off to see an aunt in Canada—expressions of her ambitions and aspirations in phantasy terms. But among these stories are many which deal with the life she is beginning to lead in reality—the life of 'dates' and teenager girls. These stories of hers do not have the excitement we find in Joan Stall's dialogue, nor are they full of incident: but there is a wiseness and responsibility about them, and they obviously help Ann to deal with the life of the youth club and cinema which she is beginning to live in the evenings and at weekends:

TWO PEOPLE

CHARTORS (characters)
Jean
Joyce

SCENE I

Two teenager girls at the top of the village when a boy comes along and ask them for a date at seven O'clock. The boys name is John seagull. The two girls are mucking about on the top road. The boy was going by on a motor bike. He stops and leans his motor bike by the shelter wall and said"

"Why was you playing on the road, haven's you got a boyfriend" (he said it to Joyce because she was the prettest) and Joyce said "No I haven't got a boyfriend" The boy said "oh" Do you want to come out with me because I haven't got a girl friend," this was about 3.30 one Sunday afternoon. in the winter. The boy said "shall we go for a walk. Joyce still hadn't anwerd his question. So he ask he again. So Joyce said I would like to. Now I will have something to do in the evening. *Joyce said I am glad I am going out with you because it was boring sitting at home in the evening doing nothing.*

Jean already had a boyfriend she was waiting for her boyfriend to come he has a car. Joyce said hear come Roy Jean.

John said. "Whos evers Roy, Joyce said that is jeans boyfriend. They never did go for a walk.

Joyce said shall we go home John said "if you like & so they went home Joyce said to Jean see you tonight." Cheere ho for now. Joyce has no brothers or sisters. Joyce prarents said who evers this with Joyce.

Joyce introduced John to her prerents they said glad to meet you. John said shall we do to the picture. Joyce said yes can Roy and Jean come if you want so Joyce and John walk down the road to Jeans house. the asked Jean and she said yes please. So Roy said shall we go in the car. So they said if you like, "John said I will pay for you to go to the pictures. Roys said "What time are we going. John. said well the pictures starts at 6.30 and ends at 10.30 so if we go about 6.O clock that will be alright. They had they tea and when it was time to go they said cheeroh want be late. They got to the pictures they got out of the car and went through the picture door they paid they man: they sat down and the film started. They put there arms around each other and John said will you kiss. Joyce said if you like. it was the end of the film they just walked out and go into the car. Jean said what did you think of the film you two. they said if wasnt too bad what did you think of it. Jean said. "I really enjoyed my shelf. They stop outside Joyce house. John went and had some supper. And then be went home. Joyce kissed him Goodnight and he kissed her Goodnight. and then he went on his Motor-bikes. When he got home he told his Mother and father that he had a beautiful girlfriend So there said "you will have to bring her to show us. Joyce said alright. I will bring her tomorrow. So John told her the next tonight and Joyce said I would love to meet your parents.

So they sent ove John House. John introduced Joyce to her Mother John Mother said Glad to Meet you, and then his father he said the same. they started to talk and and dicide to get engaged and Marrid the spicil is March 4th 1961. and they engagement is Dec 25th 1960. On Christmas day. There enagement soon came. They are enaged now. Many People gave them wedding presents John kept the present at his house. but he got two many that Joyce had to go keep some of them because John had no more room. The day came and for they wedding John arrived first and then Joyce when Joyce got up to John they both walk up to the steps. The wedding is over they had they photos. taken and they went to the hall and had they party. And the People all said Congratulations to you two they both said Thank you.

They decider to have two chidren.

The End.

In the absence of any great contest with psychic material, and in the normal, unsparkling, exploration of experience by a pleasant, warm-hearted dull little girl like Ann, what is the teacher's function? Always, I think, to seek to extend the range of perception—not by sources of information, such as films, which in the event don't extend very much, but by bringing the arts to bear on the child's awareness. The reason why imaginative art does this where, say, documentary film often fails to do it, is perhaps explained by the difference between images which convey information, and those which stir the phantasy and imagination. Unless we stir the deep areas of unconscious poetic apprehension, we don't change the child's potentialities. Merely 'knowing about' life doesn't recreate potentialities: stirring our whole sensibility may. A related point is that the commercial influence in film and television is usually seeking to confine the sensibility to clichés which are useful for the purposes of commercial exploitation, or to which the nature of the medium limits them. Thus Ann became engrossed in the phantasies of rock'n'roll success—particularly the career of a young girl singer of 14—because her own phantasy life tended to concentrate on success, because she was seeking to overcome her limitations, her 'dence'ness,' and gain self-esteem. The rock world cruelly substitutes for the real quest for self-esteem and personal success a false image of seeking the false 'top'.

Pop star

My best pop singers are Cliff Richard and Adam Faith and Mark Wryer. The song I like Cliff to sing is Falling in love and Adam best song is want do you want if you don want money and I have not heard Mark sing yet The best group are the Beverly sisters and the Everly Brothers Cliff and Adam and Mark are not married. I don't know about the beverly sister and Everly brothers I no two of the beverly sisters are married the tallest beverly sister is married to Billy Wright the football player. But I don't know who the other is married to . . .

Ann attaches her domestic interest in personal relationships even to the private lives of the pop singers: they are for her a kind of royal family, or totem symbol. What happens, then, when she reads about the love affairs or the 'good time' sought by one of the latest singers, who is to 'stay unmarried and have fun while he can'? Presumably her needs for security, and all her quest for the good future in life 'as the long days go by', will be undermined, cruelly and damagingly. The teacher's task is to fortify and nourish her imagination: on the opposite page to the above piece Ann writes her free comments on a picture by Jan Steen, *The Effects of Intemperance*.

As I looked at this picture it made me think the people were druck. The people throw the thinks on the floor. The woman put the baby in the chair in the corner so that they can have a sleep. They opened the window to let the fresh air in. This picture we panted in the olden days. *It was dark in the house but not out side. It looks to me as if it was raining. The dog is licking up the scraps. The bird is up in his cage wondering what is happing. Look at the old fashion shoes. They socks come up to the top of they legs like long grandpas pants. One of the children are playing with the fire.*

By such stimuli for phantasy the real and domestic may become merged with the romantic, so that Ann may be encouraged in her own wisdom, and come to deal more effectively with the problems of life. Here is a later story which contains much more unconscious material, and hence is wider in vocabulary and richer in drama than Ann's routine work:

When a woman looks in her Pram

One day a young woman went down the street to do her shopping. She went into the shop to order her weekly meat, of course she left her baby out side the shop. Her baby was still sitting her its pram, but the little baby was crying. *the little baby could not talk much he could say little words. He's Mum said to him "Now what are you crying for My little baby, "he keep on "Man, Man, ",* he mean't that Man which were going down the road, at first she could not understand him you see this man had a black baby in a blue pram And a woman came over the road a said "you better watch were you leave you baby misses." the baby's mothers said "why" so the other lady" said, "because you know that old man which as Just gone down the road, well he tried to take your little baby out of it's pram.

So she said "thank you very much for telling me, and said" good-bye.

So the lady walk on with her baby.

This time she went into the baker's to get some bread.

The old man with the baby was outside the fishmonger, which was just aside the baker's. The Lady went in, and while she was in the man changed babys. So he had the white one and she had the black one, of course he ran away, no one saw him. She came out of the Baker's and looked in her pram a saw the baby asleep. She went home a while the baby was a sleep she done some jobs. When she had done her jobs she said to herself. *"the babys is having a long sleep. I go and see if he is still asleep. She opened the down and she sow a black baby sitting in her pram she shouted.* after she had shouted she put on her coat and went and phone the police. The police said they would be here in a very few minetes. As soon as she had a knock on the door, she said "Come in," it was the policemen. The police said, "What can we do for you Miss.

So she said *"This is not my baby I had a white one* so the police said when did you first find out she said just a minute ago. Just be-fore I phoned you. One of the police said "did you leave it out side a shop, and she said "yes while I

87

went in the baker's. (she was crying) The other policeman said. "tell us the whole story" So she told them to sit down and asked them if they wanted a cup of tea they said yes. So she put on the kettle and then sat down and told then the story about her baby. And the police said they would try and find her own baby.

The very long days went by and still they couldn't find the baby, but afterawhile the police heard a little about the baby. The women was very upset.

And one day the two polce men came to her house.holding a white baby. So the women grab the baby and said thank you very much for finding him. I will give you £5 ponds reward. the policemen took the £5 ponud and shared it.

And the old woman lived happy ever after and all ways took her own baby were ever she went.

The end.

In her final examination she writes a story in which I find elements in the imaginative creation that make me feel happy and assured that Ann now has confidence in her own wisdom—in her own interpretation of the realities of personal relationship, and in her simple domestic and social ambitions:

Once upon a time the were a ~~little~~ girl who wanted to get married, but her parents wouldn't let her not untill she were 20 or 21. She had a boyfriend and so did he want to get married. he's parents said if the girls folk agree you can . . .
The big day came she was a bit nervous. She got up to the church and walked in with her father and stood up the alter with her boy friend. She were still nervous and so was he his knees were hitting together. churching were over She walked up to the door with her husband . . . there were all tins and shoes tired on the back of the car and JUST MARRIED wrote on the window with lipstick. All the people went back into the room and started clearing up . . .
they enjoyed living by they self . . .
one day they had a serious talk thinking about having a family of they own. One day it happen she was pregant So when she told him he was pleased *he said I am pleased you are having a baby.* So they went to they parents and told them the news . . .
he was a bonny boy, , they were both fond of him. After that she had two more, and when they all grew up they all had familys of their own . . .

What could I do but give this full marks? For here, to use Melanie Klein's terms, is 'belief in the continuity of life'.

✳ ✳ ✳

PSYCHIATRIST'S COMMENT

The dullness of the content of Ann's work may be the consequence of her excluding anything which might lead to the dramatic or romantic. Love, hate, jealousy, rivalry and ambivalence in human relationships are simply not there—everything goes too smoothly to be convincing. This produces a kind of smugness, because she has 'split off' her bad qualities and attributes them to 'other people'. The black baby in her story is perhaps the bad part of the self—a common phantasy in children—to be got rid of, usually 'into' somebody else. The theme of someone putting the black baby into her pram symbolically expresses a fear that someone is going to push the bad part of herself back into her, instead of the good one. Unconsciously she has 'got rid of' the black baby, and can be good and smug. It is noticeable that the black baby is a 'bad object'—one not worth caring for—nobody takes any heed for its fate in the story.

If Ann could accept and integrate her bad black self, of course, her stories would be more varied and interesting, and contain more feeling.

6. WILLIAM GLEBE

(I.Q. 95.)

Here is what I consider to be a good, literate, exciting piece of writing for a 'C'-stream boy. The stimulus was simple enough: at home we had a glut of apples, and I took in a box of shiny red apples and gave them out, with the instruction to write while they were munching them. I wrote the name of the apples on the board, Gascoyne's Scarlet:

AN APPLE

It comes off of a tree when you pick it is rosy red and before you eat it makes your mouth water it even makes your mouth water when you hear the name gascoyne's scarlet. when you go scrumping and when you get caught it is worth taking the chance of getting some gascoyne's scarlet apples. when you go scrumping you have got to be carefull you don't get caught if you do get caught the man will be waiting for you next time you go to get some more gascoyne scarlet apples. when I go scrumping all I go after is apples and plums, pears. when you go pinching apple you do not want to take to many people or you will not get away so quick when there are a lot of people with you a specally little boys they make too much noise. If you pick apples off of the ground you have to be carful of the wasps or else they will sting you and the sting comes up to a big bump where ever it stings you. when you are by yourself and some one comes and you have to climb over the barb wire and get caught the man will probally catch you but if someone else is with you they can unhook you. some people when the catch you they might hit you and said he will hit you harder next time he catches you. But some people say they will hit you next time but warn you not to come in the orchard again But the children could not resist getting some more apples to eat. It is best getting apples from an orchard where there are no houses. when I go scrumping I do not take bikes because the man who owns the orchard might come along and take the bikes and if you want your bike you have to go and ask for it and that is how the owner of the orchard knows that you were in the orchard. I never take a dark jacket or a red one because you will be reconnised very easy because red shows up very easy. But still it is worth getting some gascoyne's scarlet apples.

To give such clear instructions about how to go scrumping involved, obviously, a good deal of imagination: the apple touches off even imaginative considerations of how people behave, such as irate orchard owners! Gordon is known for his literary usefulness: 'when bill was in love with pauline he hired me to write his letters . . .'

But William's practical attitudes don't prevent him from writing in a definitely personal poetic mood, at other times, and short stories of a courageously imaginative kind.

The Fox

The fox is a sly old beast
He sits in his den cleaning and waiting
To make a nother savage attack
He walks the field to the farm
The smell of chickens in the passing breeze.
he's gone to collect his meal.
He makes a leap.
Chickens cackle as the fox collects his meal.

WINTER

When the snow lay round about
The robins come out to seek crumbs
Their feet are numb
But the snow still lies round about.
A tree is a place for song
That's where birds sing their sweet song.
The leaves have gone.
It will not be long before the tree has gone.

Stranden on a Desert Island

One midsummer's day at 9.30 a.m. a ship was wrecked by a corral reef so people jumped overboard. People who could not swim did not know it was a case of life or death The ship was sinking fast but some still hung on. the shore was only about a mile away so some began to swim to the shore. Getting food from the ship was impossible but some people on the ship could get down to the store room and get some diving out fits. So one man volunteered to swim out to the ship and go down to the store room. Their were dead bodys on the deck within 20 minutes of the ship wreck. Their were 1 or 2 live people on board but he was frightened to go on the island. The man who swam from the island went down to the store room. He held his breath as he went down below the surface of the water. *As he open the store room door the water gushed in very quickly.* So he had to feel for the diving suits. He brought as many as he could find to the surface and that was only 5. He got up in the crows nest and waved to the people on the island so they sent to men to help him. When they arrived they all put their diving suits on the went down to get some food. Lucky enough it was mostly tin food. They brought quite a lot up for the people on the island. When looking around the deck they saw a life boat but it had a little hole in one side but they thought it would be good enough take the food to the island in. They all had one tin of something each. *They all ate this just like pigs feeding out of a trough.* After they had their tin of food to eat people were still hungry so they started looking for coconuts. They all decided that there would only be two meals a day. most of them agreed but of course there were some who protested. There was about 35 on the island but people who use't to get coconuts usally got lost or got bitten by a snake. They had shortend done from 35 to 15. They kept near the coast so they could go in the sea if they wanted to. And they could also catch fish to eat. After several weeks ships had seen them waving but took no notice of them In september food was running short so they kill animals and drank fresh water from springs. they found here and there. they found coconuts while hunting for animals. They took the coconuts down to the shore and drained the milk out and ate the rest of the inside. They caught quite a few tigers in traps which are holes dug in the gound and sticks laide across with grass on top of them. At night they slept all together under coconut trees. *They were not surprised to see somebody dead in the morning.* One morning in december a ship was going across the sea to England they waved and waved again. Then the ship began to turn and was coming to fetch them they were all delighted. As soon ass they arrived on board the sailors told them to report to the captain's office. They all too pleased to be on board a ship again the captain said how did you get on that island they replied we were shipwrecked in June and we have been there since. They arrived in England 2 days later and how glad they were to be back in England again. THE END

Despite some illogicalities, this also has some interesting pieces of sequence in it, which shows William can think about experience, and face troubling aspects of reality bravely ('They were not surprised to see somebody dead in the morning'—a sentence that reminds me of mornings in the Normandy beach-head!).

William was also bright enough to understand exactly what it was we were trying to do. In fact, of course, he could respond to much more formal teaching than the others, and should perhaps have been moved 'up': his story above is perhaps the best spelt, and best punctuated of all the work 3 C did for me. It was written in an examination, in an hour.

More literate, but not more interesting than the others, William Glebe offers in the class a standard of efficiency which they can emulate. In organising synopses and writing notes down quickly he was most useful, and the others benefited much from his presence. He was nice enough not to feel superior to them because of his greater fluency. This is because together we cultivated his sense of humour, and his capacity to amuse, and illuminate—any sense of his superiority was swallowed up in the flow of affection established between himself and the others by his lively and sympathetic ways. For the teacher of backward children such work as his may represent achievement in essential literacy which sets a standard to pursue.

7. WALTER PERKINS

Walter was an Air Force child—that is, his parents came to the local bomber station from Hong-Kong, and before long he moved on again. Children from families of R.A.F. employees were nearly always deeply disturbed emotionally, because of frequent moves, and many were unstable children of a kind of unstable parent service life seems to attract. Walter's attitude to life was dismal when he arrived, his sole interests 'motor bicks', 'flicks', and 'girls'. His ambition was to become an RAF 'moncancle' (mechanic). His writing was prosaic, though it showed signs that he could perhaps become more literate with good teaching:

> When evining is dark
> And I am alone
> My farther's at work
> Ans my mother's at Home
> I sit in my room
> Just reding a book
> My HAT on the bed
> And my cote on the hock
> When TV is over
> and it's time for bed
> I pull over the covers
> And lay down my head.
> I have a girl
> Small and dork
> WE SIT IN THE GARDON
> AND LAY IN THE PARK.

After being allowed to write on 'any' subject (his pleasure in this is indicated by the capital letters above) he came nearer to a genuine expression, full of poetical potential, and expressing unconscious pre-occupations metaphorically.

In the two pieces that follow one can see the boy setting out on the road to greater fluency—but unfortunately he was moved away before he could really benefit from the work we were doing.

The Cheter

A cheter prouls around in the thick undergroth of the jungel. Birds clater there wings and fly away to escape from the jungel cat. Munces (Monkeys) swing from

94

tree to tree. A litel way away the lions are gathering together. the cheter rorse,
something forls to the ground, the cheter has cort its pray.

This prose poem seems to me very striking, so does the story written
in the same 'test':

Sudden Dearth

One Saturday morning wen I was haveing my brecfast a lady come and told
me that her little boy had been playing with a dog, and the dog had biten
part of the boys ear off. I got my little black bag and followed her.

She told me that she lived in Honk Kong street at number 32. she tuck me
to the river and we went on a house boat. *I thort it was a bit quere then.* In
the house boat there where fore men, one siting on a chere, one standing at
the fore end of the boat another standing at the door were I enterd and the
other laying quite still on a bunk. The man at the door said thats wat you are
here for. To see that he lives and to take the bolot out of him. I told him I
did not have the proper aquitment for the job. He told me to rite down on a
pese of paper wot I would nede. Not long after one on the men came back
with the things I started at wons to try and save his life, wen I had got the
bulete out there was mothing to do but wat and see wot hapends, Out side
there was a sound of sirens at that moment the three other men came rushing
in, I rushed for the gun one of them had he fired but it mist me then he fired
again that shot mist me to but the may laying on the bunk stoped the bulet
the police came rushing in and tuck the men and body to prisin, the man
laying on the bunk was dead that second bulet had killed him suddenel.

THE END

Part of the confidence one establishes with pupils like Walter is
gained by not responding with hostility to his attempts to 'test you out'.
Of course, one does not suppress their dealings with hidden subjects.
When he found I did not object to 'AND LAY IN THE PARK', but
rather seemed to imply that it was quite natural for a small boy to be
interested in what lovers did, he went on in his later writing to explore
his own fears of death—or, perhaps, at a deeper level, unconscious fears
about his feelings about his parents. In the passage above there is a
conflict of love and hate, wanting a man to die, yet not wanting him to
die. He writes his story, to see what happens if he does kill his protagonist. What interests me most as English teacher is the economy and
logic of his story—the way he makes it plain to the reader obliquely
that the hero is a doctor; the way a character directly says, without
beating about the bush, 'That's what you're here for.' I note also
that he spells some quite difficult words correctly, but small and more

familiar ones he can't spell. This almost certainly means that his spelling is affected by emotional insecurities within him, and will improve as he gains confidence. But from the qualities of his work I feel he is limited by emotional disturbances, and could have become very literate if his education had been consistent, secure and regular, and his family life more stable. A teacher can only do what he can in the face of such adverse conditions.

✳   ✳   ✳

PSYCHIATRIST'S COMMENT

Walter's spelling errors seem to be different from those of the other children. Theirs are confusions and disarrangements of letters. His are improvisations on a phonetic basis, some of them quite clever. This is probably a consequence of his broken schooling.

8. ROGER SCOTT

(I.Q. 84)

Roger was one of those small boys teachers find dull, unattractive and uncouth. Sometimes he was a babyish child, sometimes too much the smart alick, mimicking the sophistication of men. He couldn't read: yet he had a £30 wrist watch and a £25 bicycle. Contest with authority seemed to mean too much to him, and he was deeply humiliated by being reported and caned for riding his bicycle with someone on the cross-bar, at 14.

I donot like school I is horrible, I have has the cain because of one of the teacher got we the cain for on a Bicycle . . .
Dear Sir,
    I do not like this school because when something is done rong we get the blame for it. So it about time something was done. . .

The conflict in him came out over sex-anxiety, guilt about smoking, and the impulse to get himself in the wrong. Every Saturday he worked in an abattoir and I think this was both a source of deep fears and disturbances, and at the same time a source of pride, for he earned good money, and his future as a slaughterman was assured. His family seemed to be that of the better-off artisan class, probably very much concerned with external smartness and slickness, with an antipathy to sensitivity and tender feelings. Roger had obviously made many of his feelings taboo, but could also reveal himself at times—and was building his self-confidence round his future in the next business. This I sought to reinforce, by encouraging him to write and talk about his work as 'gut boy'.
    Here is his account of 'My Family':
There are five of us in my family counting my mother and farther . . . my father works at Concreteville as a electrician he has a firm of his own Six men work for him. I like my mother and Farther but I get a clout on the ear some time. but he is all right. he got me a new Italian suit on Saturday, and my Mum got a per of trousers on Saturday . . .

Roger was very prosaic, except for stories of violence, and some approaches to a poem:

The Bat

The bats fie by night a sleep by day, they hold on to the branches by their little fee. or in the caves and hold on to the rocks. Bats can not see, but they can hear, the bats eat fies and insects.

His imagination was best stretched round his potentialities as a stock-breeder or meat-worker, and here is his first imaginative account of his ambitions. Later I quote the last piece of work he wrote for me, a very self-confident approach to the reality of his life, and adequately literate.

The Sick Sow

My name is James Brown I have some pigs on my farm and Six bullocks, sixthone cows; One day one of my sow went sick, I did not no wot was the matter with her feet was solued and her mouth was saw, I called the vet to look at her, he said her has got footandmouth, All the sow pigs, bullocks, and cows, had to be kid in the airaear of 15 miles all of the market had to be stoped, Artair 16 weeks their had not bine aner outdrak [been another out-break] of footanmouth the markets was open I went to the market and got some pigs, and bullocks, the money I lost when my animals wher kid [were killed] I got it back by seling the pigs, the money I got for the pigs I got some more bullocks, and soled the fort lot I got and got we a castels lorry.

One year later.

One year later I got we a wife, I said to my wife I have got a nuff money to buld a slaughthouse I arsed the cousall if I cod have some land to billed a slaughthouse on the counsall replid saying that I cod, so I roat to one of the bigest billding ferman and arsed if they would billed me a slaughthouse, they replid saying that they would billd me a New Slaughthouse, 20 years later I had nuff money to retier on so I gave the farm, and the slaughthouse and all of the animl, to my son. My wife said that she would like to go around the world. Me lift England to go to Fance then to all of the mane pars of the world.

The End.

This piece was illustrated, and I was surprised by the sturdy accuracy of the representation. (Figure 3). So I gave Roger further opportunities to express himself, in paint, on big sheets of paper. He painted with uninhibited verve, as a child does at the junior school (the teaching of art in the school was lively and free, and in the hands of a most experi-enced and excellent teacher who had, in fact, returned to teaching from being an H.M.I.). Roger's recurrent symbol was the deer, standing nobly among trees, or with proud antlers and often prominent sexual organs. This symbol, I felt sure, was his vision of his own emerging potency and prowess as a man, and this imaginative work I am sure helped him to develop the positive self-possession which enabled him to be proud of his function in the slaughterhouse. (Compare his identi-

One of his cow

One of his bullocks.

Fig. 3

fication of himself with animals and his attitude to slaughtering with that of Gerald Goodchild the butcher's son and see Plates I, III, and Figure 10, p. 152.)

Gut Boy

My name is Roger Scott I work in a Slaughterhouse in Bridgebrook, I am the gut boy. I work on Saturday and Sunday morning. The first thing I have to do is to make the tea for the men. On Saturday morning we have bullocks to kill first, after we have finished the Bullocks the men go and have their lunch, and we have to clean up, and empty the gut truck and then go and have my lunch and a fag. I go back down to the Slaughterhouse after my lunch, and nose the pigs up. by then, their would by a gut on the table. I would do the gut and get a tin in side to run the guts into. Then hung the pluck up on the hook, and that goes on all Day. until they let the hot water out of the tub, all of the hair goes into my truck, by the time the tub is empty, and has been clean I have finished the guts. all I have to do is to empty the hair and guts and out go the truck and then go home.

The end.

'What a terrible occupation!' I hear my reader exclaim. Yes, but some-one has to do it, and it is Roger's pride that he can do it well. The more sensitive child perhaps could not endure it: Roger's struggle has been to reconcile his sensitivity (one can see this in his noble paintings*) to the task he has chosen for himself, and in despite of his impulse to make himself unattractive to adults. The fascinating aspect of the piece of writing above, I note as I type it out, *is that there are hardly any spelling mistakes*—pride in the description of his occupation won't allow it—and the piece was written under examination conditions without help with spelling. Roger can write a clear letter, and give a most interesting talk about his work, and with him I feel sure that free imaginative methods have helped avoid both slovenliness in literacy and a personal delinquency. For reasons of inward conflict Roger was perhaps the worst reader in the class when we began, but as he found he could write fluently, he was able to read his own writing when it was dupli-cated in the class magazine. By this method he improved by leaps and bounds, and ceased to be ashamed of his halting reading. By the end of his time with me he could read without halting or breaking down in blushes, and was beginning to make progress on his own in reading, in his own time. He was also more self-possessed, and less antipathetic to school, and began to come in to evening classes.

* see plate 1

9. JAMES CARR

(I.Q. 76)

I don't think I learnt the secret of making James Carr work, though he did in fact write some excellent pieces from time to time. James is the destructive little boy to whom Geoffrey Hawkes refers (p. 248), who would wring an imaginary bird's neck in moments of free drama, when the class were miming handling a wounded creature. It was possible that he was troubled by his inward infancy, conflicting with his desire to be manly. He was certainly much obsessed with sex, and wrote odd indecencies in corners of his exercise book. He was fascinated by contraception, and wrote thus in an examination:

The Little Mother

One day a Girl of 14 fell in love with a boy of 15. The girl Mary and the boy name was Jame.* Jame had been going out with Mary for time then one of his frens told him that she was a prostut. They were going the nest night, Jame telphoned Mary and told her he would not be see her agan Mary sed come to night and I will make it up to you. So Jame all right then I will see you at the your place at 70 pm. they met on a comon and Mary gave Jame a Durxer [Durex] and then are have a sexul intercors they sed good-by. 3 months lated Mary dicuverd that the was pregnet 6 mouths latter she had a baby boy

THE END

* 'James's' name is not, in fact, James.

James's attitude to personal relationships was as unprepossessing as this ('after having sexual intercourse they said goodbye'). And he was noticeably not successful with girls, as Gerald Goodchild eminently *was* successful. James was a lone wolf, and was happiest out in the field shooting pigeons alone with the gun belonging to his grandfather who had been a gamekeeper for 52 years and was over eighty. James would shoot, pluck, dress and deliver pigeons for a shilling each, and used to cut my grass with a motor-mower for so much an hour. He rode a very smart bicycle which he had earned himself, and was at once unattractive, as an anxious salacious-minded adolescent, but yet endearing, as a child. The only possible hope was to be kind to him, for his reading and writing were very poor indeed, and he suffered obviously from feeling this inadequacy, of stature and prowess. I cannot help feeling that these feelings of inadequacy made him shelter a greater competence behind a laziness which fortified itself by verbal backwardness.

James certainly could be shrewd and often used long words in his expression: here for instance he invents a portmanteau word between 'in disgrace' and 'indiscreet':

Smocking in the houes
One night in bed I had a puff,
wil reading literature and,
lsning to hear if the sairs would creek
so I was not cort indiscrest
not a sound I could hear
utill the door was open
as quick a flass the fag was in bed
But my mums got a bludy good Nos

I told him I was going to write this book and he suggested the following titles:

The M.1 to English
To English on the M.1.
Straight to the top of the English lader
Walk through the English book
English as simpl as ABC
Crazy mixed up English
English in a nutshell
The others tung (author's tongue)

There was a shrewd calculation within his range, and good expression, but it was often concealed or unreleased, and so I would have welcomed a little psychiatric help with James.

One night the cat working in the mill spys a moues feeding on corn. The cat scill-filly creps up behind a sack and all of a suden his musirls are tens he spring and a little squick from the mouse I herd as the cats clors sunck deep into the mouse the cat quily ete it and then cerled up on a sack to slip.

—this 'poem' suggests to me that much more could have been released in James's potentialities, had his development of literacy come earlier. Here are two well-constructed stories much more full of detail and sequence than many other written by members of 3 C:

Which Way

One day a Youth got put on Probation for a year for stealing a box of oranges in Covent Garden. His name is Bob. He is 17 years old. He had dun 9 months of his year. Then Bob straghted to get frendly with a man called Jame. Jame was about 30 years old he had been in Prisern 3 times for house braking, stealing cars, and pick poketin. Jame said to Bob will you do a job for me. What is it I have to do. take a lorry for Melton to Clare. all right I will do it. "When do you want me to pick up the lorry." "On Sunday night on the market hill, it will be a B.M.C. Austin 10 toner coloured red it will be loaded and covered up. The kees will be in the cab. It must in Clare 4 a m on Monday morning on the market Place a car will be whating there to take you back to Melton.

Bob dicided to to it. on Sunday night Bob went to the market hill and pick up the lory. He new how to drive it becaues he had drivern one befor. He was about 5 miles out of Melton and he began to think to himself "I wund whate is on this lory James semed every suspicious. thort Bob. I wund whate is on it. I will have a look when I get to a la-by. he comes to a la-by and pulled in and had a look at the lod it was stolon whiskey Bob did not know what to do he climb in the cab, and sat and thought to himself, I wunder what to do, shod I tell the police or shod I keep quiert. He dicider to tell the police so he cared on to a little village near Clare he saw a police car coming donw the road it stop the policeman wound down the window "You have not seen a man with a lod of whiskey on a Autin Ten Toner hav you." Bob said, "I am glad you stop becaues I am driving the lory the lory is round the corer I stop here becaues I was going to tell the police if you follow me you can catch the gang" The policeman said, "Led the way."

Bob niped round the croner and got the lory Bob and the police car proceded to Clare. By this time it was harfparst thee in the morning, they got to the market place there was no one about so Bob put the lory in a corner. Mean while the Police got in position. At 4 am Jame and his friends came. Jame got out the car and walked over too Bob "good morning Bob" said Jame "Good morning" said Bob then Jame said "You got the lory here" "Yes" said Bob Jame was going to give Bob a £100 so Jame told him but it was a liy. Jame intened to doudle cross Bob Jame gets a wad of £1 nots out of his pocket, he handed the money to Bob. Bob was just going to take the money and Jame dropped it. Bob bent down to pick it up. Thats what Jame was waiting for he hit Bob on the head and knokt him out. James and his frends pick him up and put him in the car. The police realise that James had found out that Bob toled them about James and the ganer. Jame and his frend drove of in their car *with Bob laying in a heep in the flor of the car.* The police had got James car number and they were hot on the trail of them. Bob was just coming to, he pull himself up and looked out of the back window he could see the police car behind. James had not seen the police car behind they pulled up at a house they took Bob in the house. The police stop near the house two policemen went round the back and know on the door when the policemen know at the door James and his frends look out back windows, Then the police went in the frunt door Jame was come down the sters the polic cought Jame and his frends, they all go 10 years for robbery. Bob had a lump on his head for a week but he got 50 £ reward.

The End.

This seems to me a well-sustained sequence, hackneyed as the material is from television and film drama. More original, and more interesting in the delineation of character (possibly because it is closer to personal inner phantasy) is this examination piece:

Caught redhanded

One day Tom an old tamp was warking up a hill, it was getting dark and it was very cold. *It must have been frizing had for there was icicles hanging for guter of houes, the snowe on ground was cresp as he wark through the village.* Tom sorw a light coming for a farmhouse it did not look far. Old, Tom jumped a dich and wark towords the light he arived at farm. He could see a bran he went in and in corner there was a heep of strow in another there was a heep of potates and he could see a rabbit loker. He wark over to it there was rabbit in it but he could not see how many there was. He went back to the storw lay down and went to sleep. Next morning he was up at 4 am it was dark then he throught he had beter go before the farmer got but he did not go emty hang (handed) he took two of the farmers rabbit and sum potates in a bag. He warked about a mile. Old Toms legs began to ack so he stoped he was in a brus [brussels] field most of them were picked, it was just get light. Tom pot the two rabbits and potatoes down. He sat down and thot to himself how can I light a fire he look round the field and *he sow to his delight a hide* made from bale he warked over to them there was somes strikes and a tin the tin had some disel in it. Tom did not los any time in making a fire he got an old tin out of the heg and put it the fire he put some snow in it picked 3 or 4 brusels and got 2 ol potatoes and pull in the tin with his brusls and the rabbit were allso cooked on the fire. Tom injoid his food* that night he went back for some more. He did not know the farm was wating for him. He went in the barn and shut the door the farm was on the loft. "Stop thif" said the farm Tom said allright right dont shoot" the farm cimed down Tom said "I only wont to sleep in here" farm said "have you been here befor" Tom said "no I have not" farm said to Tom well you get out and if I see you on my grow again I will blow your

* I.e. a hide for shooting at pigeons.

head of" so Tom warked out of the bran and back to the hide in the brust field *next day he moved on into the next.*

James has the soul of a poacher, and reveals here lively turns of expression which could have been developed earlier, had his English been related to his field-wandering interests. James could give a good short talk in the end, and is another child who was helped a great deal by the use of a tape recorder and other oral exercises, towards a fluency he found it difficult to achieve in writing, and towards greater self-possession.

10. JACK O'MALLEY

(I.Q. 75)

When Jack was given an anthology he copied out—

Swart Swarthy smiths besmattered with smoke
Drive me to death with din of their dints . . .
Such noise on nights heard no-one never . . .

His own background was as raucous. Of his family he writes:

In my family we have 8 children starting from the Oldest Robert, Stephen,
Peter, Jack, Leon, Dilys, Derek and John. three of them go to work and
the rest go to school . . . I like my family but I do not like Robert he keeps
hitting my brothers . . .

Of his family background the most revealing thing he said to me was,
'Did you hear about that woman got raped at Melton, Sir? P'lice
come and took a statement from my bruvver.' At least this revealed
why for the last fortnight Jack had been unruly, fractious and ill-
tempered. He was frightened by the violence implicit in the sexuality
of his elder brothers, and disturbed by the rough and turbulent context
of the large family in which he was one of the youngest.

His stories were therefore full of violence and death, and love which
turned into death—the small boy's obsession with his own impotence
leads him to develop phantasies of terrible motor-smashes which often
seem to stand for his fears of sexual love. His inward fear was of a
world which seemed to threaten to 'Drive me to death with din of their
dints'. Jack was much the 'top' writer of 3 C but his anxiety made him
lazy and indolent, so that his success was partial. I will not discuss here
as many pieces of his voluminous output as I would like to do, but only
say that I think the unlimited opportunities to express his fears and to
symbolise his pent-up aggressiveness helped Jack to write a piece about
death in his final examination which shows him able to look fearlessly
at human reality. He behaved badly in school after the rape incident,
and was quite untouched by punishment—indeed, caning for forming
a gang for assaults on others in the school playground made him even
more unco-operative. But I think he might have fallen into more
serious delinquency at such times had he not gained a good deal of

understanding, insight and self-respect through his imaginative work in school, and contact with a number of sympathetic adults there. Of course it is impossible to measure how much a school contributes to stability. (A doctor comments on Jack below that I am probably too hopeful about him.) But there are sometimes small indications: all my ex-pupils wave to me when we pass in the road, and are glad to stop and have a talk—this alone suggests a confidence in some adults, given them by a friendly and liberal school atmosphere:

HE DIED SLOWLY

on day a man and his wife was going for a holiday to America. Their names were mary and Paul. when they got to American paul bought a car they lived in a flat in California . . . at night paul said I am going out for a ride in the car and when paul was going down a very steep hill he could not pull up his breaks, he was going 95 m.p.h. and at the bottom of the hill was a car going across the road and just at the bottom paul hit the other car, his car was in flames and paul was thrown through the door and he landed in a field, . . . *Paul was took away in the amblance with very bad injurys on his head. In the amblance paul was dieing slowly. the doctor cave him morphine and tried every he could to safe his life. But when he got to the hospital he was dead . . . after* a while Mary got over the shock . . .

RUNAWAY BOY

. . . Bill but his gun on a nail on the table the nail was near the trigger amd Bill joged the gun and it went off in his stomach he fell to the grouned . . .

THE KILLER

One day a man and his wife went for a holiday to Greece and he did not like his wife very much and wanted to get red of her . . . he told her go and order some tea and When she had gone *peter picked up an iron candle stick and said to him self I am going to kill her.* IN Tow minutes she was Back as Jane came in the door he hit her on the Back of the head she fell to the ground. then he looked at her and she was dead . . .

THE SON WHO SHOT HIS FATHER

It happened in 1949 when a mans son aged 14 sHot his father
In the Back because he would not give him any tea so he got the gun from the cobard and loaded it he called his dad in and pointed the gun at him his father said what are you doing with that gun I am going to shot you why he said because you would not give me any tea turn round pleace dont he said again John said turn round so the father turned round and John shot him in

the back. the nabour next door heared the shot and ran round to the house she johns father on the floor with blood coming the his back . . .

DIMMOX THE OLD MAN

Dimmox the old man was walking down the road one day and when three boy's came out from the hedge and hit him in the face with a apply then they ran away Dimmox lay on the ground with blood comeing from his nose. Then Dimmox went home and sat on the chair and wippd the blood from his eyes then he went back down the road saw the three boys which hit him they were bend in down Dimmox got a stick and hit the three boys on the behind and made them run away crying thire eyes Dimmox said Ive got my own back on you at last.

Sometimes it is as though Jack is working out in phantasy his tremendous urges to revenge when his elder brother illtreats him and his younger brothers. But there is other psychic material too deep for us to discover: Jack's other recurrent themes are infidelity ('Then when Jane was getting dressed Bill asked where are you going Jane. I'am to tea with a frened I meat here when I was going shopping. When Jane met her handsome yank they kissed . . .') and a couple faced with fear of retribution ('Oh Jim what shall we do there in the next room well we just wont go out well it wasn't worth coming dont worry dear I am going to tell the police . . . when they searched the luggage [of the men next door] they found guns and pappers showing they meant to kill Jim. They were both jailed for a year. At last Jim and his wife were having a good time . . .') Many of his stories are strangely unresolved.

His writings and the imaginative power he has gained from this work, culminate in this last story which is close enough to the reality of human mortality and emotion to show that he can now help himself to deal with the difficulties life is putting in his way, and with his unconscious fear of violence and death.

SUDDEN Death

One day a man and his wife were going to america for a holiday. there names are peter and jane. they were going to america for two weeks. When they got there peter and jane went to a carage to buy a car. they got a big red yanky car. then they went of to have a look round new York. when they had done that peter and jane went to find a hotel. they got the hotel and were all fixed in just right. peter said to Jane how a bout me and you going to the pitures to night. orrigh darling we will go. so when night came they went to the pitures. the cinma was four miles from there hotel as they were going a long a stright road Jane said let us see how fast our new car can go orright dear Ill see if I can get a ton and was doing ninty five the stearing locked. the car went stright throw a brick wall and turned over four times in the road then it went on fire. there was no hope of peter and Jane coming out of the car alive. when the pople heard the bang they came running out to see what they could do but it was to late for anyting to be done they were both dead. *peters left leg was missing and Jane was burned all over. a man rang for the police and amblance when they came the croud was told to go home and dont worry about the crash.* the next there parents was told of there sudden death. then they flew the bodys over the england to be bered there near there parents home to two days after the funrel too place *peters mother fanded over the crave of here son the cofens were put one on top of the other in the crave peter mother had to be carried away by here other son and husband who were both crying with hertbreake* Janes mother was unable to atened the funerl because she was ill after she had hered the shock. after the funerl they all went home weping. it was three weeks when peter and jane got married and as they were going on honymoon peters dad said for a joke dont kill your self after six weeks had gone they still kep on taking about there dauter and son. and not long after that peters mother died with hart atack, so then peters family was the lonlest family in the world peters dad tried to stop him★ from crying but it was no use. now they were dead and nothing could be done at all. peter father took his son for a holiday to Itlay. then they son got over the shock but it took a long while peters father never went near a car since the death of his son and daughter in law.

THE END.

This seems to me a valuable exercise in studying 'what life is like', though the morbidity indicates that it probably has a deeper personal meaning, to do with Jack's position in the family, and his own needs for love. Here the clue is possibly in the father's joking remark to his son going on holiday—'Don't kill yourself.' Unconsciously Jack is fearful of sexual love as a kind of violence leading to death, and this is why he was so disturbed by the thought that his brother might have been in some way involved in a rape case. (His elder brother was, in fact, always driving smart 'American' cars.) To punish Jack for his disturbed behaviour was, of course, useless, though perhaps inevitable. More effective in gaining his co-operation perhaps were his stories, which entertained the class a great deal, and boosted his self-respect. He was

★ 'Him' is presumably the youngest son with whom Jack identified himself—though the father is still 'peter's father'—the father of the eldest brother.

the most literate boy in the class, but often used his literacy to cover up his anxieties, or refused to employ it in fits of laziness. Yet it was obvious that at times he found great relief by expressing violence in his stories, and could often be very co-operative and pleasant. But there were antipathies, and a crushed resentment that education alone could not allay. All one can say is that here again the development of effective literacy could only come by the development of imaginative power to overcome inward psychic disorder by phantasy. This most literate boy in the class was one who most needed free phantasy in his work.

✶　　✶　　✶

I would not be so confident in this boy's progress. I get the impression that he is *not* dealing with his phantasies. For instance in his short stories he leaves people dead and cannot face the possible sequels and consequences—he stops there. If his imagination stops short of the consequences (and of the fear of punishment) it seems to me to show that he is likely to act out his phantasies rather than to approach life in a realistic and responsible way.

I think that this boy should definitely have been the subject of a psychiatric investigation, for similar reasons to those given in the case of Kenneth Prime (below, p. 137).

11. TOM SULLIVAN

(I.Q. 77.)

Tom comes of a large family who were coarse, loud-mouthed, vulgar and aggressive. But his elder sister, whom I taught in an upper form, wrote some delightful stories which I have discussed elsewhere, full of vitality, and, in the end, tenderness. And Tom was one of those delightful small boys with whom one may have privately a most entertaining conversation about other people's characters. With his background he couldn't be other than vulgar and sex-anxious: yet it turned out in the end that he found he could talk about such things as a bull mating without embarrassment. And by the time I left he was a self-possessed young man who could give a fascinating talk about farm work, and read and write adequately for all his purposes.

My family

There are Eight of us in my family counting my mother and Farther. I have two sisters, one Janet one Edna. Three brothers Terry Sturt and Goef . . . I think my family is awful because I get blamed for nely everything if one of my brothers hit any own else I get all the blame . . .

Tom seems not an emotionally disturbed child: he has but the normal aggressiveness of a small boy.

I got a bag nearly ful and then I soor a man with a gun coming across the meddow after me, I put my bag over my shoulder and run, the old man come after me he seid stop or else I will blow your hed right off. *I said shut your gob and I took two apples out of my bag and through them at him, one hit him in the guts and hit him on the bonce, he fell too the ground and lay there, and I said to my self thats a good Job now I can eat my apples.*

There wouldn't seem to me to be much wrong with a small boy who can so coolly bring out this kind of homicidal phantasy such as all small boys indulge in, and happily conclude 'Good job!'. Writing this passage helped Tom a good deal with his reading, which was poor before we began using the pupil's own stories, duplicated, as 'books' to read from. He read this piece aloud, it was taped, and later broadcast in a B.B.C. programme of mine. He didn't bother to listen to the story on the radio, but the mere knowledge that he had been 'on the air' made a great difference to his self-possession.

Tom's family were most assertive ('You punish me', Tom would say, 'and my old man'll be up here tomorrer'). And so perhaps they needed little reassurance that they were 'good people' in spite of their lack of academic intelligence, or their being in 'C' streams. They were, in fact, very shrewd and perceptive, but in rural ways—and Tom's self-possession grew round his delight in farm work. He wrote and gave talks again and again about this weekend work of his, and because we found it so interesting and full of lively detail he became secretly very proud of these themes. They are attractively illustrated:

LEAVING SCHOOL

When I leav school I am going to work up the petrol pumps at Mr Sturgess's at Mording. I work up there at weekend and in the holidays.
I like working up there because I meet all kinds of people. They have a farm attached to it they keep a few pigs up the farm and a few down the road in a meadow. They have a tractor and a trailer. They are two brothers Frank and John. John is my boss. Frank has four cars two which go and two which do not go. John owns the tractor and trailer and all the pigs and a cattle lorry and Frank owns one bullock one cow and one effer.

THE FARM

When I go up the farm on saturday morning I go down the yard and start up the tractor, and back the trailer on and go up the yard, then clean the pigs out with John, then the lorry. Then we go back down the yard and unload the dung. Then I started the tractor up a gain, and went out on too the fild. Then we an cafferd some manggles [uncovered some mangolds], and loaded them up we got three loades before dinner from about 11.30 until about 1. oclock. When we come back from dinner we started the tractor up again and went for a nother load, we got for more loades before tea the last one we go stuck with. But we soon got out of theat when John put some bricks under the wheels.
This is the tractor witch I drive at week ends, and in the holidays.
You have to start it by a handle and you have to turn the petrol on and when you get it going you have to let it warm up first and then turn it on to T.V.O. Then away you go.
It is a low gird tractor it has three fowd girse and 1 reveirse.
It has for silinders and a high drollit lift [hydraulic lift]. the many fold as [manifold has] burnt out so smoke and flames and sparks fly out of the botton of it.
if you fill the radyator up with water it will last for 10 minutes becouse it has a hole in the bottom of it as big round as a sixpence.

His illustrations complete the lively record of the experience. Doesn't the whole, despite the incredible spelling, convey a sense of genial reliability and enthusiasm, and observation of detail, which are valuable personal qualities? Round the comedy and vigour of such 'free'

Fig. 4

writing one can build a self-respect in such a boy, to counteract what all 'the world' tells him about his 'C'-stream status in society. Tom left knowing he was 'alright'. Tom is learning the nous of the countryside, and one has no doubt of his absorption, and his satisfaction in the tasks of agriculture—much of his interest being in creatures, including human beings, whose dialogue he is here able to reproduce in such a lively way:

The Sick Sow.

Last week I went up the farm and Bill told me that he had Just bought a black and white sow. He said it fed all right for the first three days, but now she won't feed a tall.

So I said let me come and look at here, so we went and had a look at here, and she was lame on the here right, front leg.

I said to Bill no wonder she dus not feed very well, she is lame on her front leg.

Bill said she will not feed a tool, well let me see the kind of grub you give here then.

So Bill showed me, I said dont you give the old gell any brain no said bill well their you are that is your truble then I said.

You give her some brain tonight and then see if she will eat it.

Well I could give here some now couldnt I yes if you wish

Look at that see she will eat if now yes thank John, thats all right mate.

She is in pig in'sen't she Bill yess she sould have them on the 24th June.

Well I no one thing what you won't to do.

What is that John, you won't to clean here out and put here plenty of straw in the place where she sleeps and out in the yard.

The clue to a means of turning Tom's obsessive obscenity into acceptance lay, I thought, in a touch of the clinical veterinary attitude in his handling of procreation: see his contribution to the composite class story (p. 226). The virtue of the above is in its realism—its imaginative 'catching' of men's talk, in passing on agricultural know-how.

Could this become his clue to maturity? Thus, later, Tom develops emotionally in the farming context too. It was a moment of great triumph when he produced the following piece of self-sex-education—because it meant a great departure from his previous sex-anxious talk (he was the chief one to ask, 'Tell us the facts of life, Sir' and listened gratefully). This is a 'manly' acceptance of the sexual in animal life as something which could be written and talked about without shame. He read this passage over and over again with pride and without giggles or embarrassment—he had heard men talk thus about animals breeding, without facetiousness, and he now came to feel, encouraged by me, that this grave attitude to the forbidden subject was the best one. After this he was able to talk to me earnestly and easily about sex:

'She's a funny old girl, Sir. The boys say she's a dirty old girl.'

'Perhaps she's unhappy?'

'I reckon that's what it is. Joe says Johnny done her—but I don't believe it. Anyway, that ain't right at her age.'

This was a conversation on my last drive home, after our farewell party—and Tom wasn't trying to find out 'how far he could go'—he was being wise, and manly, with his ex-teacher. And I think he was really concerned for the girl, who was well under the age of consent. (Obviously I had to pass the information on, in confidence.)

The Old Bull

One day I went round old man Joneses farm and he and some of his work men had got the bull out in the yard. As I went in the gate the old bull started to tern on me, so old man Jones, said get behind that old cart Joe. About 4 or 5 minutes after, I came out from behind the cart. They had got the old bull back in the shed. Then he asked me if I would held him bring daisy the old cow up to go with the old bull, because he thinks that she ought to have a nothing calf.

So he put here in with old Toogey the bull he got on here back and we let him stay with here fore about half of an hour. About four to five month after she had been with the old bull she had a calf it was a bull calf. When it was about ten weeks old, when we sold it it made £15. 10s. 6d. Then the time came for the old bull to be sold he was to old and fat for the old cows. So we took him down tonbury market and he made £85. 10/ 6d alife he wade one and a half tons.

Tom was no exception to the observation I am trying to make in this book that backward children are sensitive and emotionally responsive. He answered questions on the poem by John Crowe Ransom about the little dead goose girl ('There was such speed in her little body'), and answered them well—

1. *A brown study means when some one is in a sort of dream or a sulk.*
2. *Fighting with your own shadow.*
3. *The snow which the geese drip on the ground are feathers.*
4. (What does 'cried goose alas!' mean?) *To greive like a goose.*

And then Tom wrote a 'story like the poem':

Poor Bob

It is ten years since Bob had his accident he was a bright lad I she nether forget when I and Bob fell into a river coming home from church on Sunday night we had got our cloths on.. The were coverd with mud and wet right through, when we got home mother and father niely killed us and then that night when we where all in bed, bob saw a lorry come up the road he always liked lorry's and cars he got up without a sound and hurried down stairs and opened the door and run out into the road in front of the lorry it killed him strate out he was only seventeen years old when he was killed. *I am just going to put some moor flowers on his grave are you coming with me.*

The End.

A painting followed. To choose this subject and illustrate it with care perhaps shows how much this story meant to Tom.

The last phrase, perhaps echoing Robert Frost's delightful 'I'm going out to clean the pasture spring', is a lovely touch. If it moves the reader as it does me I hope it reinforces my argument in favour of a more humane and civilised education for a million 'low stream' children as engaging as this vulgar little boy.

✻   ✻   ✻

PSYCHIATRIST'S NOTE

This boy is, I agree, the most normal of them all. He has a real interest in life and an ability to come to grips with it. His work contrasts interestingly with that of the others, in which there are so many depressive attitudes implicit.

12. ROSE JAMESON

(I.Q. 72.)

According to the school record cards Rose had the lowest I.Q. of all the class. Yet of all the children's work I find myself quoting in lectures and articles I find Rose's the most moving, most full of character, and the bravest. Indeed, she is the pupil who has most driven me to write this book, and to contest the prevalent attitudes to 'C and D' children which I regard as poisonous and inhumane. In Rose I found a brave child spirit confronting the profoundest of griefs, the most deplorable home conditions, and much brutality and indifference, with courage—and making a tender hesitant quest for good in life and for self-respect. Though she often spelt wrongly, and her punctuation was imperfect, these faults often arose simply because her courageous sallies into imaginative expression far outstripped her technical powers of handling words graphically. But she seemed to me the most literate of the children, in that her use of language, coming directly as she spoke, felt and thought, without conscious manipulation, had the power not only to move deeply, but also to express profound truths of human nature and reality, at times, in an innocent way reminiscent of William Blake.

Her spirit was that of an innocent child. But in the social world Rose attracted to herself all the difficulties of dealing with unhappy children such as I discuss in chapter 1. Her mother had died recently. The father came home late, and the children were left from four o'clock until about eight, in a cold motherless house, grief-stricken, and lonely. Rose's younger sister apparently kept the house going: Rose met her mother's death in the throes of adolescence, and perhaps found herself unable to cope. In class, when I first knew her, she was liable to fall into long periods of grief, in which she was withdrawn, and could do nothing but lounge in lassitude and despair in her desk. She was indifferent at times to any persuasion. Sometimes she would weep, without apparent reason, but then at other times she would be lively. Yet she seemed 'lazy' about work, liable to tease the boys in a 'sexy' way, perhaps. Then one day she came to school with huge black bruises on her legs and arms. I quickly learnt from the class that her father had beaten her for going out with approved school boys. It seems likely that with them she 'went too far' in terms of petting if not actual sexual intercourse.

I found it difficult to respond to the horrified disapproval of the members of the class, at Rose's beating. Of course, I did disapprove. But yet I could see that Rose was in conflict, hating her father, yet at the same time needing to cling to his authority and affection in the absence of the mother. Her sexual adventures with the approved school boys had no doubt been impelled by unhappiness—the same unhappiness which made her at times suck her thumb. One could not join the class in their disapproval, and all one could say was, 'Yes, I have seen Rose's bruises', and refuse to be drawn further: one could see in them the desperate misery of the father himself. I resolved only to wait for Rose to begin to work, without browbeating her in any way, and offer her nothing but encouragement and sympathy. The listlessness went on, though sometimes Rose tried to write a little.

One morning she came to school in a new outfit, of black stockings and a black tunic with a white blouse. She had washed her hair, and with her pale pretty face and yellow eyes she looked alive again, a beautiful child. 'How nice you look!' I said, almost involuntarily, as I would say to my own daughter. I noticed one of the staff looking at me with surprise and something of—could it be?—a leer. Later I was shocked to hear another man teacher, in reply to a remark of mine that Rose was 'a delightful child', 'Yes, and she's got other attractions'. He meant that she had a mature figure, and was sexually attractive. I registered the truth of this, but it was the way of talking about a child that shocked me—a touch of the febrile popular press attitudes. I suppose it is too much to ask for a reconsideration of 'sexy' talk about girl pupils such as one sometimes hears in staff rooms—a talk which conceals and disregards the essential childishness of the girls themselves, despite their 'sexy' appearance?

But after this I began to see the truth about Rose and her relationship with the adult world. She was called 'lazy' and unco-operative, and was often obviously unconsciously resented by some in one way and another. The reason was that her childish vitality and *sensitivity* (which I shall demonstrate) went with a flowering that was richly sexual. This aroused a hostile guilt in some of her teachers as much as in her father, and the man teacher's remark about her 'sex appeal' was a mark of embarrassment in him. She was insufficiently treated as the child she was: instead she was made something of a scapegoat for other people's sexual and other guilts. Poor Rose. I stood flabbergasted when a woman canteen worker told me with outraged disapproval of the uselessness of Rose in the home, and how she only thought of boys, while her younger sister did all the work—a point of view of this girl I found generally shared in the school and village. Yet the girl was in deeper need for sympathy and help than the younger sister, because her grief was complicated by her sexual maturity, the changes of adolescence, her conflict of feeling about the father—and by the envy and hostility that she met in the adult world—for her very creativity.

Under the surface of this adolescent girl there was a lovely child spirit, with delicate perceptions, and great courage. No doubt it is too much to demand of the world, in its clumsy arrangement of such institutions as schools, that all should respond to such qualities. But it is perhaps worth pointing out that our ideas of what education is, and of what is desirable and valuable in human achievement and human nature nowadays singularly neglect the kind of qualities Rose embodied. As a creature she was very much A1: yet it was she who asked me, 'Do you like being with us, Sir? As much as being with 3 A?' The whole school edifice, humane as it was, piled on her grief both the envy and hostility of adults, their wolf-whistle attitudes to her physical attractiveness, and the disparagement of her unhappiness as laziness and 'backwardness'.

I got her to work, and I shall quote a good deal of her writing here, to show how much finer her nature was than what was implied by her being relegated to a 'C' stream, ill-treated, or leered at. She casts light by her work on the implications of our educational system. Rose believed firmly that she 'knew nothing', that she was a 'dud' and a failure. 'Mr Holbrook make me work I don't now nothing but he still mack me work why does he mack me work I cart thinck but still I have to work . . .'

Rose's first pieces of writing were short passages in her contribution to the 'joint' story, called *The Blind Date*. The exercise is discussed on pp. 212 ff. They contained a few indications that Rose could write freely from her thoughts and feelings, and had learnt the capacity for free imaginative dialogue from her work in drama:

Audrey was a bit shiy she said halloe Rex and Rex said alloe Audrey were shall we sit here is a nice place to sit rigth at the back it is rather dark isinted Rex well you whon it to be dark dont you I will hop it will be all rigth because sothing allways happens and whot is that audrey said fore instace kissing and cuddly Rex siad dont you like it. audrey said I dont mind Rex said will you kiss me now audrey do you whant me to. well arigth then.

She lent over and gave him a kiss
And Rex said how did that feal a it was a lovely feling Rex will you do it agian.

Perhaps a teacher who was guilty about his sexual feelings for Rose, or his sexual feelings in general, might see this as simply a brash exhibition of sexiness without inhibition about enjoyment ('will you do it again'). But there are also clues to Rose's anxiety ('something always happens'), and to the fact that she writes about 'kissing in the dark', as they all do, both for imaginative experiment to ask 'what will adult life be like?', and also to find out what the teacher in authority will say. To have been angry or censorious would have nipped in the bud Rose's natural progress towards the proper contemplation of personal relationships which follows (I see no harm, I may add, in her uninhibited piece about kissing in the cinema):

Rex took audre home with him and interdust her to his mother Mum this is audre I am glad to meet you audre. audre said I am glad to me you Mrs Harison Mr. Harison said what was the pictuou lik ow it was could the five theves I lick the bit where the olddis man fell down the drian said Rex Audre said ow wastent it funney when the man took the money. he gave it to another man who he thorugh was is frend and it was The police man in his Sunday beets suit Ow that was funny. and Mrs. Harrison said that will be enough for to nigth Audrey and ow I never quite got your name . . .

Once she gets 'into' a tale or poem, Rose's phantasy—I began to see—can produce such penetrating touches—observations they really are, of how people behave—as that 'That will be enough for tonight, Audrey'. At this point Rose can unconsciously 'see' how her young pair are becoming ebullient and talkative about their experience of the film and Rex's mother reacts with a slight envy, expressed in a snub, to which she adds, 'Oh, I never quite got your name.' She knows, too, that in asking about the film the mother is trying to find out (*a*) if they went to the pictures at all, and if they did (*b*) whether they ever looked at the screen! Here is the child's mind at play making its valuable imaginings about how people behave, and pondering how people do behave. Even if phrases and exchanges are remembered, to write them down so is still an act of imaginative selection from life, such as the novelist makes.

My first impression of Rose's capacity as a writer was confirmed by her piece about apples:

On day in the autunm pick an apple and smell it and what a lovely smell it has. But when you pick it, it might have a bit of fungus you migth find a bit of spur with the leaves still on or you migth see a earwig gust coming out of it but that doesnet mind just fick it of when you whont to eat gust give it a shine and dig your theeat in it and you say what a lovely tast it has very juiciy and you feal a sort of tingle what mack you feel so jay.

Rose's progress by informal free imaginative writing towards literacy is accompanied throughout her work by a growing capacity to deal with experience, and a growing self-respect. Her spelling improves remarkably during the process, and I would draw the reader's attention to the evidence in her work that spelling and improved graphic setting out of work can improve 'by nature' (to use Dogberry's term). In the course of getting expression to flow, and with the improved reading that comes from using the pupil's own work for reading practice in duplicated form, spelling and graphic skills improve, with the aid of a few supplementary exercises. In the end (see p. 134) Rose is writing under examination conditions—i.e. without a dictionary or help with spelling—and spelling correctly such words as 'sudden', 'children', 'pillow', 'morning', 'doctor', 'hospital', 'alright', 'island', 'stranded', 'already', and 'breath'. And she doesn't flinch at having a go at spelling 'unfurcherly' (unfortunately), 'amberless' (ambulance) and 'uncoshers' (unconscious). Some of these are phonetical spellings from Rose's slightly adenoidal pronunciation: more speech training would have helped her spell better, perhaps. But there is no doubt at all that in her work we have evidence that uninhibited fluency, of which the child is made to feel proud, because its *content* is relevant to its needs to gain self-respect, is the best means to improve spelling in the 'backward' child, and the best ground on which to impose strict spelling drills. Her vocabulary is extended, too, because of a need to explore experience more deeply.

I followed Rose's delightful piece about apples as I have pointed out elsewhere, by reading the group a stanza or two of Keats's *Ode to Autumn*:

To bend with apples the moss'd cottage trees,
And fill all fruit with ripeness to the core . . .

Rose's writing is an expression of a sensitivity to experience, 'you feel a sort of tingle', 'what a lovely smell it has', 'dig your teeth in it'. She notices the mould, the earwigs, the leaves on the spur—this little girl is acutely alive to sensations, and uninhibitedly enjoys sensations—'will you do it again'. Here we have a deeper clue to the hostility and brutality with which she was treated—Rose enjoys life, and it is her creative enjoyment itself which brings out destructive envy in others.

A teacher who himself responds to creativity will be able to cherish such creativity in a child—this is why creative activity is so important in teacher training. Only by such experiences can they come to see how brave, and how valuable is creativity in the child. Here, of course, we must touch on profound and deep areas of human make-up, and I must ask the reader who is interested to read Melanie Klein's book *Envy and Gratitude* (some of which I summarised roughly in part above, pp. 38 ff.). The most relevant pages are pp. 39-42, where she links aspects of the growth of human consciousness to wide implications in the field of culture and attitudes to life.

After some weeks of withdrawal—a kind of dementia due to grief, I supposed—Rose suddenly wrote a series of seven poems all in one period. Some were childish rhymes of a nursery rhyme kind:

Silver spoon
Silver spoon
Everything silver
Under the moon.

But two of them were profoundly original:

Poem 3

Light light
I see light
On the fair
They have light
And in my house
I have a lot of light
I hope you don't have candles
Because I hate candles
Candles drop their wax
And burn you
If you get your hand in the way

Poem 5

When I think I think
I always know it will come true
I lay in bed thinking all night
Until I fall asleep
I dream of wondoful things

That will come true
Oh why do we have dreams
And think all the time
Oh why.

No wonder 'backward' children so often choose poems by Blake, when asked to pick poems from an anthology!

These poems seemed to me at once very beautiful (as they still do). Their careful word-order, measured and controlled, springs from an ambiguity (in the Empsonian sense) of meaning. The first aspect of the meaning is the contemplation of the activity of mind itself—'I see light', 'I think I think'—'I dream of wondoful things'. 'Everything silver' in the first poem perhaps means that reality may be coloured, brightened, by the mind, by happiness. We may recall Melanie Klein's reference to the 'relief' a child experiences in 'symbolising the unconscious aggressive and destructive phantasies'. Here Rose apprehends, and delights in, the relieving effect of phantasy, thought and expression, which goes on all the time below the surface and above. 'Oh why'?—because 'it will come true'—that is, the dreams are earnests of creative attitudes, the creation of constructive and positive attitudes to life that are actual in living—thought and phantasy can make 'Everything silver / Under the moon'. She sets out in this series of poems to seek to *make* the world beautiful for herself, when it is so full of pain—and she sees in this 'light' a new joy and colour in the world—the escape from dementia. She wants home to become like the fairground, illuminated with dazzling lights and gaiety, when, in fact, it is so dark and dreary without the mother.

In the second poem more unconscious material is symbolised. The candles are those associated with church, funerals and death. They are also the lights used in a state of deprivation, as when there is a storm and an electricity cut—they are the dimmed lights of home, now the mother has died. And they are also sexual, unconscious images of the phallus in father perhaps, to which she is attracted unconsciously, but in which she apprehends the pain of his hatred, envy, and his violent beating. And they are, probably, at the same time the penises of the approved school boys with whom she had been having sexual adventures, and in petting sessions finding herself alarmed by their orgasms—'Candles drop their wax / And burn you / If you get your hand in the way.'

Thus the anxiety brought about by the mother's death is indissolubly linked with the anxiety about the 'going too far' sexually in which Rose has been engaged, perhaps in phantasy, but probably in fact, because of her anxiety. Yet from the candles in the vision, evocative of church solemnity, she finds relief from her guilt in a kind of atonement. She accepts even the threats in her experience as 'light'— there is nothing persecutory here, though there is recognition of the capacity for experience to 'burn'.

These seem to me the most sincere poems written for me by any child, simple and childish as they are.

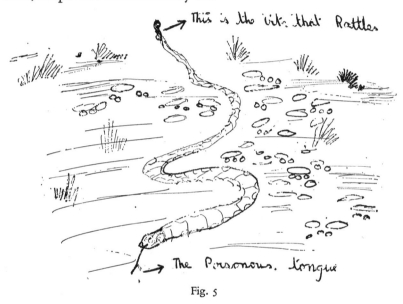

Fig. 5

As if to confirm my inward diagnosis of the meaning of her imagery in these poems, Rose went on to write about snakes, also phallic symbols, of course. This was just at the time when she came to school often beaten, and suffering much. Here is an example of where interpretation of her meaning (to her, in psychological terms) might have proved most harmful. Her relief was in the creativity. So I praised Rose to the skies for those marvellous poems—in no patronising way, for I was deeply moved by them. Praise and unfeigned glad response kept her going. Indeed she pestered me saying 'Is it all right for me to go on writing about snakes? I want a book about snakes. I want to write a lot about snakes'. She had taken the point of our work, without a word being explicitly said about symbolisation of unconscious fears. Indeed, she had said it herself—'I dream of wondoful things/ That will come true'. She stood, as it were, ready for the wind of God to blow through her. To interpret might have damaged her badly by stirring up powerful anxieties: and it would have destroyed her confidence in me and the poetic process.

Her pieces about snakes confirmed my impression that they were phallic symbols, too: 'I have pick a grass-snake up and when you let it grow a bout on your hand it tickles you hand I have never heled any other snake. I don't whant to ither . . .' And she accompanied her accounts with drawings, in which the predatory ends of the phallic creatures were indicated.

Rose next embarked on a long pursuit story of a couple who had had a wallet stolen, in which there are many anxious moments, and fears of being found out or hurt. It contains one beautiful passage in which she perceives that someone may be reassured and made happy by the way in which something is said, though what may be said is conventional in itself. A small point, but it is a gain for a child so limited to be able to distinguish between what is said and the way in which it is said:

I think I will go to bed I don't feel very well. don't stay up their very long will you I hope you are comming out with use tonigth it gust depends how I feel donsent mater you needent come if you don't want to Jean. ow thank you I think I come now you said that. Sorry what did I say. *I was the way you said it. I so sorry to upset you I sopose it all right.* Well we better get redey to go out to nigth you will need your coats and gloves it is very cold

'It was the way you said it' goes with an awareness of the need to consider the feelings of others: note the remorse of 'I'm so sorry to upset you'. Here we have a child at the 'bottom' of the secondary modern school exploring intuitively the nature of civilised behaviour in personal relationship, as Jane Austen explores it, or George Eliot.

Rose came to me a few days later, having at last managed, on the strength of all this poetic exploration of her predicament, to make a direct approach to reality, in confidence of my respect for anything she produced. She said 'Don't read that out, Sir!'. Here was a measure of the trust in the relationship between teacher and pupil:

My Family

In my family there are 5 we ust to have 6 but my mother died she died about 3 month ago (she) died of her brain shrivelling up she could of died when she was a little girl but she had all of us if she would of lived she would have been blind deaf and doum and paralised sone theme times my father crys I don't like him crying it get on my nerve when I dowing the work my little brother is a nousant (nuisance) he keep on hitting me and kiging me when he canth get his own way but is a nice boy reley and his name is steven thomes christopher . . .

From her deepest grief Rose turns to her little brother, as Leontes turns to Mamillius:

> He makes a July's day short as December
> And with his varying childness cures in me
> Thoughts that would thick my blood . . .

In her words we have a child bravely striving for 'belief in the continuity of life', and struggling for resignation to human mortality. I turned aside, fighting tears down hard, so as not to get on Rose's 'nerves' as her father did, by showing I was deeply moved.

One story does not cure a grief, and there were many aspects to Rose's problems to which she returned again and again. But the ice was broken, and she had expressed the terrible reality without increasing the pain or bringing retribution on herself. On the next page she explores the possibility of being taken in to the normal community again.

One day I went to a partey they had nice things but I did not like some of the girls they didden like me some of them but I just sat there watcheing them play games until some one ask me to goin in then I felt a bit better then The girl were beginning to like me and in every game they ask me to joine in.

—again a symbolic statement of the value of 'play'—as of thinking, 'light', imagination—to bring herself back to acceptance of the normal.

More nonsense-wiseness followed, some of it culled from childhood lore, making conscious the changing aspects of a young girl's interests:

> When Jennifer was a little girl it was toys toys toys
> but now she is a big girl it is boys boys boys . . .

This is about cosmetic rouge:

Apply it in little dots on the cheeks and blend in carefully otherwise it would look alfull, if you don't put in on properly and people will start to torck and I teel you that isant very nice. So I advise you to get the book about macke up because it teset (teaches) you how to make your skin lovyley . . .

She writes short stories about caring for abandoned and wounded creatures, and young things—one of Rose's ambitions was to 'be a vet but you don't get much money at first' . . .

One day a lady look out of the window it was very cold and weat. She saw the milk and broug it in and on the stepe was a little babby oh a baby. I wonder hows it is ill take it to the poilice I feed it first because it mite be hungrey are you poor thing don't cry you poor thing I wonder what it like I give it some milk and see if it will stop crying I wonder what my husband will say when he gets home . . .

One day I was walking down the sterret their was a little mole I pick it up and took it home it had caught it leg in a crat (trap) and brocken it is got better in a few weeks time but I set it free after a few days. It came back I bilt it a hudge with a lot of mud and grass. It liked that place very much I trid to find anther mole I fed one it was quite big I did not know whether it was a male or a feemale but put them together they did no figth after a few month she has some babyes fore litte ones they were very sweet and they neve wonted to leve me and hudge I buit for them I gave them worms and water and a few bred crumes it never eat very mush at all they live nicely in their little hudge untill they all diad of old age . . .

These stories about animal pets are only partly true, as I happen to know—but, again, there is little point in quizzing Rose about how true or not true they may be. Indeed it would be pedantic to care—the point is that she is writing about herself, and about restoring family life, and about the 'continuity of life', to allay her grief at bereavement:

I am writing a sory about what I do in the summer Holliday when it is hot I go swimming and when it isten so hot I go to find some wild insexs last year I had some frogsporn. I have some evry year and only a few diy. I is quite had to find a place for I keep my frog sporn under nethe the tank where it is very cool it thak about 3 monsth to get hast first they get long then they grow their finse and after a few weeks they get bigger and bigger. but last year their whan't very meay eggs around I went to the moat fast there whernt any there so I went down the lane but nere the withe bridge there was ony about 50 eggs. I got down and piked them up with my hands and put then in a big gare [jar] with some sea weed they must have a large tin or a larg gare not a small thing other wise when the tadpolls grows they have not mush room to move I use a big paint tin to put my frog sporn in and when they get to be frogs and at the end of my garden their is a stream I clime down the back and tope the rogs in the water and you can gust wash them swim away. I is best to tiper the frog away when they gust loos their tail then you know there will live and just one other thing you must keep them glean hand there sea wead every week and they will like a bit of rough meat to chow and that will keep them alive.

Into this flow of work I contributed stimuli from other works of art and various suggestions. Here is Rose on the reproduction of a painting by Vermeer, a woman standing in a shaft of light in a window:

as I read my letter on a cool afternoon with the window open a sort of breeze swaling round my neck gives me a sort of an refection [refreshing] I still keep on reading my letter untill I came to the end then I keept on stearing down in the teller untill some one made a nose [noise] then I cam of a sort of a drem I just stood their looking out of the window the breez started to get stronger untill it did not feal like a breez it became darck I could her the curtains started the swing in the wind I felt a bit sleepey so I just closd my eyes for a moment and open them again then I felt I was difrent form other people

Here Rose writes of her own state of dementia in grief, her 'difference' from other people, in a withdrawal state. But yet one has a sense of her true difference in being able to enter so into the awareness of a condition of absence. The same period she went on, coming closer to reality, to write of the food she disliked: 'marrow, cumumber, turnip, swed, potatoes pumckin Bred Pudding . . .'

Rose then approached the theme of her mother again, and began to deal with complications of her grief. We are told by psycho-analytical writers that when our mothers die one of our chief difficulties is that because we have unconsciously hated, in a ferocious and destructive way, the bad aspects of mother, we feel, when the mother dies, that it is our unconscious desires that have killed her. For those destructive desires we felt we would be revenged upon by the bad aspects of mother, full of a destructiveness as terrible as that we directed at her—she will return in retribution, with claws, rending teeth, and the capacity to consume everything by incantations and spells. The bad retributive mother is the witch in folk-lore and children's lore.

Rose had to deal in phantasy with the witch mother whom she felt perhaps might come back from death to take vengeance on the little girl who had at times wished her dead. She first writes a story about a wicked woman:

Once apone a time there was an old lady she was very wicked when the milk man came she did not say thank you she just said get out of here and shut the gait . . . she was very snoty . . .

This old woman swears and steals, but when she confesses in the end, is let off

'Ow now I did not' 'I know you did' aright I did it then wath if I did I was to get my own bake on you' . . . 'Very sorry I wont do it again' well this thim you can have th biccuits but if you do it again you be in trobel Oh thank you very mush . . .

At this point Rose went into a state of great laziness and lassitude again, before embarking on a long story to come to terms at this stage with her mother's death. She pulled herself together sufficiently to give us an impression of the mood of the withdrawal state, in which she dreamt:

> The wild winds we . . .
> The wild is very cold
> The sun is very warm
> When it is very hot

You see people of the shore If you lay on the sand with you eyes clous you can here people play and tork and the rusall of the sea going out and coming in soon the wind coming wery fast I feal a shiver on my bear back the sun hase go behind the couldes evry on starst to go they know there a storm coming up they get all there things to gether and go I don't mind stormes it bacam very windy and cold I put my towe round me and lay very still looking at the coulds but of, course I was dreming.

Rose then draws a very tight, close, embroidery-type pattern in her book, and begins, after a few false starts, a long story, with two very fine illustrations, called *The Mystery Castle*. This is a tremendous effort and achievement on her part—and it is an assault on the castle of her own disturbed soul, to seek out the fears and disturbances, and to come to terms with them. It is brave, and a magnificent acceptance of the true disciplines of the imagination and spirit. Here is Rose's story.

the mistory catsal

One day there were two men they were very greedy and slevish (selfish) the herd something about a catal. one day in the midal of a big lack they disided to expore it. they did not know it had a witch living in it. the borrowd a rowing boat and saled right to the middle of the lack and when they got nere the cartsel they sor a sine post sticking up from the water it had bewere of this cartal ther is a horid old wiche the men did not worry a bout the sine post they just went rowing on when they got nerer to the carlsat they saw another sing post wich had a skeleton the men were a bit frightened of this they dident know what it meant. they saw fore girls in a boat with a cloak and hood and with a marsk on there face. their names were the for spiy girls they now how to get in the mistory cartal.

(At the outset Rose 'knows' intuitively that the approach to the witch and the castle is an approach in phantasy to the memory of her dead mother and the disturbances this causes in her soul. The skeleton on the post is her fear of death, the signpost an indication of her preoccupation with the 'bad' mother. The word 'witch' when she first wrote it is written over the word 'wicked'. The girls are 'spy' girls—and they are masked. They know the way into the mystery castle, when the men don't. In this Rose is perhaps saying to herself that the way of dealing with her spiritual troubles is by masks and spies—by double meaning, metaphor and phantasy. The girls are herselves. The world of men—the adult world—doesn't understand how one has to dive into the subconscious to come to terms with one's troubles. Her whole story is thus a vindication of the poetic function, and her drawings are illustrations of how to find the solution to the 'continuity of life' one has to dive into the mysterious depths and spear one's quarry there.)

the gerls did not see the men. they hid round the other side. the men did not see wate they were doing so they rowd round a little bit untill they saw the girls on (one) had disaperd. the men wonder were she had gon the men saw bubbals coming up from the bottom of the lack they now were one of the girls were are the bottom of the lack tring to find the way in the men made a plan. to try and get ther befor the girl get ther one of the men said they might have a play how to get into the cartill. I will dive down and see were they get in then when they have gone we cane go and expore the carsell and selve their might be some hidon tresure then we will be rich recher then any on the world we can go for a month holiday in Swizaland we nedent do any work untill we die we can bouse up.
the other man said shock [shut up!] they can her you full [fool] O! shut up your sleve your making as mush nose as me watch out some one has herd we better get going other wise theile think somethick fishey arigh then will go.*
The girls never now about the two men the carrid on with their work
that night the two men whent across the lack they nowe where the hole is they had their swimming gere. they dind not like that sine post with the skeleton on it look a bit creepy a grait wind rose it started thunder and ligthing the two men were very scared the lack was getting very rougth the boat started rock and it got very dangerus the men could not swim so they were very frigtend the boat tipe overy and the men fell out of the

* Here is strong evidence of the need for the teacher of 'backward' children to have small classes and many free periods. This lively dialogue needs much careful deciphering and study, before, say, a teacher could bring it to life on a recorded tape. Yet this is an important part of his work.

boat and dround so they never got the thresher nore did the 4 spies it was only a rumer going round.

The men belong to the adult world which does not know the secret: they approach the fearful area of retribution and doom at their peril—they are not equipped, as Rose is, with the mask-disciplines of imaginative courage. They do not get the treasure. So they perish, as Ignorance does in *The Pilgrim's Progress*: 'Then they took him up, and carried

Fig. 6

him through the air, to the door that I saw in the side of the hill, and put him in there. Then I saw that there was a way to hell, even from the gates of heaven . . .' And now, the reality of the spiritual quest asserted and tested, we can go on to the second part of Rose's pursuit of the Grail—of coming to terms with human morality, to find relief from her mental agony:

but the carsal was a mistory because there was an old lady dead in it the top of the tower She had been dead for 10 yers know on now this thing but the fore spies expord the castle again they all whent down in the water this time they wern't afraid of anythink.

Now we come again and again to references to 'being brave'—indications that Rose is really reassuring herself that courage is needed to approach 'this thing' about which 'no one knows'. I am reminded of the courage of the protagonist in another little girl's story in which, on her way in to the dying mother's room the young protagonist says to herself, 'I daren't: I must.' (See *Eloping* in *The Secret Places*).

they wanted to see if there was a wich living in the mistory castle they went up 3 tower and when they went up the 4 tower their was bats big spider crowling about the girls were a bit frightend they went up the crepy stairs and up the top was a big door with a key on the floor the door was lock one of the girls pick they key up and open the door she was the bravist on she dere do anything the door was a bit stive it grete as she open it. It was absolutely horrieyfide to find some on dead on the floor on of the girl fainted. they went nere the old lady and sore it was a wich she had all black on and big finger nails nerly as big as a nail and as sharp as a pin She was as white and shrivelled up

Here we have a clue to the identity of the 'witch'—for Rose uses the same word as she uses about her mother's death—'she died of her brain shrivelling up'.

the girl left her their they locked the door and took the key with them so that no one will distrebe her they never told any on about this they kept the key for a suvenere and a memory of the mistory castle.

How brave and marvellous it is, this approach to the painful memory, and the symbolic turning of the key on a secret grief that must not be disturbed! How utterly irrelevant to such a courageous and civilised act of imaginative exploration is so much of our English work—how irrelevant it would be here to bully the child about spelling, when she attempts such long and difficult words so bravely—and gets words like 'absolutely' right! How futile even to suppose that she 'doesn't write sentences', because she doesn't punctuate! How appalling to suppose that Rose is in any sense a 'low-stream' child! What is 'low' about a spirit that can approach its inward pain thus, by questing into the unknown, to gain relief and insight? How many of us protect ourselves by mental brightness against just such brave explorations of tender feeling as Rose makes here?

It is also an important literary consideration to note how closely Rose's story echoes Grimms' fairy tale about the sleeping beauty—a tale which tells of a desperately wanted child who is yet cursed by the uninvited thirteenth guest, and who seems to die, but does not, and falls into a trance for a hundred years instead. All these themes in the fairy tale derive their power over all of us because they touch on unconscious fears in the child of being attacked in revenge by the parent whom it both loves and hates. For Rose the long trance—the hundred years' sleep—would seem, too, like the withdrawal state of her grief:

... the maiden was left alone in the castle. She wandered about into all the nooks and corners, and into all the chambers and parlours, as the fancy took her, till at last she came to an old tower. She climbed the narrow winding stair which led to a little door, with a rusty key sticking out of the lock; she turned the key, and the door opened, and there in the little room sat an old woman with a spindle, diligently spinning her flax.

'Good day, mother,' said the princess . . . . (Jakob and Wilhelm Grimm, 'The Sleeping Beauty', *Household Stories*, Macmillan, 1923.)

To confirm the value of such a piece to Rose, both as a means to emotional balance, and, going hand in hand with this, improved technical powers of writing, I will skip a few months and come to another related passage written by her in an examination towards the end of our time together. Here she shows a marked approach closer to reality, while yet writing apparently in phantasy. She writes of sudden death happening in 'another' family, though she is in fact writing about what happened in her own home. And thus she 'places' the incident, sees it from the 'outside', distanced, and held away. She can understand better what it was that happened to her, and now can feel her grief as something common to human experience, and as something with which one may come to terms.

Asked later to write in an examination on the subject *Sudden Death*, she writes once more the story of mother's death. But this time the story is not given in phantasy—but seen realistically, as in a novel. Thus it is distanced and placed—as though it happened to others. Rose thus comes bravely to accept her loss and grief as common to mankind, and at the end is reconciled to consideration of better times to come. Yet there is no doubt that she is writing of her own family loss, because towards the end the distancing breaks down and she speaks of 'us'. Here is a little girl bravely making her way by art towards an acceptance of the greatest loss, as Wordsworth does in his sonnet 'Surpris'd by Joy', and finding for herself hope and confidence in the 'continuity of life'.

Sudden Death.

About 2 years ago their was a sudden death a lady named Misses Johnes died of what know one knowes. She wosh their childrenes hire that night and her own then she went out to Mr slad the grouser and brough some frit for the 4 children then she same bake and tork to Mrs Clarke next door and after awill she came in got the children to bed then sat down and read a book calld deat on my Pillow she was lauging at some funny parts. then she desided to go to bed he slef and in the middal of the might she went uncoshers and that morning dad said good mornig love and not a sownd he said it again but know replie he got up and moved her about and she never woke up Mr Jones got worid and went up to the phone and rang up the doctor but the doctor was out some were so then he phone up the hospital the amberless came and took he to Melton hospital and doctor Nickals said she is very ill will have to thak her to Tonbury hospital their see what is the mater they rust her their and after 2 days the hadnt had the proper things their so they took her to London hospital Mr Jones when to London with amerless and stayd at London hospital for 3 days then he came home and whated for the bad *or* good news then on Monday morning at 5 o clock a lady round they other side of us and came and gave us the bad news that she had died. and every one very kind they gave us meals and two of children went and stad with some freinds for a weeke or two and now Mr Jones is getting marrid again and that will be better for the children.

Rose's father did, in fact, marry again just at this time, and she adjusted herself to it happily and well. No doubt such a story, and the whole sequence of stories about her mother's death, helped her to overcome her grief and accept her stepmother. This seemed to me confirmed by her sudden interest in typing at a suggestion of her stepmother and her attempts to improve her handwriting to try 'to find an office job'.

But what right has anyone who is as moved as we are by Rose's story to assume that *she can't write*? That mere touch, underlining the '*or*' of 'bad *or* good news', expresses with subtlety the agony of hoping for good news when terrible news is too unavoidably expected. Rose can't spell, and she can't punctuate, and I would not want any teacher to rest until he or she had done everything to help Rose to do these things properly before she left school, as we all did. But this work must not be done with the assumption that this child is illiterate, that she cannot write. *She can write*, movingly, and beautifully. And now, having read this sequence of writing by such a 'dull' child, who doesn't feel ashamed of a society which treats her, with a million others, three-eighths of the population, as a 'dud', or a 'dreg', to teach whom it is a 'bloody waste of time', and from whom we obtain no 'dividends'?

There is much else of Rose's work I would like to quote, but this book is already too long, and I must content myself with one other story. It contains those vernacular phrases from speech such as a 'dull' child will use directly and delightfully, giving character to his own style. (Elsewhere a character of Rose's says to another, 'Oh shut up, you make me feel sick, you helpless young thing!') Here there is much character in such phrases as 'What's that shuffling in that basket?' and 'She just went off ordinary out of the door'. And my favourite spelling is 'Ow crigckey!' which entirely conveys the appalling misgivings which come over the thief when she sees the police outside. With this story, obviously belonging to Rose's deep psychic theme of care for the young abandoned creature, like her orphaned sisters and herself, I must reluctantly say goodbye to one of the most delightful young creatures I have ever known. I was very glad when a reader of *The Guardian* was so touched by a brief account of her courage in the face of sorrow that he sent her ten shillings, which I passed on as chemist's tokens for make-up. But may I leave in the reader's ears her first plea, 'Do you really like being with us, Sir? As much as being with 3 A?'

Caught Redhanded.

One day Mrs morgan was going down the shop, she went in. The shopkeeper "said good morning Mrs Morgan," how is your little baby geting on". "arigth thank you," "yes and what can I get you" "I won't a lb of butter, "and half of marg pleas. "and have you got any Bacon in yet." "the shopkeeper siad yes we got it in this morning" "well I will have half a lb pleas "Oh wha't is that nose! "Some one has tipe my pram, up," and my baby has gone! "O wha't can I do" "the shopkeeper said I will ring the police up and they will help you "I wonder how could have tackon her." "That lady up the road has had her baby stowlen but they fond it dead next morning in a dich." "I hope I don't find my their. "The shopkeeper said don't worye they will find the baby don't cry." "Oh I do hope they will find it" "here come the police now." The police man ask the lady wha't happon Mrs Morgan said my baby has been stowlen." will you help me to find her pleas." The policeman said yes their has been to much of this latley babyes been stowlen." and "People killd" "We whan't to find the baby as much as you do Mrs morgan we whan't to find the killer who is dowing all this." So the police started to search for the baby they put it in the papers. The lady who took the baby saw it in the paper she became a bit worred of this and got very nerves she through the paper down. "This has not happen before" I will go and hide it before they come and look here for it" Ow crigckey! theres a police man out side on the pathment wha't can I do now" I now I will put it in a barscket of washing and cover it up with dirty clous." Then he won't now"

She just went of ordenrey out of the door. She did not now the police will ask her wha't have you got in that baskek" "I have some dirty washing I am going to thack them to the lordery. "Wh't is that shufarling in that basckek "nothing sir" nothing "let me have a look pleas" "no you can not" "your not going to se wha't I own no your not" "I cam here a baby cry "that is not your baby" "you stowl it." The lady started to run as fast as she could the police man blow his wiscell the other police men came and started to run after her She did not get very fare befor the police man cought up with her she strogald abit but they carmd her down and took her to the police stastione she made a a statmeant and she was in jaell for to years for killing babyis. and the ladys who baby was stowle got her baby back safaly.

✽   ✽   ✽

PSYCHIATRIST'S NOTE

This gives a fascinating picture of a child facing grief with the normal resources of the human spirit. She tackles her sorrow in a healthy and courageous way, and works through it. She shows compassion, a reparative drive, and the capacity to mourn in a mature way. The account makes plain the value of imaginative-creative work in such normal processes of meeting life's more distressing circumstances.

13. KENNETH PRIME

Kenneth was another R.A.F. boy, and suffered as these children all do from being moved from place to place. But this boy had suffered more than most, and was, obviously, very ill mentally. I have discussed him in some detail elsewhere in an article I wrote because I was appalled to notice the similarities between Kenneth and the man who murdered a motorist on the A6 main road near Bedford at the time. The murderer was obviously caught up in a terrible phantasy, and had spoken to his victim's woman friend, whom he later raped, of playing at gunman. The way he had spoken was disturbingly similar to Kenneth's phantasies:

Beat for the drew 'Bankg' bullet Mr Macdillon its
Mac Plester in the HEART
Dead staidght away
Macdillon fire his gun Bankg Bankg Bankg
Doc H he is dead
Kitty Macdillon yes Kitty yor Brother is Dead.
THE END
THE END

All Kenneth's stories end with the repeated 'THE END', sometimes illuminated with expanding rays, as on television, and much of his material is television terror-stuff repeated. But yet there is a more disturbing quality, which shows how a child will use commercial horror sensationalism, choosing it because he is disturbed, and employing it for his own ends, in the quest for relief. But television horror, being sensational, exploiting and arousing fears as an end in itself, offers no relief. Interestingly enough, I note among these children that those most affected by television are those who are the most disturbed or unhappy. In this there are, I am sure, implications about the inevitable weaknesses of the more trivial aspects of our culture.

To come to see what Kenneth was about one needs to study the drawings, relate them to odd touches of behaviour, and learn a little of his family background. The result may add up, as it did here, I think, to the fact that all normal human contact was broken: he was in a kind of perpetual trance. It seemed to me then, and still seems, miserably frustrating to be able to do nothing for such a child in such obvious need.

I reported that it seemed to me that he, together with four other members of his form, should see a child psychiatrist, to be diagnosed, and so that therapy might be given to these children. It seemed to me that, even if it remained unlikely that their condition could be remedied, they would at least be brought to feel that some help was available. I think that Kenneth would probably need lengthy psychotherapy before he could be brought towards integration and normal behaviour. This would require several years of regular visits to a psychiatrist, if one could be found to take him on, probably in Tonbury, 18 miles away. Parental support would have to be secured. This disturbance of his normal life would have had to be set against his present misery, for the child in a withdrawal state or psychotic phantasy does suffer a great deal, as psychiatrists have pointed out. He might have been given a little superficial help by occasional therapeutic sessions, through the school psychiatric service, and this might have enlisted a little his confidence in the adult world—even such aid might perhaps have prevented him from becoming gravely unhinged later in life. Whatever the truth of his psychic condition it seemed to me that he was much in need of examination and diagnosis. And yet nothing was done, either for him or his mentally ill classmates, even though the fact of his disorder was made plain by me in articles in the national press. It was said of him, 'I'm glad he's gone—I don't like to say this, but he's the sort who will one day do somebody in.' I don't report this as an exceptional remark —this kind of thing is said in a thousand schools daily, even by kind and good people. But the neglect of such a boy, in another hundred years' time, will seem like the chaining of lunatics in bedlam. Here is an obvious chance to redeem a potential criminal who, if he is kept in a prison later, may cost 'society' £1,500 a year. To give him £500 worth of psychiatry a year now would be cheaper, in the long run. But certainly the child is so ill that no educational experience—no degree of sympathy, no desire to do him good from the best and most ideal motives, no care by a devoted teacher could really have the slightest effect in removing the blockages to his development by the manifestations of his disorder.

I think Kenneth was much more intelligent than he seemed—indeed he was very cunning, and had many undeveloped potentialities (see Geoffrey Hawkes on his work in free drama, p. 297). He was attractive physically, as, one gathers, are many such mentally sick children, and he made at times an appeal to one that seemed full of the innocent and disarming appeal of the baby. Yet he had come to the school originally in a filthy condition, and my headmaster had to make a special effort to encourage his father to see that he was properly dressed, through the R.A.F. station commander. But Kenneth was irregular in his behaviour. Sometimes he would co-operate, sometimes he would playfully hide in the cupboards or under the desk to test out 'Daddy's' reactions. But then on other days his face was immobile, locked in an expressionless pout, not hostile, but withdrawn, turned inward. I have seen this expression also in a girl, who sucked her thumb, and needed anxiously whenever it was possible to get a boy to take her outside and pet her. ('She's a dirty old girl', a boy said to me about her). Kenneth once masturbated in class, and the fact that this could happen in otherwise normal surroundings seemed uncanny—all the other boys knew, and watched, and commented—the manifestation brought out all their guilt, too, of course. And I found it deeply disturbing, because the boy's withdrawal state made it impossible to do anything about him. He simply behaved as if stunned, before and after. And, I reflected, while his father is servicing aircraft which cost millions, and are designed to annihilate the population of Moscow or Kiev in the twinkling of an eye, this boy is thought not to be worth more than the minimum care and treatment as a human being. Reflections such as this sometimes give one an uneasy feeling that the human conduct and attitudes we assume to be normal (such as the maintenance of armaments for 'defence') are, in fact, distorted with the same maniac flaws which bring from time to time a Hiroshima, a Belsen, or a campaign of terrorism. The Canberra bombers flying over the school were 'normal': Kenneth, victim of the service life, had needs our society ignores, even taboos. Poor Kenneth was a wounded soul, and I can still see those pleading sick eyes—but he went elsewhere long before I ended my teaching stint. In face of him, as in face of the threat of war, one felt helpless, and the normal patterns of what we accept as 'ordinary life' dissolved.

Clues to the degree of Kenneth's disturbances may be found in the drawings which accompanied his writing. The victims were either killed by being stabbed in the genitals (and no doubt left in the reader's mind as to exactly where), or a naked woman stood over the body:

One day a man was kill and stabb.

Fig. 7

The rope and the man
my name is Lee Morey I work fo M.
Squad. M Squad put me on a special
cores I went to a howese in a bock
Screet. I went in the howese and I Saw
a man deed on the Floor theme was
a ~~deor~~ bear ~~wife~~ women standing by the body.
I put her in the cou. A day lact
thay cod my thot the ~~wife~~ women
bid not do it the mon thay caughe the
Man ahd thay hand him

Fig. 8

Notice that 'deor wife' has been altered to 'bear women', and 'wife' to 'women'.

Being asked to write an imaginative piece about a sculptured head, he not only draws the face with almost a classical beauty, showing his sensitivity, and adds to the femininity by adding kisscurl and earrings—he also adds a ferocious scar to the face, and a convict's number to the neck.

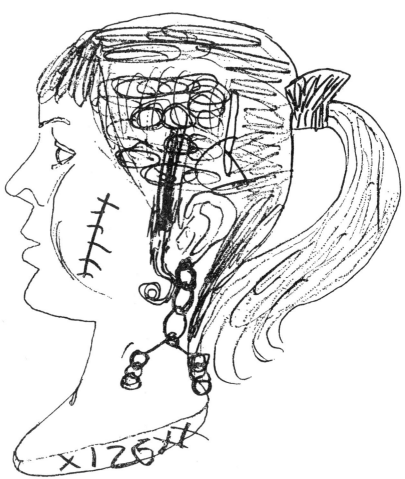

Fig. 9

In all he creates there are distorted and destructive elements, inexplicable in any normal terms.

Thus we cannot, I think, apply to Kenneth the same principles we apply to other 'backward' pupils. Of course, we can advance his inward balance a little by sympathetic encouragement, and by allowing him to obtain relief from the expression in phantasy of his inner conflicts. In any case Kenneth was with the class for too short a time to judge how much might be achieved by such means. With him, however, as with Michael Holmes (No. 19), there were disturbances which teaching alone could not overcome. There is no cause for the teacher to despair when his idealism meets this impasse—as is explained in my chapters about our responses to disturbed children above. This is a sad truth of human nature, that the sick mind is inaccessible to normal sympathy, aid and nourishment. Because of this the mentally sick used to be abused, ill-treated or locked up. Nowadays, we suppose we treat such unfortunate people better: but the public services for the treatment of mentally sick people and children are still much less efficient and more sparse than those for treating physical illness. And we all tend to try to pretend that such problems do not exist, or we are hostile, from unconscious fear. There is a proportion of 'backward' children who are mentally sick, yet when I wrote to suggest a survey to a County Education Officer who had made what seemed to me an enlightened speech on such matters, he wrote back to say that he could not share my view, and that he felt they had no children with whom they could not cope in the primary school, and bring back to normal efficiency in living by normal methods. This surely ignores a grave problem, and I feel sure that among the children in 'C' and 'D' streams there must be at least one in ten who are mentally sick enough to require psychotherapy, probably something like 100,000 in all our secondary schools. Certainly this aspect of school life seems worth investigating. As it is, it is those like Kenneth who are beyond normal access to sympathy who make the whole atmosphere of a 'backward' class disturbed and unruly, and exhausting for the teacher.*

I will here simply add notes on all the work Kenneth did for me, and then add notes on this pupil from the doctor with paediatric and psychoanalytical experience: she suggests he is a grave case. Teachers may then judge how relevant my concern is to their own proportion of unbalanced children.

Kenneth's family:

There are 7 of Us there is my mum and my sister thre is Peter and Andrew and Alan and my self and my bad. By bad is a elecenician man. Mum dus houseework. I go to the pictures kneeling every night.

* See teachers' comments p. 262 on the recurrent refusal in schools to recognise mental illness in backward children.

Asked to write on the title 'Which Way', and told this was to be a story about a man faced with temptation he writes:

There is a man in my . . . [crossed out]
Wiich way to go to the bank mate. I went in to the bank I give Him a Forged Note. And the bank man said this is a Forged Noet He said weight Here I will Be Back in 10-mine Sir. He came Back wiht to policeman they took me in a police car I went to prison.

On the next page are some scribbled pieces:

A lady is a man best fenird [friend]
A lady Fat and Fhin is a Dog best fenird a PLENTY is my best friend.
I like Lady nice and Sexy with PLENTY of bod. and not to driy [dirty] and not to rude.
I know a little mouse who said to a nother little mouse come round the corner I will show you my hole.

Many of the more disturbed children made such attempts to 'test me out' by writing as near to the obscene as they could. At least one had the excuse of pretending that the writing was so bad one didn't notice the meaning, and could concentrate on the more positive pieces of work.

Kenneth then wrote a cannibalistic piece. This was once shown to an ex-public schoolboy after a discussion at my university seminar at Cambridge on children's writing. The public school man said, 'My God! If only I'd been allowed to write like that!'

One day a man kill a womon. and cut Her Kidney out and eat them. next day He kill a another woman and cut her kidney out and eat them. and made an awful mess. He was called the vampire. He hab to horrible teeth 91 Thursday january 9161 a wamon was kill and a kidney was missing. it was getting serious. Nexe they find the body was on marshladn and foodprints in to swamp

This next piece seemed to me a direct reference to his need to plunge into the unconscious to release a hidden fear (see Rose Jameson's story about diving down to enter the mystery castle, above). When the threatening mine is released he can go 'home'.

My name is Kenneth I work in a Facttoer I have a leave comeing I wet on a motor-cruiser. hon the motor cruiser there was shm Frogmen's-suits. the captman he thc hus hot to sea we Put hn out suits we wet down in to the sea hon the bottom. there wos a sea-mine I wet to the top of the sea I told the catptman I go in the motor-cruisr. he go hon to the Radio we tod the sea Command. he tod the motor disposol thror come to the side of the ship thrar pht on the Frgmens suits and wet down thrar fo the mine thrar cut the choin which hasld the motor floated to the top thrar fired a rifle which hit 1 of the horn hit blew up so we wit home.

Kenneth once ran away from home. To the title *A Runaway* he wrote: 'One day a buy her [boy heard] is mother and Father arguing and he 2/6 he decided to runaway. To Aunty and unlce in Suothwode (Southwold).' How sad to think of a child running away who cannot spell the name of the place to which he wants to run!

I will conclude my examples with two passages written by Kenneth in an examination. I cannot claim he is literate, though for him these pieces are orderly. There are reversed letters in the spelling that speak of grave emotional disorder (*thrar, wnet, ladn*) as do some of the more extraordinary departures from correct spelling (*payer* for *played, hiter* for *hit, pit* for *picked, dan sasys* for *down stairs, holler* for *hole, saffery* for *safe, feod the pelser* for *fetched the police, cHmer* for *came* [note he marks the H which stands for A= a as definitely an 'H'!]) 'I went home' is almost the only phrase clearly written—and this alone seems to me to stand for the achieved relief!

The orphaned Family

In the orphaed Family thrar was 6 Boy. One day the Boy wnet to payer in the wood and mayd a dener and Fiyer then a Frameman he had a gon he fiyed his gun and hiter one of Boy The ophoned ~~Family~~ Boy pit im up. and wet home Doc chm and the Boy that was sot wos or rit.

The HED

As he passed the on his way home fom the Dance he heard a muffled explosion I sor that the dor was oped I wocer in wend dan sosys and sor a holler in

↙h

the saffrery I wet hover I feod the pelser and thoy cHmer I went home

the EDH

Though, as I have said, it seemed to me Kenneth was a shrewd boy with fine perceptions, his potentialities were quite locked up in his mental disorder and very little could be done about his spelling, writing or reading until he had received psychotherapy. This he will probably never get, so he will remain illiterate, through no fault of his own. However, I think our imaginative work in English may have afforded him a little relief, and a little self-respect.

✻   ✻   ✻

This boy seems to me extremely disturbed, and differs from the others in being almost certainly psychotic, that is, he seems to be really out of touch with external reality. It might well be that his bad feelings and murderous impulses were so projected outside into the world around him that he would feel himself to be surrounded by bad and dangerous people. The danger here is that he might feel himself justified in attacking these people without provocation—as if 'hitting first' in 'self-defence'—and commit some serious crime. It is possible that he lives in his inner world of phantasy altogether, with all the bad impulses and people around him, so much so that he can see nothing of the more reassuring world of everyday reality.

With this boy and 'Jack O'Malley' (p. 106) it seems possible, from what is written in the evidence here, of their behaviour and their writing, that they are too much out of touch with external reality. They are living in their phantasies, projecting a great deal into the external world, and therefore may act on the assumption that the phantasy is a fact. Such psychotic disturbances merit urgent close attention—recognition, diagnosis, and treatment if possible—so that criminal acts may be avoided.

14. ROBERT SHIRE

The child-like, agreeable simplicity of Robert may be taken in at a glance from his painting of a small castle among the clouds at the top of a small green hill (Plate II). Life for him could easily be no more than the life of the simple cliché, of a 'good time' of empty distractions, such as the popular mind, at the *Daily Express* level, might embrace at its most banal:

One day a boy stood leaning against the cafe door named rex harrison. He had Black hair with Brown eyes with red Jacket, Grey trousers with black shoes. He was waiting for Jean smith she is 16 Brown hair, brown eyes, they went inside the cafe, then they talked to each other then Jean said I am going out with another boy, but I can get audrey for you Rex, said all right. I will tell her to meet you outside the cinama at 6.39. Audrey is a blonde she is 16 they went inside the cinama Jean went in with them when the film was nearly over when Jean went of to see her own boyfreind and left rex and audrey were left a lone in the cinama the next 6 months they went to the pictures then they got ingaged. after they got ingaged. they went to the seaside for the day at Blackpool they got there at eleven oclock saturday morning they got out of the train. Rex siad should we have dinner in that fish and chips audrey said yes after they had finished there dinner they went down to the amusments they walked down the amusments Rex siad lets have a go on that thing said rex yes said Audrey it was Bingo a game like housey, housey, Rex got his card and he won a dog Audrey had a go she never won. then they went to catch the bus for home they got home at nine oclock Rex kissed audrey then they went home in the morning Rex went to work at the television studios Audrey went to work in the cafe when they got home from work the next saturday they got married.

The End.

Robert could be treated as a dumb cluck, and left to moulder away in some bottom stream, merely 'kept occupied'. Is it worth spending effort, money for books, an adult teacher's good time, on such a simple soul? Why not let him go out, at 12 years old, into a job? Yet if we persist we shall find that Robert can yield rather childish, but sensitive poems and stories about his fears and perceptions—thus he is brought out of the shell, relieved from atrophy and the limitations on his feelings—and possibly made a better lover, husband, parent, worker because of it.

The unispected trip across the sea

Once upon a time there was a boy named Peter. He went to the harbour he was very tired so he saw a ship he got on board the ship, he crept down to where the cargo was kept he got in a comvatable place to sleep. He woke up 6 hours later he got out of the cargo store crept up on Deck and all he could see was the sea the boat had left the harbour and it was due for china. he creeped back to the cargo sat, wondering what he would do next then he laid down and went to sleep again when the men came down to fetch the cargo. They saw the boy they took him for to the captain. Then the captain said to the boy what are you doing hear I run away from home I was very tired.

I see this boat so i creeped on board, and had a sleep. The captian said I will let you stay abroard the ship as long as you work for your keep. The boy said all right ile work. The captain said go with the men to shift the cargo so he went to the cargo store they lifted all the cargo to another place, then they had to scrub the deck when they had finished that they saw china in the distance he wondered what it would be like. The captain said it will be all right you will not go of this ship by next week you will be back home. The boy said I dont want to go hime, if I do i will get killed. The police will see that you dont get belted on December 10th they were in england, and the boy was home with his parents.

The End.

Robert in this explores the possibility of leaving home, which he still fears as a child. The release of fears in fictional form seems to bring with it the capacity to write more perceptively:

The Rat

The rat is a dirty creature it digs tunnels under the ground at night it goes in the chicken hut looking for meal and wheat then it goes to sleep.

The mouse

The mouse is a slimy fellow, its not very big but it squeezes through tiny cracks in wood its got very sharp teeth and a slimy tail and its little ears prick out of the hole it likes meal.

The Mouse

The mouse is a little fellow it lives amongst straw and sometimes a pile of bags or in any old heaps of rubbish etc. it makes a runaway through rubbish and into meal bins where it eats the meal and soon as anybody comes, it jumps out of the meal bins along its runway and back in is nest . . .

How varied these children are, in their approaches to experience! Some write about farming, some about mystery castles, some about animals, some about car racing. Robert is, as it were, the Walter de la Mare of the form, as Joan Stall was the Ivy Compton-Burnett.

> *The hare came running down the hill*
> *With a flash of brown its down the hill*
> *its Big brown ears prick out of the corn*
> *resting all day and playing all night with its little*
> *fluffy tail dragging behind that crafty old hare*
> *laying in the barley*

Casey Jones produces this:

The 6.45 came racing down the line with a whistle and hoot its flying high round the corner 85 miles an hour tearing down the hill but then the fireman shouted jump for it or you'll be a goner because the was a passenger train coming this way the fireman jumped out but the driver never the fireman heard a crash and a bang there was a wreck the driver was dead for he hit his head.

And one day Robert painted first a most sensitive picture of some trees and under the trees an old tramp drying his socks on a branch. Then below he wrote the poem:

> *The Tramp.*
> The tramp is a funny man
> He walks all over the place
> He sleeps under a hedge
> He has got a pair of baggy socks
> A pair of trousers with holes in it
> And a grubby Jacket not worth twopence
> He eats scraps of meat with a piece of bread
> Then he goes on his way
> Like a funny man

This catches the qualities of bare simplicity from the Chinese poem by Lu Yu which I read them to stimulate this exercise. Robert's poem is an artefact, and when read to other children, as it will be from this book, it will produce further paintings and poems about the strange tramp figure who, like T. F. Powys's Tinker Jar who is God, is always present in children's minds. All this creativity, valuable in the contemplation of experience as I hope I have shown, comes from nothing. It is made out of air—it does not exist before it is put down on the blank sheet of paper. Think of the times you have been moved or delighted by children's pieces in this book—none of this would have been brought into existence had these children been kept to text-books, or not given time to write. Consider this loss multiplied many thousands of times and you have a picture of the neglect of potential in our secondary schools. The body of created work that might be represents a potential nursery civilisation in itself. Robert's is not a great or magnificent castle, but it stands among the clouds in its aspirations, and is a fortress of his own simple sensitive individuality.

✻   ✻   ✻

PSYCHIATRIST'S NOTE

Robert does not write about feelings—only about events, as if seen from the outside, not really 'taken part in'. Perhaps he splits off his feelings because he is afraid of them, and then cannot take part sufficiently in life. This would make it difficult for him to learn.

15. GERALD GOODCHILD

(I.Q. 74)

Gerald was one of those with whom my policy of telling them forcibly and regularly that they were 'good' worked wonderfully. He was in the throes of attaining sexual maturity, and yet was backward at writing and reading, and so Gerald felt a pressing sense of inferiority. Perhaps it was the explicit statement of his problem, in words and in pictures, which first made it plain to me how much boosting and encouragement the 'C'-stream child needs. At the end of his time with me I watched Gerald, who had been made a Prefect, handing round cakes and tea in the 'governors' room' on Speech Day. He was doing this with great confidence and even grace, but without being at all prissy, and sometimes coming to me and asking *sotto voce*, 'Who's the old bird with the feathers, Sir?'. I was pleased to see the head of another school, obviously most impressed with Gerald's social ease, put his arm round his shoulder and say, 'You've looked after us well!' Gerald responded brightly, quite at his ease and self-possessed, like the proper young gentleman he was, able to think of others, their comfort and their amusement. Here we may see civilised manners without gentility, in a 'low-stream' dimension.

Gerald's need in his early work was stated thus:

MY FAMILY

There are 6 people in our family I live in Number two Bridgebrook Rd Smallerden Melton my father is a Butcher and I am one to my family is is good them are good people my Village is pump [a dump] I have to girlfriend at this school My dad is big an strong We have got a Television and 3 bciyle My sister is 5 year old My borther is 9 year old Bill is 13 year old my Dad is 40 year old I mum is 39 year old gran is 69 year old we have go a cat dog and budgerigar ther are three bed room in our house I have go a record playa 2 wirelesses our house is a good house.

This recurrent emphasis on 'we are good people' was accompanied by a drawing which showed Gerald fighting as a protagonist in the bull-ring, with all the crowd on his side (Fig. 10). This I interpreted to myself as something to do with his father, who was a butcher: perhaps Gerald secretly felt that to be a butcher's man was not to be all that

Fig. 10

I A noble stag, painted by Roger Scott, the 'gut boy' (see pp. 97-100).

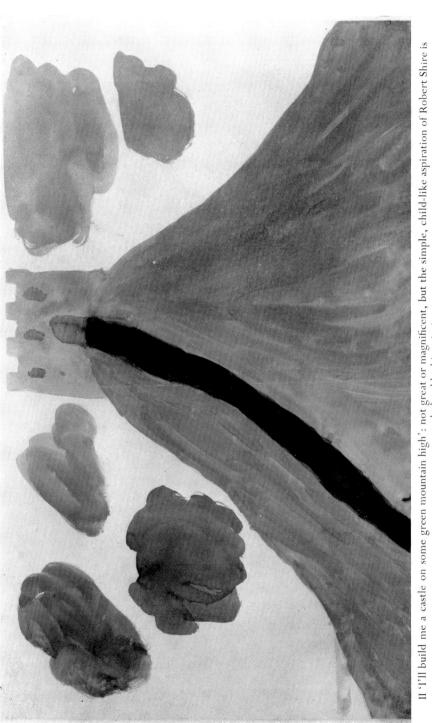

II 'I'll build me a castle on some green mountain high': not great or magnificent, but the simple, child-like aspiration of Robert Shire is symbolised by his painting.

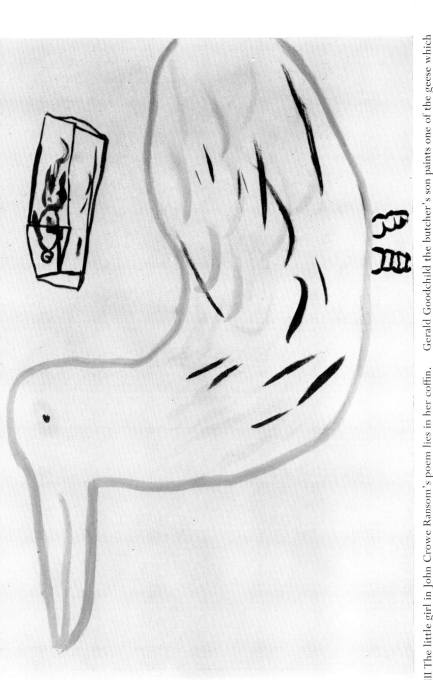

III The little girl in John Crowe Ransom's poem lies in her coffin. Gerald Goodchild the butcher's son paints one of the geese which 'cry in goose Alas', compassionate and beautiful in its flowing motherly lines.

IV By quick free brush-work Michael secures a vivid action picture of his 'sly old waesel'. When he finished a picture he would trim one end with scissors, then the other, then the first, until he was cutting the whole picture up. This one was rescued by force.

'good', and this became involved with his feelings about his father. He has to prove his worth not only by his prowess in sexual adventure and learning, but by bull-fighting, as it were, the image of his father's trade. This may be wide of the mark: but what may be quite simply accepted is perhaps that all boys grow to maturity in unconscious contest with their fathers, in an Oedipan way. They grow to their stature as it were against the pressure of the father's felt existence, as the rival to the mother, on whom they must practise loving. Gerald's work has much to do with such psychic processes. To know this gives us a little more sympathy with Gerald's strange mixture of childishness, romantic nature (his book is full of hearts bearing the slogan 'G.G. loves . . .'— but the initials of the loved girl change on virtually every page. The strange thing was that he seemed to be able to love several at once and they did not mind this!). Here is the theme again:

There is a man look for a job is name is John WIGGLE is hair is Black is eye are Blue he is a big strong man he is walking down the street he is going into the lorry department he has just come out of the lorry depatment. he look very Please he start work to morrow. he is going home to tell is wife and kids. morring come he get up at 5 am he get realy for work he has go to be there are 6.30 am and he get to work the Bos said to him take some thing down the my house and put then in the garage and he went the lot of time with load he go suspicious and he went to the poicle and they gave him a Reward and the poicle we will go up ther to get him and the poicle go him and John became the bos of the lord (lorry) departent.

Gerald's work is monosyllabic, because he finds it difficult to read much more than one-syllable words. Having his own work 'printed' in the class magazine helped a great deal, and this combined with the release of free 'psychic' material helped a great deal to make Gerald's writing fluent and self-possessed. Instead of being ashamed of his halting reading he found himself able to enter into the spirit of his work and use his considerable richness of character to entertain. Typical was his reaction to being asked to write a letter in reply to my critic in the newspaper: he wrote to his uncle (see p. 186).

The pieces of work I shall quote from Gerald's quite voluminous attempts are chosen to show that the loosening up of his phantasy, still rather infantile in its modes, together with his approach through imagination to more adult reality, helps to turn this inarticulate young hobbledehoy, as he was at first, into a young man of character, who is not at all illiterate. Again, had the process been developed earlier in the primary school and the early stages of the secondary school Graham would not be handicapped as he still is by bad spelling and punctuation. Too much preoccupation at these stages with spelling and punctuation, neatness, English exercises and the rest had made him halt and lame in his expression. By the time I left he could give a very good account of the work of a butcher, and was always amusing to talk to.

The jungle

In the jungle there are all kinds of animals. There are snake apes etc. One day a little white boy was with is Mother. And the boy said to his mother can I go for a walk. She said yes but dont go into the jungle. and he yes mother and he was walking along the path and he see a chimpanzee and he went to play with it. and he was play with chimpnzee. and suddenly an ape pick him up and carried him a way the and the little boy was shout help help and the boy mother was getting worried it was getting dark and there Husband came run and he said were is Gerald I don on (know) he went of for a walk and has not come back oh john I am worried. I will gett a party of man and go and seach for him. and they went to look of the boy and they look evry were they find him sleeping with the ape and the boy father said come on home Gerald and the little said cane I take ape home Dad and is [Dad] say on [no] and the little said I won come home all right then. ['I won't come home!' 'All right then.']

This is perhaps a symbolic story about Gerald's desire that his parents should accept the Caliban side of him in his adolescence—his need, as it were, to play with the chimpanzee side of his nature, that of the jungle of sexual and other adult feeling. He wants to show his parents that they must take this part of his life into the home, because he still needs them. This seems to me a very beautiful story.

Gerald suffered from deep guilt over his sexual career, and asked me in our discussion of 'the facts of life', 'Is it true, Sir, that if you get that disease called V.D. you have to have a great needle shoved up your penis?' Here is a poem about his masturbation guilt, ostensibly a poem about death—a Blues:

> He lay on the bed in a dream
> he like cold ice-cream
> went (when) he was alive he jump up and down like a machine
> he white in the face
> cold in the eyes
> he lie waiting for his long box
> hear (it) comes slow has can be

they slowly put him in
slow slow slow he goes
down down deep under the earth

This poem obviously had great 'relief' value for Gerald and represents a considerable freeing of associations and phantasies in him. So does the following story, which probably symbolises his 'Jack the Ripper' feelings—his sexual feelings in which he notices strange depths of aggressiveness—towards girls: his expression now is sometimes very lively:

THE HEADLESS BOdy

One dark night in midwinter There was woman walking down a dark ally and suddenly someone jump one her she screamed. But it was no good there was not any one around she fell to the ground she was dead dead as door it was a man that jump on her he was mental. He took her to is house he took her in a dark room switch on the light he cut of her head and arms and legs. He got a big trunk and put the body into the trunk he put the head in the park morning came not one had miss the woman two boy were walking through the park one of the boys run into the three senddly he shout Bob come hear "what want" "come hear quick" "I am come" "got and get the police quick" Be Back in a minute" he came Back with the police. the police said it was a murder case a head with out a body. HE sent the trunk to Melton station it had no name or nothing it stop there for six week no one came for it so at the station they had a talk and said they would open it. they opon it they saw the body with the arm and legs of they call the police the police came the body was naked this must be the body that the head belong to they took it down to the station and had it examined the body they found jack the ripper finger prints on the body so they started to look for Jack the ripper they look and look every were and one day they go a lead and they look for him and they went up to room 19 and the police said Jack this is the police out the door they knock the door down Jack has go out of the window there he go half him man they go him down a back ally he call not get away ther was change with murder he died in prison 6 year a go it was 1897.

By such phantasies Gerald is able to come closer to and accept his own reality, with some self-confidence:

Work at Butcher

I work at a Butcher shop in Bridgebrook. I work for Mrs Tate the paid it is quite good. I go out on a round saturday I still at school I work two night a week and all day Saturday I can drive I turn the van round in the yard my mate is Stanlay he drive the van round. I can cut meat up there are a lot of different meats. There is stack [steak], frying stack, stawing stack, Pudding bf, kid, lamb chop, pork chop, etc. My Dad work were [I] do. he is a big hefty man went I go two night a week I wash up. Mrs Tate has a abattoir to I have some good frend at the shop there is Tomy, Gordon, Andrew, Gordon has and Ariel colt, Andrew has Ariel Leader. I have go a bluestreak pusbycile [push-bicycle] I was go to work to night but we have go a party a school I will go THursday night we get paid Saturday night.

This piece led to two most self-confident five-minute talks by Gerald on Butchery. He doesn't go out into the world unarmed: if this is thought to be a limited aim, may I remind the reader of my first experience with a 'D' stream—45 boys like Gerald who could not even write a postcard. Gerald's handsome, neat and manly self-respect can be perhaps finally demonstrated by his railway engine painted as an illustration to *Casey Jones*. This painting seems to me to have a poise, balance, assurance and sensitivity that imaginative work helped this butcher's little boy to develop—compare it with his first picture, in his uncertain contest with the wounded and tangled bull (Figure 10. See also the goose and dead goose girl painted to a poem in Plate III).

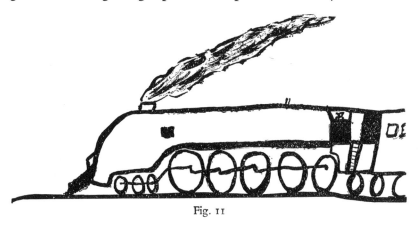

Fig. 11

☆   ☆   ☆

PSYCHIATRIST'S NOTE
It would seem Gerald's 'secondary' feelings of inferiority have been much helped by imaginative work.

16. JUDITH WARD

(I.Q. 80.)

In James Joyce's *Ulysses* he writes a whole chapter as if in the language and modes of a low class child of limited intelligence, Gerty Macdowell. Gerty is the Nymph Nausicaa, and the temptation of her exposed undergarments lures the hero Leopold Bloom (the modern Ulysses) to self-abuse. The girl is lame, and Bloom is an *homme moyen sensuel*, an ad canvasser, cuckolded, impotent and a *voyeur*. Thus, in his portrayal of Gerty Macdowell's 'stream of consciousness', Joyce assumes her romantic view of life is limited to the modes of *Peg's Paper*. And so he writes the whole chapter mostly in the language of the kind of romances he supposes Gerty to have read, which condition her attitude to life.

As an exercise in pastiche the chapter is brilliant and entertaining. But in a sense it is also an implicit disparagement of human nature—because it implies that a whole sensibility *can* function, thus, in the modes of sentimental hack writers: or at least that a girl can be wholly immersed in such idioms. In fact, this is impossible, and as we find in children's writing, only a small part of their outlook is ever wholly subject to television, the cheap novelette, or the popular song and magazine. Human nature continues to strive for a better truth, even when the mass media seek to head off and debase the striving. There would be no point in objecting to the lowest common denominator of the content of mass media if it were not far below the potentialities of each reader.

I write this digression on James Joyce, because often in low-stream classes we have girls who are the kind of girl Joyce was thinking of for his nymph—simple in their attitudes and interests, much taken up with romantic stories and dreams, a little dull and unenthusiastic about life. We are as likely to fall into error about these children as Joyce was, when he gave us so little of Gerty Macdowell except her fascination with masturbation, menstruation and aberration, and her extreme romanticism derived from the penny novelette. Such an attitude misses out the larger area of the mind of such a girl in reality, which is largely concerned with seeking the best in personal relationships, and which, if it is diverted from this quest, can suffer considerably.

Judith Ward is the nearest among my children to a Gerty Macdowell. I once taught 40 such girls, in an L.C.C. evening institute, in which these girls were learning typing—and had to 'do English'. In the end I abandoned everything except free writing, inspired by a series of vague drawings belonging to an outfit called a Psychological Thematic Apperception Test—designed to provoke responses from inward fears and obsessions. The girls wrote copiously, and we fell at once into exploring the snares and terrors of personal living, sexual and other, in which they were plunged. And all grasped eagerly at imaginative expression as a means to explore the troubling reality of their lives. It soon emerged that behind the Gerty-like exterior they suffered a great deal. Thus some of their work was deeply moving—and in mode, language and theme it was vastly superior to the stories in *Woman* or the cheap pornographic pulp book: it sought the truth, avidly, by imagination.

And this we find from the very beginning with Judith. She writes stories of the romantic kind, endlessly. But there are always moments at which she transcends the romantic dream and its clichés, reveals something of herself, and gains something of truth.

Here are fragments of Judith's first piece, her contribution to the class story, *A Blind Date*. Here may be seen the positive influence on her (as in the work of other girls) of free drama:

One day at a cafe door stood a very worried young teenager, his name was Rex harris, he had black hair, and was very tall, he was lonely, every evening because he didn't have a girl to go out with.

Then he saw his friend in the distance, he name was Jean Smith, she was very attractive but she already had a boy so there was no good ever waiting for her, when Jean got to the Cafe door, she was very surprised to find Rex there, and she said *my goodness you do look glum today whats the matter*, said Jean. Well I haven't anything to do of an evening now said Rex", Well never mind, come on into the cafe and have a cup of coffee, all right said Rex,

In the Cafe

I have a wonderful plan, I have a girl friend, who you could take out for an evening, said Jean well, that's just splended, Jean your a doll, "OK, OK, Rex don't go to far, I'll tell her to come with me to the Cafe over the road at Eleven oclock, so tomorrow that you can meet her, said Jean, by the way Jean whats her name, oh! I nearly forgot to tell you, "her name is Audrey Smith and she has blond hair, well I'll see you tommorrow at eleven then Jean Right by . . .

. . . in the Hall,

"Well" were in here now, lets go and get a table, ah theres one over there said Leon, OK lets go and sit down, I'll go and get some drinks said Rex,

After the Drink

Well that was good, shall we have a dance, yes Ok Audrey would you have this first dance with me, yet I would be delighted, the only thing is I'm not very good at dancing, never mind neither am I, right shall go, see you later Leon, OK have a good time, "Audrey" I" I" Love you, your eyes are like silver, and your hair is beautiful, yes, I Love you to shall we go out on the balcony, yes if you like, Rex, Lets go over here, "Rex" isn't it a beautiful night, with the moon shinning as well, yes it's beautiful Audrey, darling I really love you "I" "love" you too "Rex" darling. Well I think it's time for us to go now Audrey, yes I'm getting rather tired, I'll take you home Audrey . . .

If we feel sternly that young girls should not have their heads stuffed with romantic nonsense, then we will seek to divert Judith from such imaginings. But if we look closer we may see here a contemplation of mature personal conduct that is valuable ('let's go and get a table—ah! there's one over there'), and a quest for enjoyment and the good experience on which we may build all kinds of perceptions—of adequate use of leisure, concepts of love, parenthood, family life—sex education in its deepest and fullest sense.

Judith's ambitions are a combination of magazine taste, and genuine aspirations:

When I leave School

When I leave school I want to be a children's nurse, I shall most probably got to London to get a really good Job, but I will have to be away from home, but my parents said they don't mind me being away from home, as long as I like the Job, and am very interested in the work, of course I will be able to come home for a few days. I am going to leave school at 15, at Easter, 1962, and I shall work for two years at least before I think about getting a boy. I want to get married at 20, so that I will have about three years to get engaged, and to get to know each other. I wand two children, one of each or twins. I also want to live in a bungalow I want a man with lovely black or brown wavey hair not much taller than me. I want a man that likes children and takes them out, and plays with them. Then we will all be able to go out and enjoy ourselves. I shall stop nursing when I get married, after I have had a child, then I may do part-time work. I want to get married in white. I want to go abroad for my honeymoon. For the first summer holiday, I would like to go to Butlin's holiday camp.
For my children I would like a blue and white or Black pram.

There are intentions here not to be despised—some, indeed, which can be underlined in reading her piece to the class: 'I shall work for two years at least before I think about getting a boy', 'I will have three years to get engaged, and to get to know each other', 'I want a man that likes children'. These are not empty half-baked notions of a common dull child: they are decencies by which, in fact, most working-class people sustain the strength of their family and community living.

Nor are Judith's imaginary love affairs enacted in the modes of the 'heaving *embonpoint*' school: her relationships with boys, tenderly revealed here to my confidence, are still sweetly childish:

Stephen asked me if I would like to go, so he bought two tickets for him and me, and we went in and Pauline and Trevor were sitting in there holding hands. So we went in and they called us over to go and sit with them, and we did and when the film started all the lights were put out, and it was very dark in there, then Stephen was sitting there next to me, and Pauline said go on Stephen hold Judith's hand, and after a while he did, and he didn't let go of it until the film was over. . . the best boyfriend I ever had . . . he's father was posted . . . and so Stephen left. But we still send letters and post cards to each other. So that we still remember each other . . .

There seems to be growing a rather hostile assumption that secondary modern school children are brash, brazen and engaged in gross sensuality in their leisure time. But the immersion in sensuality is true only of a minority, and is a sickness perhaps produced by the anxiety they feel about the world we have brought them into. Children before 15, whatever their physical development, are still children—and it is not natural for children to be engaged in physical sex with none of the security of marriage or emotional maturity. They are mostly playing at being adults: the trouble is that our commercial popular culture drives them too far towards the adult. I make this point only to imply that the last thing we must become is hostile—and the difficulty is often (as some of my correspondents among teachers point out) that some adolescent girls are more self-possessed than their teachers. And although they are still children, they have looked after the family, coped with an aggressive dad, dealt with a drunken assault on their virtue from boys or uncles—before coming to school to sit at the feet of a young woman teacher to whom none of these things has ever happened, and who perhaps could not cope if they did! But the girls are not by any means adult, even if strangely mature before their time. They have only been cruelly flung out of childhood, and made sophisticated on the surface, sometimes by circumstances, sometimes by fashion. The teacher's function is to bring out the child, and foster the inward creature's growth towards becoming adequate to the level of the external sophistication. This I found possible, with my L.C.C. class of 15-year-old girls—and the secret is to allow and prompt the free expression of all inward experience in phantasy. In the end one finds imaginative explorations of truly tender themes, domestic and positive, such as the following:

One fine morning I got up, and went to bring the milk in to make some coffee, but *at my disaster* I found a young baby lying in a basket fast asleep, so I grabbed it quick and brought it in, it was a baby boy with light hair and blue eyes, *well of course I would have loved to keep the child but I knew that wouldn't be right*, so I telephoned the Police, and told them everything that had happened, and told me to take the baby down to the Police station. So I got ready and set off to the station. Of course I liked the baby and didn't want to give it to the Police. They said that they would put up notices about the baby. They let me look after him until someone owned up.

A month later.

A month went but nobody owned up and the Police were tired of looking everywhere for the parents that they said I could adopt the baby if I wanted to, if not they would put it in a home. I soon got married and talked it over with my husband, and he said it was OK, with him so, in a few day's time the baby was ours and were'nt we pleased. So we all lived happily ever after.

The End.

I think nearly every girl wants to write such stories, and finds them much more satisfying than the partial truths of commercial culture. Such interest in the 'continuity of life' is primal, and we should encourage every expression of it:

When I am a children' Nurse

When I get the Job of a children's nurse, I shall be very happy I'm sure, There will be lots of other nurse's there to help look after the children we have to put the children to bed, and get then dressed, give them there food, and toys to play. I like looking after young children, I will be able to get home now and then, and see may parents. If one of the children decide that they want to run away then of course we must go and look for them, and bring them back.

But Judith is still a child, and it should please us if a 14-year-old 'C'-stream child is still willing to show herself as childish, because in doing so she admits her emotional needs, and her need to develop emotionally by imaginative work:

> Tick tock, slowly,
> Tick tock,   ,,
> That's my dadies big clock,
> And my granny's little clock,
>   goes tick, tock,
>   tick, tock,
>   tick tock.

Of course, another life invites:

IN THE SUMMER HOLIDAYS.

One day, about the second week, I was going shopping, and takeing my friend for a walk. When three boys whistled at me and they asked me to come and get a rose which they had put on their lunch bags, for me, of course I went as red as beetroot, but when I came back they called me again so after a while I went and Picked it up I started talking to ~~him~~ them every day . . .

And as Judith reveals herself we find much more here than anything limited to the empty clichés of *Peg's Paper*: there is an exploring realism:

Betty went down to the shop to get some groceries for dinner, they got 2 lb of potatoes, 1 large tin beans, and ½lb ham, and 1 large peaches and 1 large cream which all came to 6/- 10d, when they got home the girls cooked the meal . . .

. . . and there is a deepening sense of beauty:

they started out and the sea got deeper, but it was lovely, the sun was shining like a star glittering at night, the sea was calm and bright, as we looked ahead at the deep deep sea, it was just like a dream which has come true . . .

Judith remembers here the intense glitter of light on the broken surface of the sea: and note that she begins to write verse, with rhyme, as her imagination carries her away in the middle of this story about the seaside. The seashore seems to have a special symbolism for Judith, who wrote answers to questions on Browning's *Meeting at Night* that are themselves almost like a poem:

Because its night time and dark. Because the wind is wild. Because the two waves are a ring. It's where the sea has washed away

The side of the rocks.
The front of the boat
Where the sea ran up the beach.
Because there are trees in way
There whispering to each other
The sun is hot with wild animals roaming around.
The beach is so hot and the sea is calm, animals are roaming, here and
   there.

I think the sea must have brought her a deep sense of animal life and wild experience. Such stimulation as that provided by the poem of Browning's can take such an 'ordinary' little girl into strange regions— where she proves how unlike the Gerty Macdowell cliché, or the 'teenage girl' we have in our minds as a type, she really is. Judith even essays a piece of writing in French:

A love story in French.

JEAN   Comatalevous (i.e. Comment allez-vous?)
LEON   Comatalevous.
MUM   Jean would you like a sweet.
JEAN   Yes please ma ma
LEON   J'aime you
JEAN   Oh! Leon j'aime you.
LEON   Jean you beau belle, J'aime you.
JEAN   You are beau belle.
LEON   Oh! Jean will you marry me, missiour [she means mademoiselle]
JEAN   Yes I will senour.

the end.

And she writes poetry, of a simple kind:

My girl
I have a girl
In love-day street
and she's as preety,
as can be,
She's got a hat,
that's white and black,
She's put it on,
when we go out,
and she's the pretiest
little girl I have,
   ever seen.

163

Shades of the prison house begin to close on even Judith's modest aspirations, as Dad arranges her future:

My work

My dad has got me a job for when I leave school, I am going to work at Bridgebrook [RAF] Station, as a privait secutery, I will work in an office. I have to be there at 8 oclock in the morning, and I leave off at 5 oclock in the evning. I will work five days a week from Monday to Friday, I have Saturday and Sunday to do what I like. I will work for six pounds a week which is worth it.

But there is a good deal now released in Judith's potentialities and attitudes to life which she did not have when she wrote her first piece, the contribution to *The Blind Date*. Her piece in the last examination is long, interesting, sensible and positive—and something she has made of the romance story out of her own small girl's wisdom. She caps it with a good reference for me—and the work we have done which she hopes will be 'of use in later years':

They ran away to get married

In a little country called Lawton was a huge house with seventeen rooms and in it lived mother, father, maids, and four children, the eldest, was Jenny who was 18 years of age, she had 3 other brothers and sisters who were all under the age of 12, Jenny had a boyfriend who live a few yards a way from her, his name was Jonnhy he was 20 years of age. Jenny and Jonnhy wanted to get marreid, they had known each other for 6 years, and were very much in love. They had got mostly everything to start with, they had a double bed, curtains, dressing table, crockery and lots of other things to start a married home. But thee only trouble was that their parents wouldn't give their consent, to the marriage. So the two young children decided to ran away and get married. So they packed a few clothes and Johnny got two tickets on a train to London they had some money in the bank about £30. So one bright sunny morning they got up about six oclock and made their way to the station. they were two hours early so stayed on the platform and had some breakfast. Soon they were on the train. Now we needn't worry about anythink my darling, said Johnny. No we can get a job in London and live in a flat for a few months until we can get a house of our own, said Jenny. yes then we can go back home, tell our parents, the news and get the rest of our things together and come back to London.

2 months pass

They got a flat and were now thinking of getting married, so they got married in a registery office and after the celebrate until 12 oclock that night, then a week later they got tickets back to Lawton, they got home and went and rang on Jenny's doorbell first. he father came to the door, and took one look and "slammed!" the door in their faces, and shouted out "I don't know where you've been, but I don't want you to lay a step inside this house, you're an absolute disgrace to our family, but dad, shouted Jenny I've only come home to tell you the news what's that he "said" I am married thats why I and Johnny ran away we got married in a registry office. so "said" her father, Oh! well I wish you the best of luck in your marriage, but I do wish you'd told us all—because I think you are old enough to be man and wife, well my daughter and son in law, welcome home. you can live here both of you, until you get a decent place of your own, thank you dad, and thank you sir, said Johnny, don't call me sir my son, you're one of us now so, you may as well call me dad I must go and fetch youre parents Johnny, and we will celebrate said her father, all the family got together and celebrated. and later they got a place of their own and a couple of years later they had twins a boy and a girl, and they all lived happily ever after.

In detail this may be callow and inexperienced, but as a larger 'picture' of the need to strike out and leave home, returning later as an accepted adult, it is very real—and new-found land for a child's apprehension. There are some touches which are much more realistic than romance stories—her apprehension of the father's reaction, mingled shame and jealousy, for instance. And how well she spells: of course, her punctuation is bad, and this would have been my next care. But the construction is excellent—and Judith has a system of her own sometimes of indicating progress in a story—here for instance is a dramatic moment pointed by hanging footnotes:

Down on the beach

Sunbathing. Oh Teena my love I love you with all my heart, me too,
they kiss m "m" that lovely
he proposes. "darling! will you marry, yet Peter but I don't thing you'll want to marry me because I'm an orphan, so what, I'm an orphan too, and nothing's going to stop me marrying you . . .

The reader who has never indulged in such a day-dream at 14-plus may throw the first stone. And here is Judith's report on me:

28 Field Path Way
Oakwell
Nr Melton
21.11.61

Dear Les,

I hope you are O.K. just a few lines to write about our English lesson with Mr Holbrook in the last 12 months. He has taught us how to write good letters, stories, and poems. some of the work he has taught us will be of use to us in later years. But some work hasn't taught us a single thing, we have to learn a fair bit of English to help us as we get older, and out to work.

Love and best wishes,

Judith

xxxxx

xxx

xx

✻   ✻   ✻

PSYCHIATRIST'S NOTE

I think this mode of taking refuge in romantic unrealistic stories comes from looking at the outside of things only. Many people seem to feel that other people have a much less complicated and a happier time than they because only the external appearances of the situation are apparent to them. The novelette situation leaves out the real complications of feeling, the inner experiences of life—and so they can escape from their own situation in which they feel lonely, or not like the boy they have, or feel that he may not like them, and so on.

A colleague says that the adolescent is confused between feeling still a child and playing at being grown up. This is, I feel, what these children are doing when they write stories about their aspirations—they explore 'being grown up' 'from the outside'—not having experienced it. They seem to feel that it is likely to be something quite different from their own existence as a child, as though grown-ups never had bad feelings or difficulties.

AUTHOR'S NOTE

The reader may reflect on the possible harm done when adolescents who are 'playing at being grown up' are stimulated into actual adult modes of behaviour—e.g. in sex—by popular commercial culture before they are ready for these, being really still children.

17. PAT JOHNSON

There is little I can usefully say about Pat except that she seems to represent the complete breakdown of school medical services, of liaison between school, the authorities, and paediatric services (she has already been discussed above, p. 26). There must be many children in 'backward' streams who are (as my correspondents suggest below, p. 254) virtually *lost* children—not really backward at all really, but deaf, mentally ill, or damaged in some way, so that they cannot use their potentialities. And because we all fear disabilities everyone unconsciously conspires to cover them up and hide them. The effect can really amount to a kind of grave neglect by default, and I think this was so with Pat.

She was put down as 'deaf', and wore a *hearing* aid. Her two elder brothers were stone deaf, and all attempts (I gather) to encourage the mother to send her children to a special school had failed. Pat was accepted in the school as a deaf child, and 'carried', as it were, through the work. She was actually very good at crafts, and even won a school prize for handicrafts. But to facial expression, word, gesture, and communication she was deaf—she did not smile, *neither did she understand language*, or hardly at all. Yet in her reports teachers had written, 'Pat tries hard', and such general remarks of appraisal. No one had written, simply, 'this child does not understand a word of her instruction and therefore it is impossible to make any comment on her work. She needs special instruction.' Why not? Why keep up the pretence that 'Pat is doing well'?

The problem was a complex one, the solution of which may be in better routines for the diagnosis and treatment of such children. The child's mother would not let her go to a special deaf school. She went to the hospital for lip-reading. The teacher there said to her absent-mindedly one day, 'Fetch me my handbag, Pat'. And the girl went to get it! She was not deaf! She wore a hearing aid, but was not deaf, only partially. The trouble seemed to be that her mother had had two deaf babies, and when the third arrived, this girl, she did not prattle to it. So the child did not develop verbal concepts, and powers of speech: her brain was now at the age of 14 lacking in capacity for these functions. More and more she defended herself against the world by refusing to respond, smile, speak, listen. Her disability was really a mental sickness. At the time I taught her the lip-reading teacher was making a little progress, and the girl was speaking a few timid whispered slow words.

There is little to say about her work, except that it was virtually meaningless—yet everyone seemed to be deceived by the apparent meaning in it. Pat's actual verbal powers are represented by the following pages, written at the *end* of her time with me. Under drawings of a cowboy, a waggon, etc., she wrote:

> he is cowboy
> he is wagon
> he is inded (Indian)
> he is pens
> he is car
> he is house

It is, I suppose, the verbal power of a child of three, and is unrelated to speech, so that she does not know it is proper to say 'The cat jumps on the chair', or 'The cat is jumping on the chair', but writes 'The cat is jumps on the chair'. In Pat we have a child who has failed to come to learn the functions of language from everyday use in speech.

This explains why I was so frustrated when I first began to examine Pat's work. For some time she wrote what appeared to be adequate responses to my stimuli—until I discovered that in fact she was simply copying from her neighbour. But then I also noticed that she simply did not understand what was required of her. Asked to write a story 'about teenagers' she wrote:

I am going on holiday on Saturday. I watched TV on Monday we looked at wagon train.
Denis and Alec and Keith and I are went for a walk on Sunday. See Auntie Phillis . . .
I have a picture of Clint Eastwood and Robert Horton and Russ Conway . . .

I wrote 'I don't think you understand what we are doing. I want you to write about things that you are interested in. I want you to write a poem, or a story, or about your family. Anything you like.' She wrote:

I am going on holiday on Saturday
I draw a picture of wagon train and horse and pigs.
I watched TV on Saturday we looked at Tenderfoot.
. . . some of the low-lying areas, however, have a naturally high water-

table which, in the absence of a proper drainage system . . .
I went to work the bedroom.

It began gradually to dawn on me that Pat understood nothing of
what we were doing. She had a few sentences in her visual memory ('I
have a picture of Bob Horton'), and others which she either took from
books under the desk, or remembered from magazines at home.
Others were meaningless. We tried again.
   'Write me a story—make it up yourself . . . or tell me a play you
have seen on television . . .'
She wrote

I watched TV on Sunday and Friday on Saturday we looked at Maverick and
the Long Rango and Tenderfoot
I have a sitting the knitt . . .
I am very pleased with my phto and the photo of Russ Conway and Robert
Horton . . .

I was lost. There were 18 others to cope with. I ignored her for a
while wondering whatever to do. All kinds of things turned up, and
judging by the errors I think this child memorised things in *Reader's
Digest* and other magazines at home, to unload them, *without understanding a word*, in class (her errors, that is, are errors in external, visual
memorising, not in forgetting content).

When we connot be with loved ones at the Festive season or for a birthday
anniversary or other 'Occasion'—we appreciate to the full the joy of a
service like interflora which lets us say "merry christman" or "I wish I
could be with you" by a gift of beaufiful Fresh flowers—sent across the world
if need by!
Here's how interflora work you simply give your order ~~the interflora mem-
ber~~ to say florist dispiaying the interflora member (one of 20,000 over the
world nearst your delivery dewy-fresh-perhaps 10,000 miles away. it say
almost as well as you could youseff "I am Thinking of you today.

Cambridge
King' is the product of two plans conceived successively within a faw years of
each other . . .
   The Revolt in hungary "means the beginning of the end of communism,"
for it "blazed a path white sonner or later other communist countries must
follow,"
After hunger, ses is our strongest instinct and greatest problem, toensure the
continuation of the species, nature decorates the woman with beauty and

give to us males such sensitivity to woman's charms that we can go quite mad in their pursuit . . . our ancestors played down this exual impulse. we have simulated it unwisely with advertisement and display, and have armed it with the doctrine that inhibition is danger-ous. Yet inhibilion—the control of impulse—is the first principl of civilization . . .

What a shock it was to read such windy pieces of Christian Science advertisement or American digest journalism in a child's book! I still cannot tell whether the mistakes are there because Pat is copying out something she doesn't understand, or because she fails to remember the shapes of the sentences exactly from memory.

We never managed to discover whether she had some system of hiding or switching books to appear to be 'writing' work she had, in fact, copied out at home. But we returned inevitably to: 'I am very pleased with my Photo with the photo of Bob Horton. I watched TV on Monday we looked at Wagon train.' And her work now began to include pieces from television books: 'Ty and Andra Hardon—a picture taken soon after there were wed. new they're proud parents of twis sons. John and Jeff.' But this gave me nothing of her, and she did not, in fact, understand it. I tried giving her drawings from which to make sentences. But these were too advanced—Pat writes

The boy is path the bike
The man with a pump is wheel down the car
The asleep is sitting on the chair
The pie is on the cat the table.

Only occasionally, and with my help, does she get it right.

But then meaningful sentences appeared, which she had learnt with her lip-reading teacher:

We are going to have our lip-reading room. One of them [i.e. one of the patients] is a funny policman and the other is a boy with a for [i.e. fur] hat and coat. He lives at Huntigdon and come to Tonbury on the ambulance.

At about this time Pat began to respond, and, after I had met the lip-reading teacher in her presence, could haltingly answer questions I put to her. She could then begin to write sentences about what others were wearing. Having made contact I became part of a simple break-through:

Mrs P [the lip-reading teacher] has just been speaking to Mr. Holbrook on the telephone we thought Mr Holbrook was coming to see us this afternoon

but he has just telephone to say he is not a bus to bring him. Mr Holbrook is wearing yellow tie and brown shoes black and white ~~blouse~~ I am wearing a white blouse and grey cardigan.
I have black shoes on.

Among the new phrases of expression recur the stereotypes of old:

'I am very pleased with my photo and with the photo of Robert Horton and Robert Fuller and Ty Hardin and Adam Faith and Frankie Vaughan and Clint Walker'.

The saddest thing about Pat is perhaps that she is the perfect victim for television, with the mental age of about three, no linguistic capacity to speak of, hardly any responsiveness to personal relationship, and an almost incurable withdrawal state from the real world: she reels off the meaningless bromides of the TV system and the 'pop' papers making only occasional connections between their crude simple phantasies:

This encouraged me to try again, and I left New York for California—for a few minor parts, and eventually the role of Kookie in the television series, 77 Sunset Strip. no harm is meant. people are so taken with the characte they cannot believe that off the seveen I am neally. Edd byrnes who enyays driving a small sports car and does not have the slightest desire to passess an £8,000 hot rod or to use veracular every second word. Luck was with me . .
I have a picture of Adam Faith and Cliff Richard . . .

Never did popular journalism seem more inchoate than it did through Pat's broken relays of its worst. In her 'examination' papers Pat writes fragments of things seized desperately from her unopened mind, from the instructions on the question paper itself, or things from displays on the wall beside her:

Note:— When you have neally.
    I made a camp once with big logs
    Cover used for protecting plants in the garden
    all you can you may illustrate your story
    it was not her Baby there, but a black one. to begin a man at the
        back began to shout.
    The Roof was made of straw.
    The ore shaw wheele.
    Hells George I'm just going to london."
    You need a pump a lever and a puncture out fit.
    We have not got a bath room but are getting one soon.
    You will be given made for This.

One woman's persistence and courage—the lip-reading teacher's—have saved Pat from total and permanent isolation from the world. The teachers were kind to her, and some did good: *but they mostly pretended that her disability did not exist*, and ignored the terrible fact that, in fact, this child was verbally blind. I suppose had she been really blind they would have had to recognise her condition,* but the fact that her illness was passable as 'mere' deafness, but was really a mental deficiency, led them to the unconscious conspiracy of pretending, in that falsely respectable way, that Pat was 'trying hard'. Yet her verbal capacities were chaotic and impotent. There could be no stronger indictment of an educational system and a supposedly effective system of medical and psychiatric care in which many thousands of children like Pat are lost to sight and damned for ever, for the lack of thorough diagnosis, in the early years.

* But see p. 191, where a teacher records similar neglect of a blind child.

18. DAPHNE BADLAND

I have no I.Q. rating for Daphne, but she was probably the dullest of all the children in 3 C. She wore thick-lensed glasses, was very shy, freckled, plain and giggled a great deal. Her mouth was ill-formed and she looked stupid. It took a long time to gain any kind of confidence from Daphne, and her work was disorganised and unco-ordinated. Her drawings, for instance, as Figure 12 below, were full of disorientated and

Fig. 12

disconnected figures, without pattern or relationship, her heroine doll-like, floating in space. She was being brought up a Roman Catholic and joined me in the mornings from a session of priestly instruction: I used to wonder how much she took in from these spiritual lessons, from which I saw phrases like 'immaculate conception' written on the board. Members of staff, I know, spoke to one another of their fears for Daphne: for she was becoming a young woman physically, yet obviously had a very low mental age, and little understanding or morals—they feared she would 'get into trouble' easily.

Yet Daphne, by the time she had written a number of imaginative pieces for me, showed that she had some understanding—enough, at any rate, to desire the good things—her last examination paper ends 'So they got married and lived happerly ever after'. And in this she was fortified against what seemed, from a distance, a very strange, and sometimes threatening environment.

At first she wrote very simple, hesitant, childish pieces about adolescent relationships:

The Blind Date.

Ones a apen a time there was a boy named Rex. He was handsome and he had black hair. but one night he came down stairs. He went to wacth the Television. he got fed up, he went out for a walk and he met Jean his friend. He was so sad that Jean asked him was the matter. He said wants a girlfriend. Jean says she will take him to a girl called audrey watson who works at the greenhouse in Melton. So after he had met her he said to her alone whats are you doing tonight and she said she will have to do a job for her maneger. he siad well perhaps wel go to the pictures tomorrow and she said yess Ill be there to meet you.
The next day audrey came to his house. Then they were both ready so they set out to go the picture. When they get to the pictures they saw a lovely picture they say it was a very nice picture but when they came out of the picture. they had an argument.

Then, as children seem to do after the first loosening up, she wrote a good deal about her home and her ambitions:

When I leave school I am going to ask my mother and father if I can be a nana. And if I do I am going to look after little children and when I am 15 or 16 I might even get a boyfriend. But not until then I am going to take my dog for a walk when I get him around the village.
My mother father and my brother and I are going to mass tonight because it is Holy obligation. I hope we get a bungalow soon because the house what we're in is a dump. We don't like it. I hope we do because a bungalow is better than a cottage. well for one thing it untied anyway it is not ours it belongs to Mr Lyons. Evey time my father goes in the Bake-house he sneezes evey time.
It is my birthday on Monday We went out on Saturday and my mother bought me a new pink coat and high heels. To wear and go out in for best.

I confess that until this piece was written I found Daphne irritating and unattractive. If asked to read aloud she would writhe, snort and giggle. She would stubbornly refuse to take part in group activities, and looked stupidly defiant. But then she looked unhappy, too, so I didn't storm at her: I simply didn't like her and thought she was an ugly little thing. But then she began to chatter in her book, and to write, not as she had been taught in school, but as she thought and spoke. One could hear phrases of her mother's and childish chat of her own, and at times her work was amusing because of its quaint outspokenness. Her spelling is good, and I began to feel that the immaturity and the apparent stupidity were some kind of defence mechanism—and that others were wrong to assume that she would 'get into trouble' because she was so stupid. There were more positive potentialities lurking in Daphne, and I began to warm to her.

First of all she needed to be accepted as a child, and explore things a little more as the child she was. She enjoyed my book *Children's Games* and found herself a piece which appealed to her devotional patterns:

Ashes to ashes and dust to dust
If God won't have you the Devil must

—which she copied in her book. She then wrote, at my request, a game rhyme from her experience in the playground:

down in the valley where the green grass grows
theres little Margaret washing her cloths she grows
she grows so sweet and she calls her love one in Beryil Beryil Beryil will you marry
me yes sir yes sir half past three ice cake sugar cake all for tea and therell be a wedding
at half past three

We enjoyed this very much, and this brought forth further confidences, when she came to see how much I shared her enjoyment.

My family

I live in Melton and I am in a cottage and *it is horrible we dont like it but still we have to Persevere till we leave.* Bernard is ill in bed and the Docter is coming to see him on Wednesday Morning he felt sick on the football ground on Saturday afternoon. *Our dog Tobe has been Excited but its a very cute dog.* I have got a bunk which I sleep in. my brother has a singl bed and my mother and father has one to. we he havn't any cats but we used to do we used to have roundabout 12 but they all disapeared. I shoud think we will be leaving some time my Mtoher will be glad when we do leave this cottage we all do *we dont no about the dog it might be different for him because he is used to that but never mind he will get used to that as well.* We all want to go were our *Relatons* but my mother dosnt want to go to Leiston but I do I like it very much. I dont now know about my father and my brother but I know that they would like it. Ther are six in my family counting the dog and the bird. we have a garden and it has only grass on each side Well on the left of the garden was a hole in the middle and there was mice in it down the bottom of it. *Well one of the cats meant to go outside but somthing happens he sees this hole and he puts his paw into the hole and the mice come up a little and they grabed the cat. then it tried to get away but it was know use it was killed they they all came out and then they all were killed. Then there was my mother and father and I came out of the house that night and saw that the cats were in the hole making a noise but we count d anything about it because it was to late. But have got over it.*

I never managed to get out of Daphne the exact details of this story of how the mice caught and killed all her cats. Perhaps the hole was an old well. But we found it a great joke, and I introduced Daphne to everyone as the girl whose cats were all eaten by mice. This moment of childish notoriety was just what Daphne wanted—her incredible story was read out and talked about, and it gave her the sense of being the centre of attention. More revelations came:

My mother and father have been married for ten years and they have been happy ever since. When they started to meet. They said shall we go to the pictures and my mother said yes well do that said my mother it is a very good idea. But some times they have a fight they had a fight last night but they made friends again then when we went out last Saturday afternoon they started to have a fight. My father shouted at my mother and than my mother shouted at my father then when my father went to the meeting we went to finish our shopping . . .

I discovered that far from being involved in sexual adventure, as are Gerald Goodchild and some of the other girls, Daphne is still involved in the earlier childish stages of normal homosexual attachment—she writes about her girl friends, and when she writes about a bit of horse-play is guilty enough to cross it out:

When the children went out to play after dinner Linda and I went on the field and sat down for a bit there were Mary Smith and Linda and I Linda said something (and then I went up to her and got on top of her and so we had a little play fight)* but we are still friends with each other. we go together every day. I like her to come to Guildwell some day but she said no she cant there if she could she would come and see me and we would have good fun together and go up to the meadow and climb trees

And after her summer holiday Daphne writes a revelation of a fear that she might have trouble from her uncle:

* Crossed out between the brackets.

Went I went on my holiday I had a very nice time we played on the bikes and went shopping and when my Auntie went to work but when she went work Joan and Derek started to have a quarrel but I did not take no notice of them and carried on what I was doing then Joan said something to me but I did take notice of her and then she said I always startes a qurral but when we were friends again. Well on one Saturday when my Uncle desided to go to the pictures with Joan and Derek well when they were in the pictures I was in a room watching Bronco Layne on T.V. it was better than watching the film but I mean that Bronco was very good. Well when they came home that night I was still watching the T.V. and Derek and Joan came in and said that my Uncle was drunk and Joan said that he nearly got run-over and als Joan had guard him back to the house where was safe. Well that same night when we were watching Deadline—midnight my Uncle came in and sat on a chair and watched part of the programe and then came up and switched the T.V. of and to us to go to bed we ran up stairs and Derek and I went into my bed-room so we stay in the room and I heard someone coming up the stairs so I went and I peped out side the door and saw that my Uncle was coming up the stairs so I told Derek so we went round the bed and I got on the bed and went straight down stairs and went into the kitchin and told my Auntie but she said that she cant do anything about it so when he came downstairs again we went up stairs to bed. And when I was in bed I lisinid out for my Uncle because sometimes when he is drunk he comes up to my room door but not always but it stopped me from going to sleep because sometime he gives me the creeps but before then he very nearly hit Derek and I but I dont know what for and then we went to bed and went to sleep but when they all were asleep my uncle got up and came out of the room and went down stairs I dont know what he was up to but still I kept awake a very long time because I wasnt tired so I stayed awake for a while and when he came upstairs and stood outside my door I got a bit scared because I thought he was going to come in my room so I kept so still and quiet and a bit later he went into his own room and got in bed and went to sleep and he woke my Auntie she was awake for a little while and then she was asleep in a know time and I couldn't go to sleep at all but still I kept awake to listen out for my uncle just in case he came into my room but a bit later on I fell of to sleep and I got nice and warm. Well thats all I can say for now.

This long piece must have been an outpouring of the memory of a night of terror which had haunted Daphne all her holiday. What the child has to live with! What evidence there is in this book, among only 18 children, that children have to live with some of the most sordid aspects of human nature, daily—yet most schools try to ignore the fact.

Perhaps freed by such unloading of disturbing experiences as a kind of short story, Daphne began to write at length, and to write really fictionally. She gets the idea from her friend Joan Stall and writes seven pages of dialogue:

ROSEMARY I dont surpose you want me any more so I wont come with you any more
BERNARD come of it I love you very much
ROSEMARY do you realy love me
BERNARD of course I do then they started to put their arms around each other and then Rosemary kiss Bernard.

Her last piece is a pathetically telescoped love story, but it shows Daphne beginning to consider personal relationships in a way needful for the adolescent. There is some indication that now she is in a little more command of herself—her lovers make decisions, give their orders for food, and accept their responsibilities. And Daphne is able to consider the needs and sadnesses and joys of others:

they ran away to get married.

Ones upon a time there was this man standing by the shore and when all the people came pass him Well it all happend when he was very sad he decided to go for a walk until a lonely woman came along.

MARY whats the mater with you
DAVID *Oh its nothing really its just that I am very miserable because he had no one to talk to*
MARY *ah you poor thing*
DAVID will you come with me tonight
MARY yes Id Love to where shall we go
DAVID Well we'll go to a Restaurant and have some lunch shall we
MARY yes alright that will suit me find but for the time being shall we go for a walk.
DAVID alright then come on
MARY shall we go to the Restaurant now because I am getting hungry
DAVID alright come then

at the Restaurant

MARY waiter could we have some lam and some Roast Potatoes Carrots and also chops.
DAVID I am enjoying this arent you.
MARY yes its very nice indeed
DAVID what do you want for your afterwards
MARY Oh Ill have ice-cream and what will you have
DAVID and I'll have steam pudding
MARY Waiter could we have one ice-cream and one steam-pudding

DAVID   Well that was very good wasnt it, Mary
MARY   yes it was I enjoyed it very much
[DAVID] [impetuously?] lets go and get married and get a house somewhere
        but the point is will you marry me Mary I love you very much
MARY   yes Id love to pet Ill have to think about it first
        I have thought about it I will marry you
        So they got married and lived happily ever after.

This seems to me very beautiful, positive, and a great advance towards reality, and the use of her potentials, in Daphne, for all its sudden leaps through time (justified perhaps by examination conditions?). It is perhaps interesting that she finds this satisfying mode by way of Joan Stall, rather than drawing directly on her own experience of free drama —though she is, of course, able to draw on that valuable experience too, once she begins in this mode.

Her final comment is in the reasonably literate if brief letter:

Jessamine House
High Street
Guildwell

Dear Maureen,
    I thought I had better write and let you know what we do in English with Mr. Hollbrook

we write story
love Pat

19. MICHAEL HOLMES

(I.Q. variously given as 82 and 102.)

Disturbing matters emerged in our discussion of 'the facts of life'. How much did we know, from medical reports, about Michael? Were his difficulties congenital ones, or were they due to a deep obsession with 'that disease' he had heard of? Why was it that such a neat and charming boy, obviously brighter than his school record showed, should at times go all to pieces? How was it that when one grew angry with him he lost control of his feelings, turned white, trembled, swore, and became utterly unable to control his body, so that co-ordination was impossible for some hours afterwards? How was it that he maddened one, but, at the least show of aggression on one's part, such as taking him by the collar and threatening to take him to the headmaster, became a cringing, weeping, terrified baby? (I have just been told—*six months after the end of my teaching* Michael—that he has only one lung.)

He writes of a poem 'I do not like the poem (*A Boy is A Boy* by Ogden Nash) because it is to babbish for us sieonas (seniors)'. Yet he himself is a strange baby in trousers, who has somehow 'lost' his mother (though in fact his mother was not dead).

> And all the Heavens cryed
> And all the babys sighed
> But mamma did not cry,
> She died.
> and all the Babys cried
> "Chorus"
> O Deary O Deary
> she felt so weary
> We put her in a box,
> and we sunk her down deep.
> The village all did weep
> And the heavens cried
> "Chorus"
> O Deary O Deary
> She felt so weary
> I never felt more like singing the blues

I never that ought I never lose you love dead
You got me singing the blues
The moon and stare no longer shine.

There is little I want to say about Michael. I reported him for psychiatric investigation, but again nothing was done. I can only feel that a teacher of English—or of any subject—could do nothing for Michael except show him kindness, give him a little relief, and help him to find a little beauty here and there in phantasy. I can only say that he seemed to me a grave medical case, and that his lack of co-ordinating power in writing was something that teaching alone could not overcome. I will quote some of his work to show that here again under the surface was a brave and lovely child soul: but his hand-writing speaks for itself, as the mark of his distress.

Encouragement, discipline, care—none of these could alter his fundamental incapacities without some medical aid, and that this was not forthcoming represents a grave deficiency, not confined to one county, in our school services.

Some of his pieces I liked very much, and they helped his reading a good deal:

Racing COMENTARY

Come in Lamont, over, Now, we are at Lamont the Farrari are in the leeding Phil hill is lead them Barham, and Moss are four five Moss is four and Barham five if you listen now you will hear Barham going thruogth eeeeargghbrooo-mghrrr gying very well now barham He is 15 sec fast then the last lap O! what heap (what's happened) to Moss Wow! I can haer a car miss fireing it is Moss in his Copper he is going into the pits Philhill is going round Gatwick Corner that is a right and left hand corners Phil hill has cage down to three gear the car is siding eeeckgggherum sh sh sh hey I am sill hear the raceing is sill now over to Gatwick Corner meet you there is Richard Bullard this is Richard seking there is quit a crush hear Phil hill is quit all right but the race divers behed him was kill and theer spectatoes two fire egreers (engines) One ambulance the ferrary were sill in the led but there was only one in the race

From such material he was later able to give an adequate short talk on go-karting. He could write poetically.

. . . Apirl the spring is hear May and Apirl are where the tree do blossm with flower so gay June Jluy both those mouth are bright and gay corn is coming to ripe in fields August we cut the corn and reper September and October we see the nigth draw in, the trator has a busy time ploughing the feild . . .

181

The Waesel

The wasel is a sly old thing The gamekeeper saw him run so he aimed his gun And he fired a shot the 2,2 went off and the weasel fell to the ground the gamekeeps picked him up And pinned him on a treee

This is what the latter piece looked like:

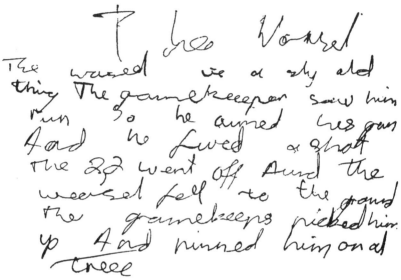

Fig. 13

Michael had a sense of order and beauty somewhere, as his painting of his prose-poem about the weasel shows (Plate IV). Yet when we combined writing and painting Michael often had to be restrained from tearing his paintings up or destroying them in some way, so little did he trust his constructive impulses. In him these difficulties were not accessible to the healing power which imaginative work in school may exert on a child's unhappy self—they were too deep, and required medical treatment.

✳   ✳   ✳

PSYCHIATRIST'S NOTE

I agree about the difficulty of helping a child like this by normal educational methods, or even by the best imaginative approach. The way this child breaks down suggests possible serious neurotic disturbances, requiring individual prolonged treatment. He obviously has considerable capacities and could probably be helped to a normal and useful life if such psychiatric treatment had been available. As it is it remains possible that when he gets into the world and has to stand on his own feet he may break down seriously, as a young adult.

EPILOGUE TO THE SECTION OF EVIDENCE

As an indication of the efficiency of this informal work, and to help anticipate a certain kind of criticism, I would like to quote here some letters by members of 3C, written towards the end of our time together.

I have, as I have said, known a class of 4D boys only two of whom could write a postcard. After much phantasy work 3C coped with such a practical test with ease and comparative success—they took it in their stride. The exercise arose when a reader of *The Guardian* wrote in to criticise my work—on the familiar lines, that it was impractical, and unrealistic. Here is the letter, from a Manchester teacher:

Sir,

Mr. David Holbrook's sympathetic devotion to the handicapped children he teaches was readily apparent in his article 'Literacy for Backward Children'. Some of the views he expressed, however, and the methods he described are, in my view, not merely misguided but dangerous, the more dangerous, because such views are becoming widespread in education today.

Mr. Holbrook is misguided because he is (though he disclaims it) taking over the role of the amateur psychotherapist rather than that of the teacher. He is accepting without question the outpourings of an intellectually limited child and, having adapted himself to the child by interpretation of those outpourings, he arrives at the verdict that the child's work is 'complete and satisfying'. Three and a half pages of barely decipherable scrawl may have a therapeutic value for the child. If, as I believe, education has as its aim the development of the individual to take his place in society as we know or envisage it, they have little educational value. His boys will sooner or later be faced with the necessity of writing a letter, a postcard, or a telegram.

My experience has been that young backward boys are often desperately anxious to improve their spelling and grammar. Because some of them are so handicapped that they may never achieve a high standard is no reason for not helping them individually to make the attempt. With regard to handwriting I doubt very much whether this has a very high correlation with general intelligence. Some of the neatest writers at the secondary modern school where I teach have been in 'C' classes.

In choosing the word 'dangerous' to apply to Mr. Holbrook's methods I do not do so lightly. His discovery of himself in the role of a 'father figure'

· is common to all perceptive teachers. The danger for both teacher and child lies in an over-indulgence which is every bit as crippling as too much harshness. Mr. Holbrook is deluding himself, but what is worse, he is deluding George, the writer of the virtually unintelligible essay. That boy when he leaves school will no longer have the benefit of Mr. Holbrook's protective 'interpretations'. He may well become bewildered, bitter, resentful in a society in which it is he who has to make the adjustments, and not others adjust themselves to him as his teacher had done.

An over-protective teacher, like an over-indulgent parent, bids fair to produce an adolescent misfit in the outside world.

Yours &c.

R.W.T.

The letter is worth quoting here for many reasons. For one thing it represents a common misinterpretation of the creative approach to the training of literacy—that it is 'amateur psychoanalysis', and consequently 'misleading'. (Presumably, such teaching makes people too human for the 'lower echelons of industry'?) Helping 'the development of the individual to take his place in society' is a matter of preparing him (according to this letter) to 'make the adjustments'—otherwise he will become a 'misfit'. To 'accept' children's 'outpourings' is 'over-indulgence'—the words reveal the writer's fear of what emerges from the freed imagination, and the fear of the adjustments a teacher must make to them. The hostility of the letter (Cf the tone of 'barely decipherable scrawl') reveals a refusal to accept the nature and reality of the children who find themselves in low streams, and a fear of teaching as a creative process. Creative work should foster creative attitudes to experience. A child who has been helped to develop true literacy and fluency—which means helped to feel and think—sets about the world to see what he can make of it. It will be his *world* that will have to make adjustments, to his creative energy: why not? Isn't this how civilisations grow? And he can even take a creative attitude to his own necessary adjustments in terms of acceptance—as, say, to a new condition of his existence as a husband, parent, or factory worker. In some circumstances a creative attitude will certainly produce misfits —such as those who go on strike over a real grievance, or challenge unfair privilege, or protest against racial discrimination or hydrogen bomb warfare: the more my pupils were such 'misfits' the happier I should be. But I don't think that such critical attitudes to society produce bewilderment, bitterness and resentment: the roots of these are in deeper states of inward disbalance and the lack of a felt sense of significance, in life at large. Sympathetic teaching that pays attention to the needs of the imagination certainly doesn't make such kinds of alienation worse: once a child has learnt that there are some benign and tolerant adults whom he can trust he never forgets it, even when the pressures of adult living seem aligned against him. All this is much more important than spelling, grammar and handwriting.

But to return to the simple issue of efficiency. I wondered how best to test Mr. T.'s points for myself. Then I decided to read his letter to 3C.

They were furious. This perhaps was no more than a demonstration of loyalty. But John Young, I think it was, took things to the next stage:

'Can we write to 'im, Sir?'

We had as yet done no practice in letter writing, though 3C had done some with other teachers. But now they *wanted* to write letters. So I produced some single sheets of paper for them, and they began.

'Can we tell 'im 'e's a clot, Sir?'

'No,' I said, 'you must write carefully written, proper and polite letters saying what you think.'

All the letters were neat, and set out in the proper way. (See the typical facsimile, p. 80.) Nearly all were postable. Every letter had its own characteristic way of putting the arguments. What surprised me most of all was that they not only wrote with efficiency, but showed that *they knew why we worked in the way we did*: they understood what I was doing. Far from being deceived about the world, they were very realistic, in the way a child can only become by attention to the needs of the realities of his psyche. As for 'adjustment', some of them even agreed with Mr. T.

Here are some of the letters and extracts from others:

Sir,

Mr. T. says Mr. Holbrook is to soft with us by not teaching us spellings. I agree with Mr t because you can not write a good story without knowing how to spell, I am the best speller in 3c and do not find some words diffcult but people who get under 40 find words very diffcult. If you do not practise writing letters you will find it very hard when you leave school. I think Mr Holbrook has difficulty in reading our stories if we do not write neatly so I think it is essential that we should write properly. I have written a lot of stories in the term I have written a lot of stories because spelling does not slow me down so I find it quite easy . . .

William Glebe

Sir,

Mr T says that Mr. Holbrook, our English teacher is too soft, and does'nt teach us very good English but I don't believe one word of it, it is absolutly nonsense, he is a good enough teacher, for any child to learn from.

We write a lot of stories but we nearly all enjoy writing them.

Mr T said it will be, be harder for us when we leave school, but if we consantrate, and listern to what we are told in English we will have no trouble when we go out into the world.

When we write stories, I think the story is much more important than the spellings, and puntuation.

Yours faithfully
Judith

When we have Mr Holbrook we have to write a story, and sometimes we write 4 pages or more and we plenty of the idea your tinking of.

Jack O'Malley

we have to work hard, and it tacks hard work to write thoese story and it very hard when people say he soft on us . . . .

Joan Stall

I think Mr T shoold come and see Mr. Holbrook teaching us we do a lot of writing we have even made a frame [form] magazine . . . .

Michael Holmes

One indefatigable individualist, however, refused to have anything to do with the flyting with Mr. T., and gaily wrote to his Uncle:

Dear Uncle Ben,

I hope you are well and aunt Sue to and Kim we will became up in the August hoilday will you come down for a holiday to hour house this year I am writeing this letter in school it is a hot day our Sally is on heart [heat] did I tell you my new girl friend Name her name is Pauline Howlet I fall out with her own [once] and she went with a another boy but she does on like him much now she is geting back with me we have go maths now . . . .

Gerald prefers life to letters. His letter draws attention perhaps to what was to me the most encouraging characteristic of these letters: each was the child's own, and despite the technical inadequacies, each has his own voice and an effective one (even to such phrases as 'absolutely nonsense': and note how William Glebe learns to spell 'difficulty' at the third attempt!). The letters answer the criticism in more ways than

186

one. Judged by the level of attainment in those 'C'-stream children who have spent all their school life doing 'practical exercises' these letters had a fluency which should enable them to cope, at a minimal level admittedly, with the kind of task Mr. T. has in mind. It is not commonly admitted how many of these children leave school simply not able to do this, because their English has been based on such unrealistic and inhumane attitudes as those expressed in his letter, and the springs of their literacy have been dried up by boredom.

PART II

CLASSROOM PRACTICE

. . . putting the lemon-peel into the kettle, the sugar into the snuffer-tray, the spirit into the empty jug, and confidently attempting to pour the water out of a candlestick . . . I saw that a crisis was at hand, and it came. He clattered all his means and implements together, rose from his chair, pulled out his pocket handkerchief, and burst into tears. 'My dear Copperfield,' said Mr. Micawber, behind his handkerchief, 'this is an occupation, of all others, requiring an untroubled mind, and self-respect. I cannot perform it. It is out of the question.'

(Charles Dickens, *David Copperfield*.)

4

RULES FOR ONESELF

A proportion of the million children in secondary school low streams is taught in old sheds, corridors, basements, crowded cloakrooms, with few books, and no equipment, lucky if they have one sympathetic adult who understands them. This picture is common from letters I have received such as the following:

Nowhere have I come across any feeling that anything can be accomplished with these children. They are labelled 'backward' and apparently only God is to blame. And nothing whatever can be done about it. For three years I and a number of these boys were hived off into a remote building with rotten floors and ceiling. Mice would come out and play if we remained quiet for long enough. I took thirty boys in a room measuring 16 ft. by 15 ft. complete with desks, and heated by an open coal fire. We were starved of books and equipment, and most of what we had I made myself. One boy was nearly blind, and for the three years that I had him he spent the whole of every lesson staring blankly at some object 6 inches from him. Nothing was ever done, and now, four years after he has left school, he is still unemployed and unemployable. I have raised cases at that school of boys who were persistent bed-wetters or what have you—and never once was anything done for any of those boys . . .

In many places, of course, things have improved, and there are many teachers making great efforts to help backward children. But the average condition of schooling for backward children still suffers from a lack of genuine understanding of their nature, their needs, or aims and values in their education. There are hardly any books for the teacher to use, or for him to translate directly into classroom practice. Thus the teacher with them is in isolation, and this feeling of isolation is reinforced by the whole context and the circumstances of his work.

I hope my account of 3 C and their work in the section of evidence above will itself help others to approach their own work with less of a sense of isolation, knowing that the nature of such children and the low standard of achievement is common to thousands of classrooms. I hope that what I have told about 3 C will help teachers to teach in their own ways with more confidence, even though they don't use my methods. And this brings me to the problem of making suggestions for classroom practice.

The teacher at this level needs many suggestions, devices, tricks, books, gambits, openings and devices up his sleeve. One needs books—because books can bring the escape from isolation into a common culture: one knows that other children are doing these exercises this very morning. But the teacher cannot work well in his own way unless he understands with some confidence what he is trying to do.

Mere practical suggestions, therefore, are useless, unless there is some definite goal. I have suggested that with 'low stream' children this goal is the release of personal potentialities in each child, its self-respect and élan, rather than the 'putting across' of a subject. But even to do this the teacher requires aims, and some knowledge of means whereby the aims can be achieved.

Here perhaps I may mention the relevant sections of my *English for Maturity*, which attempts to state the aims of teaching English in secondary education, and to outline some of the methods by which these aims may be reached. The aims are discussed in Chapter 2 of that book, pp. 16–28. Apart from the general chapters on teaching poetry, drama, reading and writing, there are also suggestions for practical oral and written work on pp. 129–132, and I think there is no point in reprinting them here—many are relevant to work with lower streams, and it is for the teacher to decide which he can use with them.

This will leave me free here to give suggestions which I regard as of particular relevance to work with backward children, to help the teacher face his solitary task with a little more confidence. In some cases he will, in fact, be employing these procedures and methods already, and has come to the same conclusions. All I am doing here is setting them down in print for him.

The first rule exerts on us the most difficult of all human obligations, and yet unless one can learn to put it into practice little of one's work will succeed, and the teacher may consequently become frustrated and disgruntled while the children remain alienated.

Rule 1. Strive not only to see the children as human creatures of great value, but treat them as such.

This cannot be achieved by hypocrisy, of course. One can't *pretend* to 'love' the children. But there are some disciplines by which one may come to understand these children better, and by which one may prevent oneself building up cynical defences against them. These disciplines are useful in other directions—not unrelated, for instance, to wider matters, such as racial relationships, or marriage, or creeds and policies with which we disagree, or teenagers, and other aspects of social living, in which we tend to find solace in prejudice. It will be difficult not to be smug here, because it is difficult not to imply that one has solved these problems oneself simply because one is able to discuss them explicitly. I once felt so remote from and afraid of a group of unruly adolescents that I called them 'yobs', when they threw apples at the windows of my house. Fortunately I got to know them better, by forming a youth club for them, and becoming involved in other youth work with them such as canoe building. And when I did get to know them, it seemed ridiculous that I should even have been hostile, or full of spleen, about boys *who were so much like me when I was 16 or 17 myself.* Fortunately the word 'yobs' became a joke between us. But there was an awkward moment when I was trying to get them a County grant for their club, while they were still shouting the word back at me in the street. A verbal slip, revealing an inward hostility and fear, can thus begin to create a situation that leads, in some circumstances, to actual violence and disorder. This kind of irrational situation can be circumvented by disciplines which restrain some of the angry impulses that seek to punish in others the weaknesses one fears in oneself.

I think teachers should deny themselves the common terms of antipathy to the less able child. From my own experience and my Appendix of letters from teachers, it is obvious that if unfortunate things are said in front of such children (such as 'he's ineducable') they understand more than we believe. If they hear occasional references to their supposed inferiority this will deepen their unconscious self-distrust and their damaging depressed sense of being unwanted and incapable. I spoke strongly in *English for Maturity* against the head-master who said, 'We only get the duds here': now I know he was helping to make his work harder. There is no doubt that the more we use terms such as 'dregs', 'dim', 'duds', 'useless', and the rest—whether or not these terms are overheard—we are making our work more difficult and frustrating. Of course, there may be something to be said for a kind of relief gained by ironic facetiousness about one's work, in the privacy of the staff room. But the worst kind of irony is destructive of the better attitudes to limited children, and reinforces harshness to them.

Besides being careful about the terms one uses, and the way one thinks, one has, I think, to cultivate a positive attitude to these children deliberately. We must also study to understand children who are different, as these children undoubtedly are, from those with quicker intelligence, and freer potentialities. This is part of the art of teaching. Perhaps the best training for developing this attitude is the experience of having children oneself: one only has to know the fierce total needs of a baby to see that in 'backward' children the strong baby-need for love, security and attention is still powerfully with them. The baby conveys the primal claim for contact, nourishment and attention without which it must die. Its urgent plaint for attention is the voice of the survival over many aeons of the human embryo which is born so helpless. Babies which didn't fear separation from the mother, and abandonment, as death, *did* die: those that survived have bred a race of babies which clamour relentlessly to survive. This explains the force with which a baby's cry works on one's emotions. In 'backward' children—perhaps because their minds remain rather infantile, because their infant soul has failed to grow up, and because in some the home background is not happy—this fierce demand for 'love' which seems to guarantee to them, unconsciously, *actual survival*, persists. They want us to be Daddy to them. And if one is irritated, perhaps one should think of what it would be like to be dying in the Sahara of hunger and thirst, and to see a man passing in a helicopter. He would seem to us a little like God: and if he saw us but flew on indifferently, how would we feel? Or, say, suppose we were badly injured and needed immediate treatment in a hospital—how would we feel if the surgeons and nurses decided (obviously to us) that we were too dirty, unattractive and unintelligent to be bothered much with? Supposing all the equipment and attractive nurses went over to someone much less in need, who happened to be, say, a film-star who kept up bright conversation and was tremendously handsome? Wouldn't we protest loudly? But isn't this just how many unattractive, dull, unhappy children feel for ten years in school—having psychic, and cultural, rather than physical, hurts? The attitude we can perhaps consciously cultivate without hypocrisy is to seek to be like a surgeon, or a nurse, or some other kind of therapist, who works for human beings according to their need for help.

One has to be careful to resist the invitations (they come even from the children themselves) to disparage those with unawakened or limited faculties. One has to be prepared to meet their probing enquiries into whether one 'loves' them or not, and consciously strive to build up their self-confidence. This can be done without hypocrisy. It simply requires understanding. If the children hide in a cupboard or under the desk, trying a trick on you, then you need to exert your authority—as discipline. But the way it is done will be helpful and constructive—and more efficient—if the teacher can say to himself inwardly, 'Look at John now! He's behaving like a child of two—playing "Come and find baby". How sad for a boy of 13, to need to make out that I am "Daddy" to him! I suppose if I speak sternly he'll go white and tremble for an hour, because he feels he's going to die or something. What a life it is with these kids! How can I get out of this one? I know! He wouldn't let anyone else prepare the tape recorder for use, and so, damn it, I'll have to think of some exercise which needs that.' 'John—I can see you're there—get the tape recorder for me. Sit down, Billy, James, Bobby. There's a job for you later. Right, quiet, everyone.' This is what one says: with luck it will prove effective.

This isn't to say that at times one isn't going to lose one's temper, and even do good by doing so. All I want to suggest here is that one is less likely to make a fool of oneself, may gain more co-operation, and may be more efficient, if one resists all temptations from within and from the children to browbeat, denounce, assault, sneer, bully, even in small ways. The children often want you to be unpleasant, because this will enable them to find relief, by explaining their inward torment by attributing it to your beastliness. Or they may unconsciously wish to enlist you in destructiveness which confirms their lack of confidence in their constructive and creative capacities.

Sir Cyril Burt is valuable on this question of attitudes to these children, in his great work, *The Backward Child* (p. 624):

Make the best of each one's strongest points and compensating aptitudes. The dull child will have failed so often that he will always be expecting to fail again. Give him something at which he can succeed, and keep him happily as well as usefully occupied. Avoid reproaches, and remove the ingrained sense of failure by giving him some special kind of work in which he can quickly achieve a conscious improvement and taste the triumph of a personal success. Never let the child lose heart, for once he has lost heart he has lost everything.

Combined with such resistances to their attempts to 'test' him and to force him into bloody-mindedness, the teacher needs to give explicit assurance to these children that they are 'good'.

Because I was fortunate in having a small class in a good school, with encouragement to work as I pleased, I could, without hypocrisy, tell them that I did enjoy being with them—and this became increasingly true as our relationship deepened. As I studied their work I found that I grew to like even the less attractive ones, because I came to understand how brave they were, and how much they suffered. The more one understands, the more one finds how like oneself these children are.

If we are able to reach such an understanding, then we can honestly tell a 'backward' class that their stories and poems *are* 'as good' as those of 3 A. They are doing the same things, within their powers, as any of us when we write creatively. Their awarenesses and perceptions, as I have shown, can be as fine and as valuable, if in a narrower and different dimension. Thus creative work is a means of dispersing the 'low-stream' child's sense of failure and inferiority—the needs of the sensibility, and the perceptions of the psyche unite all, and such children understand this.

The problem remains how to frame the explanation. The teacher will find himself perhaps saying something like this, if he can:

Your stories and poems are as good as anyone's—at least, I find them as interesting as I find those of any children. Why not? You want to find out what life is like: so you write stories of poems about things you know may happen to you. They're like dreams, really—dreams written down. All these are very interesting, because they are just like the story books and poems I read myself—and just the same as the stories written by 3 A or 2 A. They may write longer stories, or write more easily than you, but you're doing the same thing. And I find your writing just as interesting as theirs, or my own. That is, if the stories and poems are good—entertaining, moving, true, lively.

These aren't the exact words I used to 3 C: but they may convey the kind of attitude I strove to develop in myself, and sought to communicate to them. After a while they stopped asking, 'Do you really like being with us?' though they never stopped their babyish tricks to test out 'Daddy's' limits of affection, nor their maddening habits of restlessness, swearing, and eccentricities of scribbling and ill-treating their books—all of which belong to the same impulses to find out 'how far they can go', where the limits of their freedom are and where your secure authority begins.

Another aspect of the poignant sense of being 'dregs' in a C or D stream is in the sense of shame the children have at being unable to read as well as primary school children, or, if they are literate, being in the same class with those who are quite illiterate. Once the sadness of this shame is understood the teacher can take rigorous measures not only to exclude from his own remarks any comparison between them and 'higher' forms which implicitly denigrates them, but also to stamp on any face-grinding developments among members of the same low-stream forms. Often when 3 C were proving particularly taxing I found some such remark rising to my lips (remembered no doubt from the kind of thing that used to be said to us in my grammar school) as, 'I don't have this trouble with 3 A', or, 'It takes me a term to get a page of writing out of you: I can get that out of anyone in 3 A in half an hour!', or, 'Oh, it's so boring working with children who don't bother to look and learn the words!', or, 'I wish you could spell like 3 A!'. But such remarks need to be resisted—there are some comparisons which may be made, however, such as, 'There's only one difference between 3 A and you: when they sit down at the beginning of a lesson, they work. You try to create a disturbance'.

'But they've got more brains than us, Sir'.

'No they haven't: everyone has brains and can write good stuff. The only difference is that they don't need to be told, so often, to get on with it.'

This exchange produced fifteen minutes of quiet concentration.

But a much more disturbing tendency is for the class to exclaim in derision, when I ask George Green to read, ''E can't, sir', 'No good asking 'im, is it, George?' And when George stumbles even over 'the' and 'and' for the rest to express their shame at being classed with George by 'Tuts' and 'Pshaws' and 'Dohs'. This kind of thing has to be firmly suppressed. It is likely to be a trouble when a large group is reading, and I met it first when I was 'reading round' to discover who could read and who could not. The solution is to divide children up into small groups in which each will read aloud to the others. I find these children like helping one another to read—particularly if they are reading one another's work in a class magazine. But with a small group such as the 19 members of 3 C it was possible for us to 'read round', particularly when we were reading things they had written themselves or knew well and could thus read with confidence, without anyone becoming bored. More will be said about such arrangements of the work later (p. 236). But it is always important to prohibit any jeering at poor readers for this can become gravely inhibiting—the abused child comes to believe that he cannot master reading and will never make progress with it. Perhaps because of the children's emotional disturbances, their lack of adequate ordering power and weak feelings of security, they become at times cruel to one another thus, almost trying to climb up over the weaknesses of others, as if trying to make themselves feel, 'Well, at least I'm better than *him*'.

This cruelty one to another, and making scapegoats of the very inarticulate for their own weaknesses, can be eliminated by a teacher who feels compassionately and who seeks to relieve suffering wherever he finds it. Here is life, he conveys to them—we all have to deal with it—let us help one another.

Much of our capacity to deal with life centres round our faculty for oral expression—reading, writing, talking, listening. There are perhaps deep reasons for this, bound up with the immense importance in our psychic growth of the primal satisfactions of suckling at the mother's breast, and the associations of oral satisfactions, aggressions and lusts, with both sexual impulses and creative and altruistic ones. With 'backward' children one can see how the activity of word-expression relates to the whole being; and, as in stammering, disabilities in the whole being are embodied in verbal incapacities. By contrast, a rich sensitive relish for life comes out in great poetry such as, say, Keats's *Ode to Autumn*, in a richness of verbal enactment, of sounds, sights, rhythms, bodily satisfactions and raptures of soul. We share the 'feel in the mouth' of the ecstasy of being alive: in saying the words one's mouth-muscles enact the delightful sensations of hearing the sounds of natural life and the movements of creatures.

Conversely, trouble in the soul can inhibit these areas of verbal expression, and destroy the capacity to relish life through language, to speak 'with the tongue of a ready writer'. Encouraging a child to think better of itself, helping it develop its perception by praise and love and the exercise of its imagination will release its oral-verbal powers and also its relish for experience. This is the secret of our 'raid on the inarticulate'. Yet we need say little more to them than 'good', 'excellent', 'marvellous', 'Listen to this splendid piece', 'what an exciting poem', and know that the natural poetic process will go on in them and strengthen their living powers, as well as their powers of expression.

But before I conclude on this theme I must digress for a moment on the fact that, if the teacher seeks to follow my advice in trying to see 'backward' children as 'good', and to tell them they are 'good' and fine creatures, he will find himself sometimes striving against prevalent common assumptions as to what is fit for these 'low-stream' children. In *The Secret Places* I analyse some of these assumptions, in the content and illustrations of books designed for them. The teacher's touchstone will be their own best writing, and the sad but tender images they draw for us of their world, like Rose Jameson's portrait of childhood:

Fig. 14

The Second Rule I made for myself was: always be flexible and spontaneous. Don't be alarmed or uneasy about working sporadically and opportunistically. Rather, accept this as an inevitable condition of the work. Backward children can't be expected to concentrate for more than a few minutes at a time—and one needs to prepare about four or five different activities for each period.

I made this rule after missing a chance. One morning the sunshine was bright, and some of the children asked if they could go for a walk. I said, 'No, get on with your work'. Then, though there was no going back, I regretted the decision, for more reasons than one. I found myself actually thinking in those old-fashioned terms which imply that children must not *enjoy* education except for occasional rewards for doing unpleasant and tedious things. (The pieces written in my Section of Evidence about walks round the grounds show how valuable this exercise can be.*) It dawned on me as the morning progressed that, in fact, my children would have been helped more towards literacy by going on that walk than by staying in the classroom. They

* See also the expeditions described in *An Experiment in Education* by Sybil Marshall (C.U.P 1963).

would have observed things. They would have talked excitedly and would have been prepared to write about them in their excitement. They would have come closer into my personal confidence. But I missed the opportunity, and I felt there must be many such chances which one lets slide because of one's unconscious fuddy-duddy tendency to resist growth and change, and informal methods, perhaps because one is uncertain of one's ability to keep control in the informal situation. But the worst enemy is sheer laziness and inertia. Flexibility and spontaneity must govern the work of a backward class. A teacher with an 'A' form can work through a series of topics. For instance he may say to himself, 'This month I will deal with the following: (a) what is a noun? (b) the poetry of John Keats, (c) the uses of the comma, (d) *Huckleberry Finn*, chapters 1–6, (e) writing a ballad.' He will adjust pupils' expectations and rhythms of work to these subjects as they come round.

There is no point in making such a series or syllabus with a 'C' or 'D' stream. All one can make is a series of personal notes about one's aims, e.g. (a) Hope to get from each a complete small poem, (b) Hope to get a story written by the form all together and a complete personally written story from a few others, (c) Hope to read them a couple of good poems, (d) Play them some folksongs, or perhaps co-operate with the music teacher over this (and they could learn some?), (e) Make a form magazine, (f) Hope to read them one exciting story or chapter from a novel or at least an episode. But there is no point in trying to take these in an orderly sequence—children of lower intelligence simply do not adjust to a schedule, and cannot easily look forward to long-term satisfactions from a project which takes a substantial time to complete. They have small powers of concentration. 3 C's interest in the first form magazine I prepared for them began to flag as the weeks went by and they hadn't copies of their own: they would be just as likely to abandon their copies half an hour after looking at them. But in the end they don't forget the general impression of many small successes. They will even follow an exercise, but obliquely, and often not exactly in the way you meant. For instance, you may ask for a poem, and even describe what kind, and what subject. But some children will write a story instead—albeit inspired by your stimulation, if not to conformity with your intention. In an 'A' stream the teacher couldn't accept this—but with a 'low' stream the only thing to do is to be glad, and even praise the digression as originality.

Progress in this work is a matter of small, brief achievements, which evaporate as soon as grasped—leaving, one hopes, some slight advance in personal maturity, together with some slight gain over words. But even then we must be willing to have no result from our efforts: this demands our resignation to an occasional futility. Much worse to accept the alternative, to make all the work a futile bluff by 'practical' exercises which merely 'keep them quiet'!

But often a gambit, devised on the spur of the moment, will have remarkable success. Here is an example. There being an unusually prolific apple crop at home once I took in a box of apples. I gave each child a large red apple, in class. I realised this was something they would take, having souls with infant needs, as symbolic of a gift, or love, say, as in so many nursery rhymes and folk-stories. There is also something evocative about apples, as in the poetic story of Adam and Eve: and children associate them with 'making something'—i.e. 'scrumping' (see above, p. 90). Apples are food, sex and sin, unconsciously: they are also free (when stolen) and beautiful. Apples are very poetic objects altogether.

I said, 'Write about apples'.

'What about apples'?

'Anything that comes into your head.'

Up to that occasion I had found their imaginative power needing a degree of constant stimulation which wearied me, and made me despair of ever striking a spark from any of these children. But the apples did it for me and Rose's passage (p. 120) was a turning point.

When I had read it I exclaimed how lovely a piece of writing it was: then I fetched Keats from the library and read them the stanza from the *Ode to Autumn* about the 'moss'd cottage trees'. I said how someone that had said those words made you feel you were biting an apple. (I didn't, of course, tell them it was F. R. Leavis in *Revaluation*!) But I said, 'that's what Rose's piece makes you feel, too'. This was a sheer piece of opportunism: and yet it brought to them a genuine literary experience, as deep a one as they could stand. They liked the Keats I read to them about Autumn and apples because it was like the things they could write, only better. It did them good to suppose they could write things comparable with poems in a printed book. I might have taken William's piece on scrumping just as well, and compared it with passages from *Tom Sawyer* or *Huckleberry Finn*.

In my eighteen months with 3 C we have, at odd times, done the following things, many on the spur of the moment, some planned, some not.

(1) Looked at the material, tools and plans for Making a Canoe and tried by word of mouth and in writing to compose instructions for making a canoe (Boys only).

(2) (Girls only.) Tried stage make-up (with mirrors), and looked at leaflets about cosmetics, then written about make-up.

(3) Discussed a story about young people, tape-recorded it, duplicated the results, and written, each, the story in our own ways. (This is discussed in the next chapter.)

(4) Written about apples.

(5) Written poems, after being read some simple poems.

(6) Listened to folksongs on gramophone records, and American folk tales (on a record obtainable from the American Library, Grosvenor Square).*

(7) Written stories, 'about anything', stimulated by being read stories by other children and fragments of T. F. Powys and D. H. Lawrence.

(8) Written about 'my family'.

(9) Written, after a practical demonstration, how to change the wheel of a car.

(10) Read our own stories aloud or into a tape recorder, and heard them back.

(11) Compiled form magazines by reading aloud our best compositions to the teacher who typed the stencils. These were then used for 'readers'.

(12) Illustrated our stories in indian ink or paint.

(13) (Boys only) have been told the 'facts of life' and discussed sex and love.

(14) Heard some of *Porgy and Bess* on records, and heard the story.

(15) Conducted imaginary interviews of 'candidates' for jobs. (I found the children astonishingly smart and quick in repartee about wage-rates, and here the conversation even ran away with the pupils sometimes:

A. What wages did you think you might start at?

B. 'Bout £5.15 a week.

A. Well, you'd better b—— off then. . . .)

(16) Making a 'BBC programme' on tape, of members of the class being interviewed about what they were going to do when they left school. This went very well.

(17) Played oral guessing games in teams, e.g. whereby one member of each team in turn draws something on the board as it is described by a member of the opposite team (without giving the game away by using

* The catalogues of this Library are obtainable free.

words like 'spout' or 'handlebars'). The drawers' own team have to guess what it is he is drawing in a limited time.

(18) Had talks and debates on subjects drawn out of a hat.

(19) Worked at free drama, working in groups with one of the best writers and organisers in each group. Synopses were worked out and written as notes in everyone's book before the plays were 'performed', while the rest of the class watched.

(20) Had spelling tests.

(21) Done written exercises in punctuating, and setting out properly on the page, taking as subjects pieces of writing from the stories of members of the class.

(22) Selected books in the library to browse in, each book choice being supervised by me.

(23) Written stories or poems from various visual stimuli—reproductions of paintings, an oil painting of an Irish donkey cart, a skull etc.

(24) Written stories or poems or passages from music (e.g. Varèse, *Ionisation*; a March by Sousa; some Red Indian war dances; a jazz record; ballet music).

(25) Listened to poems and stories read by me for amusement only—and also plays—e.g. many poems from *Iron, Honey, Gold*, the verse play *Death in the Tree* (by Hans Sachs, put into modern English by myself in *Thieves and Angels*), T. F. Powys' short story *Only the Devil*, and so forth.

(26) Written comprehension exercises of a simple kind on poems—questions on the meaning (e.g. *Stopping by Woods on a Snowy Evening*, Frost, *Meeting at Night*, Browning), from anthologies such as *Tom Tiddler's Ground*, *The Poet's Tongue*, etc.

(27) Chosen poems to read out, or to copy in their own books.

(28) Read prose and poetry extracts (typed out) to write 'reviews' of them —i.e. whether they liked them or not.

(29) Illustrated poems in paint—e.g. *Casey Jones*; 'Hast thou given the horse strength?'; 'I'm a poor lonely soldier', and their own poems.

(30) Read them *A Boy is a Boy* by Ogden Nash, a long piece of light verse.

(31) Had periods of enforced silent reading (while I heard some of the slow readers read to me individually).

(32) Listened to tape-recordings of stories and poems written by other forms—4 B and 2 B (this was very popular).

(33) Written descriptions of classmates for identification purposes and heard a tape of such descriptions by another form, as a guessing game.

Some of these were invented on the spur of the moment: 'my family', for instance, because for two or three children a certain stage in their self-realisation had come which made this necessary and useful for them. And if the children became bored with a subject—as the boys did of grappling with the complications of the canoe-building project*—I abandoned it. It is, I think, a great mistake to feel it is 'morally wrong' for such children not to complete a task. They can't tackle complex or long-term enterprises any more than a two-year old can. Perhaps we all have that motto so often printed on the covers of exercise books in our minds: 'If a thing is worth doing it is worth doing well'—strange that this injunction should become a slogan in public education when millions of factory tasks for school leavers have been reduced to dreary meaninglessness. This is not to encourage abrogation on the teacher's part of his concern for quiet, for neat writing, for tidy work, or for re-doing work badly done and all such disciplines. It is simply to say that to succeed with these children we must study their natures realistically. And it is not in their natures to concentrate on tasks as we can, nor to complete every task.

Children—as one may observe in infants—often pursue a task only for as long as it has value for them. When they have exhausted its particular meaning for them at that time, then they drop it. Infants do this all the time in, say, sand and water play. Of course, brighter and more capable children become, at later stages in the primary school, able to master tasks, such as making a basket or learning long division, many of which are at some stage tedious. They become able to find the deeper satisfaction of completing a total undertaking in which self-discipline was needed. They *can* concentrate. But secondary modern school children writing stories often exhaust their interest long before they have finished it; half-way through, perhaps—after one particular episode or theme has served its turn.

With less intelligent children the first development of any staying power itself only comes after many small short steps each bringing a satisfaction. Perhaps after many opportunist occasions a pupil will suddenly excel himself—as William Glebe did, suddenly writing some eight pages, crying as he did so, 'I've written six pages, Sir!'—'I'm on my seventh, Sir'—'Look at me!' This cry is better known to the Primary School teacher, but the teacher of less intelligent children in the secondary school will hear it often and will need to respond. Respond-

---

* Here their powers of speech and writing were too slow for the work in hand, whether they were to do the woodwork, or (as actually happened) I did it. I think for such children much English work could relate to craft work, but the stages of construction, planning and writing would have to be very carefully coordinated.

ing in an opportunist way to such moments is far more effective than
seeking to drag backward children through a rigid 'planned' syllabus.
The attitude to cultivate is one of glad responsiveness to success. This
is a matter of emotion, and it can be taxing. This is perhaps why we
sometimes protect ourselves by avoiding it. Other teachers have told
me that they, too, share the experience of sometimes being so moved by
a child's work that they have had to turn away, in tears. This is, again,
one of the joys, but also one of the exactions, of teaching-as-an-art.
This emotional stir and its satisfactions leaves one sometimes a little
flat and irritated with the outside world after school. But a teacher
involved in these turmoils knows he is *teaching* at the level where it
both hurts and is being humanly effective.

The need for children of 'lower streams' to have odd, frequent,
quick and short satisfactions, requires us to be more opportunist and
spontaneous with them than with brighter children who can follow a
protracted course or syllabus. Each child in a 'C' or 'D' stream needs
to feel from time to time he or she has done something remarkable, and
is the most important, funniest, most lovable creature in the room. It
is a perfectly proper observation of their uniqueness—of the 'mystic
now' of each of them. And it takes many forms of behaviour—
my children would sometimes hide in cupboards while the others
said, 'Gerald Goodchild's not here today, Sir', or a child will be
particularly naughty or noisy until he takes your angry attention. All
these are common features of children's behaviour. But in these
respects 'low-stream' children remain childish longer. To attempt to
suppress or defeat these manifestations beyond the bounds of reasonable
classroom order, particularly with 'C'- and 'D'-stream children, is to
reduce the child's development of order in himself, by social experiment,
by his own opportunism in exploring experience, and by his cultural
interest. To deny children their experiments on you as teacher,
emotionally, and to deny them the opportunity for imaginative
exploration might even, I suppose, unbalance them. A child psychiatrist wrote to me to say that if the child's mysterious imaginative powers
are ever driven underground or are lost—against all the natural impulses
which are to keep them functioning—then the child needs a psychiatrist.
The child of low intelligence, or one who is emotionally unbalanced,
needs to indulge his phantasy more than a bright child, often recklessly,
and totally, becoming quite involved in his own imaginings. He benefits
from a context in which a stable adult holds the ring, respects his

expression, stimulates it, and helps him towards closer apprehensions of reality. Only good can come from this controlled and sanctioned phantasy. (My psycho-analytical adviser comments that the benign toleration of even the weirdest expression is most significant in the work described in my Section of Evidence.)

But this restless experimental force in the less intelligent, less orientated, child requires from us a spontaneous, opportunist readiness to turn to whatever suits them most, as with the infant teacher, at the sand-and-water stage. Like small children they lack staying power, and they need variety: in fact the best free primary school methods are suitable for these pupils whose mental age is 6–8. Again, perhaps it is worth saying that you cannot expect a man or woman to cope satisfactorily with the fatiguing demand of working with such children if he or she has more than twenty of them at once to deal with. On the other hand it is perfectly possible to be happy with twenty such children for long periods—even a whole morning—given plenty of resources. But, again, to enjoy this work a teacher must be trained and refreshed in creativity, and have enough free time to prepare for it, in study and finding materials, and emotionally.

This brings me to my next two rules for myself:

3. *Don't expect any but the slightest and most intangible of results.*

BUT

4. *Be prepared to jump for joy at the least success, and show it.*

A kind of paternal (or maternal) benignity, I have said, needs to be cultivated together with a capacity for constant encouragement. We tend, of course, to fall into negative injunctions—saying all day 'Stop talking', 'Be still', 'Quiet!'. Teaching is an artificial thing, and it is artificial for children to be shut in a room all day, learning in abstract ways. So they are restless, while we become nags. There is no way out of this, though one aims at a mean of mutual respect, and a minimum of noise in an atmosphere which yet allows some free exchange of conversation at times. Less intelligent children can never become as quiet, still and absorbed as brighter ones, and their disturbed souls make their feet wriggle more and make them need more than others to test your affection by falling off their seats, spilling ink or trying to break up the lesson.

For these reasons we tend sometimes to become negative in self-protection in our attitudes to them. In anxiety and desperation we even come to feel we must fall back on 'discipline'—on formality of layout, cleanness, neatness, text-book exercises and the appearance of 'proper' work. This can be unfortunate, for it may easily mean the abandonment of the only work worth doing, the real fostering of their true small achievements, in favour of an empty pretence of 'keeping them occupied'. At worst, of course, this attitude is rationalised as 'keeping them quiet so they don't disturb the examination classes'.

Rule 5 must therefore be: *endless and unflagging encouragement.* A mother says 'clever, that's clever!' to her baby in arms fifty times a day. Only because of this devoted praise in love, *can* the human creature make its extraordinary journey, so far beyond any other animal, to speech, consciousness, and its marvellous use of limbs and sense organs in co-ordination with language and thought. Take the 'lowest' child in the 'D' stream: you can find someone who will say, 'He's just an animal'. But consider what he can do that an animal can't: talk, cook, foresee tomorrow, remember events of last week, fall in love, write, believe in God, know right from wrong. If an animal wrote as well as George Green it would be the wonder of all time, and the world would be topsy-turvy for decades with excitement: thus greater than all other creatures is the most inarticulate human soul. And the marvel is made by care, love, praise, attention and devotion by the mother and father, uncritical, unquestioning love—where it can be given.

Love makes us what we are, the love at mother's breast and on her lap. For some reason children in 3 C are still in need of such a degree of approval. This is nothing to be despised, for many of us are to some degree in much the same condition all our lives, requiring approval, backing and unconditional love from our wives or husbands, secretaries —and, if we are authors—from our readers. But perhaps the children in 3 C did not get it from Mum, perhaps Mum stopped giving it too soon, or perhaps the less intelligent mind grows slowly and remains in the condition of an infant longer.

Whatever the reason, it is true they need unlimited approval and that only endless approval produces results from such children. And the simple act of approval works wonders. The teacher only has to cultivate the habit of saying and writing 'Good!', 'Excellent!', 'Well done!', instead of 'Bad', 'Fair', or 'Slovenly'. Many teachers mark work down in the mistaken belief that if children 'have it too easy' they will slack. I am not sure about this with brighter children (though I'm all for a good slam on a really lazy, bad, insolent piece). But with

'C' and 'D' stream children it does not work at all. They are 'marked down' already, and have been for years. They are rejected and despised by men. Negative criticism merely reinforces their sense of failure and disables them. They did not 'pass the eleven plus'. They are not even in the 'B' stream—they are in 'C' or 'D' or (worst of all) 'progress'. If, in stream 'D', your work is called 'Bad' or 'Poor' you may wonder whether life is worth living at all, or what point there is in staying in this damn fool game anyway—and come to develop a ruthless antagonism to everything good or handsome. Here the sense of being rejected for lack of 'brains' combines with the neurotic fears of being unloved: the effect is a gathering, inhibiting insecurity and a pathetic plea for love which may even be expressed in violence or destructiveness. The 'D' streamer is sometimes crying out against the agonies of mortal weakness, like an infant King Lear on the heath in the storm.

But say and write 'Good!', 'Excellent!', 'Well done!', when these children have sweated a little to write a line of prose, and their lives will be visibly enriched. It is almost pathetic, at times, to see how they respond to encouragement—how they swell their chests, and go back to scribble away, when their laboured little achievements have gained 'Daddy's' full approval. Yet to be able to give this approval uncynically is the means to give these children their small measure of literacy and the related inward order and power. For us to hear or play through some of Bach's *48 Preludes and Fugues* will be to experience the establishing of a new order, the achieved revolution of temperance in the piano, as an instrument in history on which to express human experience as art, and as a new grasp on human potentialities of soul. Their equivalent may be to write one story or poem of six lines successfully.

Besides these major rules I made for myself, there are a few minor ones, notably:

Rule 6. Do not bother overmuch about spelling and punctuation in creative work. (And don't consider either as the chief mark of 'education'. Disabuse yourself of obsession with the points of graphic layout.)

Read their pieces as you would read Marion Tweedy Bloom's soliloquy at the end of *Ulysses*, or *Finnegan's Wake* or the poetry of E. E. Cummings, or the rich wild prose of Dekker, or Nashe. Listen to its rhythm and voice. The more technical points of how it is written out can be corrected in those pieces which you type out for class 'readers' or magazines: then the children can see how it should look.

Encourage them to ask you to write a word on the board *before* they use it, so they see it correctly from the beginning; or get them to help one another with their spelling. Give them dictionaries. By such means, again, they move by positive holds, not by correcting error—they cannot bear much error, for it is emotionally too discouraging. 'Mankind cannot bear very much reality.' Encourage them to struggle with the reality of experience, and don't substitute for this the struggle with mere problems of graphic layout.

Of course, there is no harm in giving positive *very brief* accounts of how to use, say, the full stop (though this will come to a pupil more easily if he dictates to you while you type a stencil, or if he is allowed to try to typewrite his own piece). And, of course, one needs to have many spelling bees and tests. What I made a rule against for myself was *any kind of marking* of children's work *in the text*, on the creative page—marking errors, or corrections. I simply wrote general comments, approving ones, at the end. I wanted to leave their achievements—full pages, complete poems—clean and unspotted, without that critical cavilling which might destroy for them their feeling of being 'loved'.

All these rules were a reduction for the purpose of teaching 3 C of the aims and principles I set down in *English for Maturity*. The best principle I found I had set forth in that book where 3 C were concerned was that a child's expression must above all be *respected*. Sometimes children appear not to respect their own work—they damage their books or crumple their copy of the form magazine, write four-letter words and draw obscene pictures. There may be something in this explainable in terms of the psychology of disturbed or low intelligence children—maybe they are making a final test on themselves and you. But, in fact, though they will often cover the fact by elaborate forms of apparently disowning their work by self-depreciation and off-handedness, children care very much indeed for their *words, even if they show no care for the books or paper they are written on*—for the words come forth from the mouth, the centre of many forms of oral-psychic preoccupation and creative life, and a source of nourishment. The off-handedness and carelessness may even be a self-protection, a readiness to dash underground if attacked. They are willing to bring aspects of their tender selves to the surface only if they feel safe to do so: to do so is a great need in them, for once the matter is explicit it stays 'out there' as an artefact, as a poem, play, novel or book does for us, to contribute to our lives and the lives of others for better or worse. They find relief in the expression: if the expressed creation is hurt, so may they be. But this tender exposed part of their immature selves we must treat with the greatest reverence and respect: this is not to be sentimental about 3 C: self-exposure for them is almost a matter of life and death, of the psyche.

We may find some light cast on the underlying problems in the writings of child psycho-analysts. For instance Melanie Klein says that 'technical' capacities are inevitably linked with deeper fears and anxieties.

It is well known that young children's attempts at constructive activities are often hampered by their lack of skill. For instance, when children begin to paint, they are likely to make a mess. They tend to take this as evidence that their destructive impulses predominate over their constructive and reparative ones. It can often be observed that when their efforts go wrong they tear up the paper, or make an even bigger mess. One of the deepest causes for this attitude is that distrust of themselves and despair reinforce their destructive tendencies.

Teachers of backward children will confirm from their experience this observation, which Melanie Klein is making, of course, of much younger children, in her *Narrative of a Child Analysis* (Tavistock Press, 1959). The other side of this struggle is the success each step in creativity may be, in the child's brave struggle with his inward self.

In ordinary play, where the child remains largely unconscious of the content of his incestuous and aggressive phantasies and impulses, he nevertheless experiences *relief* through the very fact that he expresses them symbolically; and this is one of the factors which makes play so important for the child's development.   (*op. cit.*, my italics.)

Creative activity is a constructive quest for a sense of meaning in experience. But with the child, as with the adult artist, the 'relief' goes with a sense of triumph, and lessening in inward pain. To fail to achieve expression goes as much with the deepening of anguish and anxiety.

Hence any discouragement or disrespect is harmful and damaging to the child's powers to live fully and well.

Fortunately children are quick at detecting disrespect and protecting themselves from it. But we are unlikely to get satisfactory imaginative work toward literacy unless we do gain their respect. Proper respect, of course, depends, again, on our own feelings about and understanding of art, and our own experience of its mysterious powers of illuminating our experience and giving it significance. This awareness may be given teachers by training colleges and Institutes of Education, through many forms of work to do with the creative imagination, including their own experience of creation in free drama, painting, mime, dance, and the writing of poetry and prose fiction. Once one has experienced the disciplines and rigour of creativity oneself one should be able to give others a sense of the gravity, value and satisfaction of this process, and convey an attitude of respect to what emanates from it. If one does convey such attitudes, then good work will come—because the child will trust the teacher and the impersonal complex for creativity he has established. Unfortunately not nearly enough training for such work is given. We still despise what Bacon called 'the theatre of the mind' —imagination and fancy—in favour of the 'effective' intellect. The connection between essential literacy, imagination and civilisation are not understood: in this way our whole society is as illiterate as 3 C. If we understand that this is so, we may begin to make our 'raid on the inarticulate' together with them, even though we come to be convinced of the value of the imaginative late in our work, and have painfully to keep ahead of them by nourishing our own creative powers and creative interests in our own leisure time.

The rules, then, for work with 'low-stream' children are few, but they demand a radical shift of dimension and approach to be efficient. Then we need to plunge into this dimension—and convince ourselves (and the 'low' stream) that we can swim in it. Our first piece of work is crucial, like a young boar's first mating: if he fails he may never take to the sow again. The young teacher's first experience of a bottom stream is rather similar. So perhaps it is worth describing our first exercise in detail.

5

LIMBERING UP

All my principles and rules may be very fine, but I realise that the crucial moment for many a young teacher, or a teacher entering a new school, or a teacher of experience who wants to take a new direction, is the first lesson or two. Supposing the class he takes over seems dull, resentful, antipathetic—dare one start? Dare one mention 'poetry' or 'stories' to a band of swearing and hostile toughs from the local bad area? Perhaps at this moment one loses one's nerve and gives up the possibility of free and informal work for ever. So it may perhaps be worth giving in detail an account of our first step towards free and informal writing.

In the first few talks with 3 C I noticed at once how sluggish were their powers of imaginative creation. Mention a subject or produce a stimulant, with 3 A—an old top hat or a picture of a donkey, and from 35 children you would get 35 different responses—original opening gambits, fresh tangents, new themes. From 3 C I got perhaps one cliché response only: and then I found I had to work for it.

So, I decided, we needed to do some limbering up of phantasy powers. Some of the class were obviously nervous of me—the plain little girl Daphne Badland couldn't stop spluttering and giggling—and others became sullen and rigid ("'n't going to do nothin'", they would say).

I set up a tape recorder, to try to get from them a discussion of the kind of story they were interested in. I told them we were going to write a story, and then duplicate it, so we could all read it. This was received with little conviction. I asked what kind of story would interest them. We tried several. They had no idea of orderly discussion, and I did not want a stiff hands-up and speak-when-you're-spoken-to affair. For a time there was Bedlam. I recorded the Bedlam and played it back. They were a little ashamed. Then, with the machine running, we began a more orderly discussion—only one voice speaking at a time. Now notions began to emerge. Then someone mentioned the word 'teenagers'—a word for which I have no great liking, because it is associated for me with the pretend-world of the commercial rackets which exploit the young nowadays. But it was in their idiom and touched their genuine preoccupations with growing up and sexual adventure. Suggestions began to come, not exactly thick and fast, but so that at least they produced one each.

At last I managed to tape-record each child saying what kind of story he or she would like. When this was completed I took down and duplicated their statements. We then played the tape back while they read (and corrected) their own statements. By now they were reading their own words, aloud. We could now see between us what they themselves were like (that is, they were, under the surface, still very much children), and we could accept their interests (which were very much in sex, romance, love, marriage and parenthood, among other things).

We had thus established a foothold on the word used imaginatively and according to their interest. And we had made a link between talking, listening, writing and reading. Here is the list of proposals:

OUR STORY BOOK

JACK O'MALLEY. I would like this story to be about teenagers . . .

JAMES CARR. I would like to see in our story two teenagers, one female blonde with lovely long hair and a lovely figure. The man or boy a short chap with a chubby face and curly hair like Mr. Gulliver's and a nice long beard right down to his knees.

GERALD GOODCHILD. Two teenagers a boy and a girl. The boys think they're great Teddy boys and the girls think they're teddy girls.

JOHN YOUNG. I'd like the characters to be (in this story) a tall thin chap with spectacles and long hair coming over his ears and I'd like the girl to be about seventeen with dark hair and very high heeled shoes and a real fat tummy [he means bosom] and short thin legs and to be going out with men and getting to know each other.

JOAN STALL. I would like this story to be about teenagers: girl with long black hair and a short man.

JUDITH WARD. I would like this story to be about teenagers. The two characters taking part in this story are a boy and a girl. The girl's name is Joan with long black hair, blue eyes, and she's short. The boy dark, with green eyes and tall, John.

ANN BARLEY. I'd like this story to be about teenagers: a girl named Jean with long black hair and a boy Richard with his hair over his ears and they both went out together for six months.

ROSE JAMESON. I want this story to be about teenagers . . .

TOM SULLIVAN. This story's about teenagers. The girl's name's June. She's got black hair down to about her shoulders and she's got browny-green-coloured eyes fairly tall and tight skirt and nylons and about 3″ high heels.

The boy's name's James and he's round about five foot tall. He's got big black long hair, teddy boy suit, and side-boards coming right down to his chin nearly.

ROGER SCOTT. I'd like my story to be about the Larkins. When the old man's told not to go down to the pub, and he disobeys the old woman. She goes down there with a broomstick after him. She finds him lying on the side of the road drunk, singing. So she grabs him by the scruff of the neck and drags him home into the house and sends him to bed.*

ROBERT SHIRE. I would like my story to be about a policeman who met a girl.

NIGEL THRUSH. I would like a story to be about two young teenagers. The girl named Mary, boy named John. Mary's got ginger hair, long, and the boy's got flat hair in a crew cut. Mary's got blue eyes and John's got brown eyes, and Mary's rather small and so is John.

Now we had some cultural artefacts, created by ourselves, from nothing. Now each child was told to get on and write his own version of the story. Here are some of their own subsequent efforts to write a complete story, with my notes on their efforts:

The Blind Date

1. *Nigel Thrush*

One day a young boy nam Rex Harrison was waiting for a girl of 16 who he know This girls name was Jean Smith. Jean Smith had got a boy friend. So Jean was bringing a girl name Audrey Watson.

Rex was waiting outside the Red Lion. Rex had Blue eyes, Black Jacket Blue Jeans. Audrey had blue eyes, Red Blazer Full dress. Jean had green eyes, Full dress, and a blue blazer. Then they all went into the red lion. Jean and Audrey had cherry ciderette Rex had beer. They were in the red lion from 7 till 10 o'clock, Then they came out. Jean and her boy frend went off and left Audrey and Rex together. Rex said when shall I see you againe Audrey said on saturday. Then rex took Audrey home. The next day Rex and Jean went to work Jean boy friend see them go. When Jean got home Jean boyfriend come. Jean went to the dor. Jean boy friend said 'who were you with today' O only a frend.

You will have to let me meet him Yes we will see. Jean boy friend said I will have to go. Jean saw her boyfriend off.

Saturday night Audrey and Rex went out they went to Melton pictures they talk abouth there Honey moon. They went home at 10 o'clock. Audrey said do you love me Rex said yes the Rex kiss Audrey. Rex put is arm round Audrey when the lights went out the pictures was cald G.G. [Gigi] when in

* A television story.

ended Rex took Audrey home. Rex said when shood we get engaged Audrey said on Saturday, it was monday know. Res and Audrey went home Audrey kiss Rex then Tex went home When Rex went to work Jean said how did you get on Rex said OK. Jean said do you love her yes said Rex. Jean said I do not Wy said Rex because she speaks big well, I like her so thats that. We are going to get enagaged well I do not like you this is Jean wot said I do not like you. then Rex went to his room at work he thoruogh about wen he was going to get enagaged they were going to get engaged on saturday 24 August it was the 20 of August. Soon the day came and Audrey cam to Rex house, they kised and then they went to get the Ring Jean saw them go she through about her boy frend. Audrey and Rex went to London they had a lot of fun they got marid at London Jean had a baby boy & they lived happy evry hafter.

Nigel writes a long story, but it is pedestrian stuff, and he himself is persistently and methodically tedious. But the interest in his work is in his desire to grow up into adult emotional life himself, and the consequent contemplation of difficulties—here the brush between Jean and her boy-friend, and Jean's 'I do not like you' and 'she speaks big'. These more interesting moments could be mentioned when his story is read out aloud to the class. It is a mark of the less competent child to skip over huge areas of incident and compress a meeting, courtship, engagement, marriage, and two babies—into a few lines. The improbability of the precipitate engagement provided some stimulus for class discussion of this story.

2. *Joan Stall*
   One day Rex Marrison was waiting out side the cafe waiting for Jean Smith Jean was a nice girl fair hair & not very tall. She was wearing a pink drees and green coat. Rex Marrison was tall. black hair and white coat and black trousers. now comes audrey she is a quiet girl with black hair fairly long.
   "Jean I sorry I am lat I have got to go to the offis at two o'coolk
   "Rex have you what for

JEAN	I dont no whots up.
REX	I don't no I havent got a thing to do execispt to whosech the television at nights so he said is there any nice girls in your village.
JEAN	Well I don't no said Jean theres Auder
REX	is She a nice girl.
JEAN	Well why don't you get 3 ticks to the pictures to night, and I get Auder to night to come
REX	Well I don't no, all right then it whont matter but don't forget I reling on you

JEAN   all right then I be there don't yow worry at 7 o,clook. It got round to 7 o,clock.

AUDREY   I scred [I'm scared].

JEAN   you will soon get over that.

AUDREY   I hope so too.

Rex was standing out side the picture wating for Jean and Audrey. then he sor Jean and Audrey coming. What a girl I hope I be glad I meet her.

JEAN   Hellow Rex This is Audrey

REX   Hellow Auder Jean

JEAN   Well are we going in the picture or not.

REX   Of course we are let go in.

JEAN   What a nice picture well I have to go now I almost forgot to tell its yow day of aurder the boss told me to tell yow

AUDER   thank yow Jean good night Rex

REX   see yow tomorrow auder yes all right then tomorrow good night.

Then auder got into a taixi

Rex walk home that night think about auder when he got home his mother said had a nice evening.

REX   yes thank you.

MOTHER   How did the blind date go dear.

REX   all right thank yow.

The teacher who expects a less intelligent child to cope with the technical problems of writing 'before she can use language' might well be in despair at picking this up from the myopic Joan. But if we can penetrate the difficulties of her code we may see two things. Firstly, Joan has been trained to invent dialogue, and secondly, this dialogue can come to life ('don't forget I am relying on you', 'How did the blind date go, dear?'). Note particularly the touch 'Well, are we going to the pictures or not?', which suggests that the other two are awkward and somewhat struck by shyness: it also suggests Jean's firm way of handling the situation. To bother her about the technicalities of spelling and punctuation with which she can't at the moment deal *as well as* invent dialogue, might be to inhibit her. Her later work still looks awful graphically, but dramatically it has much greater power. In this first piece we can trace her discovery of her dramatic voice which she was to use later to such effect. So this was a useful piece to read to the class.

3. *George Green*

Jean said to Audrey has a sweet and Audrey said to Jean we are this Rex is

ecited and Jean and Rex wetn two the house of Me mouthr and Rex said to
Jean is it my house and Jean said to Rex it is a nis.

This for him is something of an achievement, in terms of imaginative
self-realisation. He imagines himself as Rex. The girls are talking about
him, over their sweets ('Rex is excited at meeting you'). He takes Jean
home to his mother's house, and says, 'This is my house', and she says,
'What a nice house'. (See above George's piece on *The House of Love*,
and other work (p. 69).) There is no point in discouraging George
because he cannot dream of adult life more thoroughly or with greater
articulateness than this: the only value education can have for him (he
doesn't often come to school) is to give him three or four experiences of
affectionate approval in a term. And, of course, it is important to find
a place for this piece by George in the final composite class story.

4. *John Young*

Rex Harrison was a dark handsome young man, he had fair hair and a
smart suit. He was waiting for his blind date, he was just outside the Regent
cinema. But he was worryed, would his date by ugly or cheep and dirty or
would she be preety and smart. then he saw Jean he new her by her walk
and her fair hiar hair then he saw Adrey she was a petty as could be she had
dark hair and a smart suit. Rexes knees were shaking when they were close
Jean said "Hallo Rex this is Adrey, Adrey this is Rex. Rex said how do you
do. Adrey said Allo. Jean said, "well I better be going Ill leafe you to It
tata. Rex said d d do you want to go to the pictures. Adrey said "yess if you
want to. Rex lead Adrey to the cash desk tow 4/- ones please. the got hold
of Adrey by the arm and lead her into the seats the Film was a Weston half
way frow the ice cream girls came round, Rex said would you like an ice.
Adrey said yes please cholate ice please. so he went to get them to choc ices
please he said to the ice cream girl I shilling please she said Rex gave her the
shilling and went back to his seat with Adrey he gave Adrey her ice and sat
down. At the end of the film Rex lead Adrey out side he said "can I take
you home Adrey said "yes please Rex put his hand out for a taxe, a taxe
drew up and Rex openèd the door for Adrey. but she slipped of the curb
Rex let go of the door and caught Adrey round the waist. they both fell to
the ground. Rex jumped up put his own arm round her legs and the other
round her shoulder and lifted her into the taxa and said to the driver "queen
mary hospital please and make it snappy. The driver made the taxi go 40
mile per hour he got to the hospital 10 minute later Rex helped Adrey out of
the car he lifted her in his arms he gave the driver a ten shilling note and said
"keep the canch he looked at Adrey and begain to carry her up the steps
to the hospital, the taxe driver yelled out ere mate it twelve bob from the

ride, but Rex had gone into the hospital. He came out 5 minute latter looking sad and worryed.

Here may be seen the great benefit behind writing of the drama work
which Geoffrey Hawkes describes in Appendix I. John is able to realise
scenes with great particularity. This produces both good things—such
as the record of thoughts ('would his date be ugly cheep and
dirty?') and bad things such as the somewhat protracted and tedious
accounts of a character's movements (as with Rex buying the ice-cream).
But the details obviously help him fill out his day-dream, answering to
himself the questions about growing up—'What will it be like to take
a girl out to the pictures?' and so on. The accident he invents, to bring
out in himself all the feelings of cherishing, being an escort, being a
lover. In this, 'carrying Audrey' has a value for him, in contemplating
what it is like to be a man and lay one's hands consort-wise on a woman.
These aspects are to do with the deeper value of the story to John—part
of his essential literacy being developed. They need not, should not, be
discussed. What can be discussed are some of the unsatisfactory episodes
—why does he make Rex give the taxi-man less than the proper fare?
Why did Rex say 'Keep the change'—did he know it was not in fact
enough? How did Rex know? Could Audrey not stand? If so should
this have been said? These moral points and points of episode and
sequence are what children like discussing most in their classmates'
work. Here one could have a good class discussion on Rex's conduct.
Out of all the stories the most obvious choice for discussion is the way
each child delightfully tried to render Jean's 'tackful' withdrawal from
the scene! Only after he has written two or three such stories need we
begin to bother him with details of proper punctuation of direct speech.

5. *Ann Barley*
One very dark night Rex stood out side waiting for a blind date with
Jean Smith. he was waiting out side a cafe alby himself. Rex was dressed in
Red Jeans blue shirt, and a black and white jacket, white socks. and black
shoes.
Jean and Audrey are with Rex now outside the cafe.
AUDREY   Jean is this Rex.
JEAN   Yes this is Rex.
Rexs says,
"How do you do Miss.
So Jean and Audrey said,
    "How do you do".

Rexs said,
 "shall we go in and have a drink"
They all three went and had a drink and something to eat.
 Jean intoduct Audrey to Rexs. Rexs. said to Audrey "Glad to meet you,
 What would you like to drink and eat.
 "Jean said".
 I will have to go now to meet my boyfriend.
 So Jean went off and left Rex and and Audrey alone.
 The time is about 7.30 p.m. Monday night.
 "Rex said"
 Shall we go to the pictures because there is a nice film on at Melton.
 Audrey said If you like so they paid for the drink and food what they had.
And they both went to the Pictures. On the way they met Jean and her boy
friend, so the all four went together. Jean and her boy-friend sat to-gether and
Audrey and Rex by they self.
 "Rexs said"
 I do not like the film very much
 "Audrey said"
 Shall we go now then.
 Rex said
No we will stay because when we get home we have not anywhere to go so
we'll stay here, so they stay at the pictures.
 Days and months went by and Rex said"
 Shall we get engaged at the weekend.
 Audrey said
 Yes if my parents will let me.
 She was very happy indeed.
 So they both asked they parents.
 Audrey's parents said yes and Rex's parents said if your girlfriend Parents
agree with it.
 So they got together and told each other what they parents said. So they
went and got the engagement ring.
 And still the long days went by, and suddenly the had an argument and
Audrey throwed her ring at Rex and Rex said are you going to fall out with
me if so I am going to go home.
 Audrey said well you wont took me anywhere. So Rex said well where
shall we go.
 Well Audrey said
 will you forgive me I am very sorry we had a row.
 So they both kiss each other and for got it. and Rex gave Audy the ring
back, and the went for a walk, they put their arms round each other and went
down the road. Nobody will never know they had a row because they

both were so happy. When they came back Rex's house and his mother and father had gone out so they sat on the settee and arranged they wedding the wedding is 4th of November.

Audrey said.

I am glad we are going to get married I hope my Parent will agree with it. It was time for Audrey to go home so Rex took her home in his car. They both kissed each and went in.

Audrey told her parents and they agreed with it.

So they ordered the food and a big wedding cake.

It is Saturday morning. They are going to have three bridesmaid, one was Audrey's sister, and another was Rexes sister and the last one was they friend they got married and went on a honymoon to spain.

This story has some delightful developments of episode, and it is possible, in reading through it, to see how such a child develops her powers of being articulate—if left to use them freely. I am sure that had I fussed about her extraordinary use of inverted commas she would have dried up. The fact is that she had been taught about inverted commas, but was never able to grasp the idea in the abstract. Thus she uses them with delightful irrelevance, as a kind of gesture in the direction of proper punctuation round the name of the character speaking. Left to herself she will, perhaps, when the day comes, see how they 'work' in a book, and correct her own. But the fact is that here already she begins to become more and more fluent. Her hand-writing becomes 'worse' from the graphic-minded school-teacher's point of view—but more 'adult' (more like our own, dare we say?) in dashing to keep pace with her invention, where it gets going. The more childish, 'proper' handwriting goes with matter which is conventional and uninspired— of the 'and then, and then' kind which teachers have to suffer so much. At 'when we get home we have not anywhere to go' Ann approaches reality, reveals her actual life. How true it is that these poor children stay in the pictures 'because there is no other place to go'! 'Six-pennorth of dark' can mean everything to a childish courtship, for village children. The subsequent passage, all written on the same inspired morning, is a lovely one—'days and months went by', 'and still the long days went by'—and the point of interest centres on Rex's parents saying, 'Yes—if his girlfriend's parents agreed'. This has taken Ann into the realm of social *mœurs*, and she is quite subtle about it all. She recognises the underlying reality of human feelings, too, despite all the conventionality of her attitude to romance. 'Audrey throwed her ring at Rex'—we have here an echo of Mum and Dad ('you won't take me anywhere'). Ann spends much of her time wishing for a life with a nice husband 'without argument' (see p. 83)—and possibly a better time than her mother is having. ('They are eight in my family . . . my Dad works on a farm.') This attempt by Ann to develop for herself, in the disciplined conditions of classroom English, concepts of happiness and family love, in the possible absence of these in her home, is an integral part of her total literacy. My concern is not merely for her 'mental health', but for her personal integration, without which she can never become literate. Thus, as an English specialist trying to improve her general literacy, I find her work more exciting when it is untidy—and yet springing from the true feelings of her heart—than when it is neat and stilted and cold.

6. William Glebe

One dull night Rex Harrison was standing out side of the cinema and in the distance he could see Jean and Audrey so he straighened up his Jacket and Jeans. Jean said to Audery, 'this is Rex' 'Hello' said Audrery. Rex said 'shall we got to the pictures' 'yes' replied Audrey Rex said 'will go and sit at the back and reserved a seat for thursday Then a few weeks later they arranged their wedding date for Nov 4, so when 4 nov got there they arranged the food for the party. They envited up to a hundred people so they had to get enough food for the people. They went on a honeymoon for 2 weeks and while they were down in Devon they stopped in a hotel. And then about four months after she was pregnant.

Rex said I am glad we will have a baby in the house and they were even more joyed when they heard it was a boy. Rex said to Audery shall we go to the pictures and then Audery said we can not go because of the baby. Rex said lets see if we can get a baby sitter. The girl next door said she would baby sit when they wanted to go out. One night when Rex and Audery went to the pictures, and when the girl from next door was baby sitting the girl heard a shot out side and she ran out side and found a man laying on the pavement so she ran to the nearest telephone and phoned up the police and ambalance and after she had phoned up she ran back to the man lying on the pavement until the police and ambulance came when the . . .

The difficulty these children chiefly face is that of acquiring sufficient grasp and perception to look at life as a whole, to see things in terms of their place in the larger patterns and rhythms, to see the significance of small incidents in terms of a whole life. This is possibly because they cannot carry much experience in their heads as abstract concepts: certainly this limitation has to do with their bewilderment and difficulty over moral questions. Here we can see William's difficulty of being clear as to the relevant significance of vastly different happenings: a date, a marriage, a pregnancy, a birth, need for a baby-sitter, a murder—all are presented without relative discrimination. Something of the same inability to see one experience as more important than another appears in their drawings, in which scattered fragments of things seen tend to be unrelated. Teaching William to be literate is a matter of teaching him to develop a sense of proportion as between the various aspects of experience—love, death, birth—with which he is striving to deal here. The more he can relate episodes to a whole, the more confident and fluent he will become in reading and writing.

7. James Carr

One day Rex was standing out side a caff wating for his blind date up came Jean and Audey and Jean said 'I will haf to go now'. So Audey and Rex went in the caff. Two years latte there were mared.

One night Audey said Audey said to rex I went to the Doctors today and he siad at I am pregnant. then rex said 'O good I am glad'. You will have to stard knitting some close for the baby. a munt latt Audrey siad "My baby sud come today' rex said 'Will you go the dace tonight.' No I can not come you know that.'

rex said 'I think we sod have a ely night to night dont you' Auduey said 'a good ider'. Audrey goes to bed she daid 'dont for get to put the cat out Dear' rex said 'come on pussy nice pussy swiss pussy you would go in there if you dont go out in a minit illy keck you out Dam the light gon out now ow! are got you out you go' rex goes to bed.

The End.

James Carr's last little story about the cat gave him great pleasure, and indeed it has a comic, human quality—as of something observed at home and recorded, father chasing the cat to put it out. It is like Mr. Leopold Bloom and his cat in *Ulysses*. In some strange way the domestic comedy helps James to contemplate the sexual experience behind his story—he was anxiously furtive about sex. But here, after the daring reference to pregnancy, he eventually makes the sexual (his hero and heroine going to bed) familiar and domestic, real. This obviously helps him with his developing awareness.

These notes show how I approached each piece of writing, as each child embarked on this story. On such analysis I based my comments and encouragement. Here follows the complete story as put together from fragments from the efforts of each pupil. This was duplicated, and by reading it out and re-reading it in groups we discovered, in discussion, the need for link passages and other expansions, and these were written in later lessons.

Spelling and punctuation are corrected and here the children have a proper, complete and orderly story to which everyone has contributed at least one element.

THE BLIND DATE
(Initials indicate which child wrote the passage alongside.)

J.W. One day at a café door stood a very worried young teenager. His name was Rex Harrison. He had black hair, and was very tall. He was lonely every evening because he didn't have a girl to go out with.

Then he saw his friend in the distance. Her name was Jean Smith. She was very attractive, but she already had a boy, so it was no good even waiting for her. When Jean got to the café door she said, 'My goodness you do look glum today! What's the matter?'

'Well, I haven't anything to do of an evening now,' said Rex.

'Never mind. Come on into the café and have a cup of coffee.'

'All right,' said Rex.

In the café

'I have a wonderful plan. I have a girl-friend who you could take out for an evening,' said Jean.

'Well, that's just splendid. Jean you're a doll!'

'O.K., O.K., Rex: don't go too far! I'll tell her to come with me to the café over the road at eleven o'clock to-morrow, so that you can meet her,' said Jean.

'By the way, Jean, what's her name?'

'Oh! I nearly forgot to tell you! Her name is Audrey Smith, and she has blonde hair.'

'Well, I'll see you tomorrow at eleven then Jean.'

'Right! Bye!'

R.J. Saturday came. Audrey was a bit nervous. Jean said, 'Are you ready yet, Audrey?'

Audrey said 'Yes, and I am a bit nervous.'

Jean said, 'You will get over that because when I went out with my boy friend I was a bit nervous to start but I got over it quickly.'

A.B. Rex was dressed in red jeans, a blue shirt and a black and white jacket, white socks and black shoes.

M.H. Rex brushed up his Italian shoes with his handkerchief, straightened his bright red tie and his hair.

J.Y. He was worried. Would his date be ugly or cheap, or would she be pretty and smart? Rex's knees were shaking.

'Hey there!... Why, I beg your pardon, I thought you were someone else,' said Rex.

'That's all right. I'm waiting for my friend Jean. She has just gone to the bar to get a drink. My name's Audrey Watson. What's yours?'

'Why, my name's Rex Harrison,' said Rex.

'You must be the man Jean said we were going to meet here.'

'Yes, I believe you're the girl Jean told me about,' said Rex. 'Here comes Jean now.'

J.S. Jean was a nice girl with fair hair and not very tall. She was wearing a pink dress and a green coat.

'Why hullo Rex! You're right on time,' said Jean. 'Rex, meet Audrey. Audrey, meet Rex. Hi! Shall we sit down and have a drink?'

'Rex, would you like a drink?' said Jean.

'No, don't bother. I'm not thirsty.'

N.T. Jean and Audrey had cherry ciderette.

'Well, Rex, this is the girl I told you about. She's very pretty like I told you.'

'She sure is. Hey, Jean!'

R.Sc. They went to the pictures.

G.G. Jean said to Audrey, 'Have a sweet!' And Audrey said to Jean, 'Here we are. Rex is excited.'

R.Sh. When the film was nearly over Jean went off to see her own boy friend and left Rex and Audrey alone in the cinema.

P.J. He said how pleased he was to meet her and she said she was pleased to meet him, too.

R.J. 'I hope it will be all right because something always happens!'

'And what is that?' Audrey asked.

'For instance, kissing and cuddling,' Rex said. 'Don't you like it?' Audrey said, 'I don't mind.'

Rex said, 'Will you kiss me now, Audrey?'

'Do you want me to? Well all right then.' She leant over and gave him a kiss.

And Rex said, 'How did that feel?'

'It was a lovely feeling, Rex. Will you do it again?'

D.B. When they came out of the pictures they had an argument.

M.H. The next night, they met together in the park.

'Hello Rex. Let's talk serious.'

So they talked serious.

J.O'M. Then they went home and Rex introduced Audrey to his mother and father. His mother and father said, 'We are both very glad to meet you, Audrey, and I hope to meet your mother and father soon.'

Jean and her boy friend Leon came in, too.

'I nearly forgot to tell you—there is a dance at the village hall tonight and I got three extra tickets because I thought you would like to come. How about it?'

J.W. 'Well that suits me all right,' Rex. How about you, Audrey?'

'That's O.K. with me. And how about your boy friend coming too, Jean.'

'Yes, I'm sure he would like to come.'

'Well that's fixed then. See you all tonight.'

'O.K.'

'Bye bye, Audrey.'

At the Dance

Ding Ding!

'Oh hello—Jean. I thought I would come and pick you up. We can all go in my car, instead of going by taxi.'

'Right! I'm ready. I'll see if Leon and Audrey are ready.'

'Come on then, hop into the car. Isn't it a beautiful evening for a dance, Rex?'

'Yes, it is, Audrey. Ah, we're there. Come on, hop out everybody. I'll go and see about the tickets for going in,' said Leon.

'O.K. Don't be long. We'll wait for you out here,' said Rex.

In the Hall

'Well, we're in here now. Let's go and get a table. Ah, here's one over here,' said Leon.

'O.K. let's go and sit down.'

'I'll go and get some drinks,' said Rex.

After the drink

'Well, that was good. Shall we have a dance?'

'Yes, O.K.'

'Audrey, would you have this first one with me?'

'Yes, I would be delighted. The only thing is, I'm not very good at dancing.'

'Never mind. Neither am I.'

'Right. Let's go. See you later, Leon'.

'O.K. Have a good time.'

Later

'Audrey. I . . . I love you. Your eyes are like silver, and your hair is beautiful.'

'Yes, I love you too. Shall we go out on the balcony?'

'Yes, if you like, Rex.'

'Let's go over here.'

'Isn't it a beautiful night, with the moon shining as well?'

'Yes, it's beautiful, Audrey darling. I really love you.'

'I love you too, Rex darling.'

'Well it's time for us to go now, Audrey.'

'Yes, I'm getting rather tired.'

'I'll take you home Audrey, because Jean and Leon are getting a taxi home.'

'O.K., Rex.'

At Audrey's gate

'Well here we are, right outside your gate, Audrey.'

'Thank you, Rex, for a wonderful evening.'

'Yes, it was a lovely evening, wasn't it?'

'Well, bye! See you tomorrow.'

'Hey, Audrey, haven't you forgotten something?'

But he was too late, because she had gone in and closed the door. But she had left her handbag in the car. He knocked lightly. Audrey opened the door. He kissed her. Next day they got engaged.

A.B. And still the long days went by, and suddenly they had an argument and Audrey threw her ring at Rex and Rex said are you going to fall out with me and if so I am going to go home.

Audrey said, 'Well, you won't take me anywhere.'

So Rex said, 'Well, where shall we go?'

'Well,' Audrey said, 'will you forgive me? I am sorry we had a row.'

So they both kissed each other and forgot it and Rex gave Audrey the ring back. They went for a walk. They put their arms round each other and went for a walk down the road. Nobody will ever know they had a row because they both were so happy. They became engaged again.

W.G. They arranged their wedding date for November 4th and arranged the food for the party. They invited up to a hundred people.

G.Go. After the wedding they went to the airport. They were on the plane for three hours. When they got to Spain it was hot and they went to their hotel.

T.S. When they came back they had a new house and a big garden was all round the house. Then they decided how many children they were going to have. Two years went by and then it happened—she was pregnant. When Rex came home that night Audrey told him. Rex was mad.

Audrey said, 'Well it is not all my fault.'

'I hate kids, Audrey, but don't upset yourself my dear, when it is born we can give it away to be adopted.'

'The doctor told me I will be having it in two months' time.'

'Yes, well, you will have to rest, won't you?'

She went to hospital and had a baby girl. Rex was happy to hear this and went as fast as he could to the hospital. Rex got a new cot for the baby and clothes. And every day Rex used to take Audrey and the baby for a ride in the car. Soon the christening took place and after they had a party and Rex and Audrey lived a happy life after all.

J.C. So now they are a happy family. Every night as Audrey goes to bed, she says, 'Don't forget to put the cat out, dear.' Rex says, 'Come on Pussy, nice Pussy. You would go in there. If you don't go out in a minute I'll kick you out! Damn! The light's gone out now. Ow! Ah! Got you! Out you go!'

And then Rex goes to bed.

THE END.

The value of this first effort was, I think, in the following:

(1) It dealt with subjects they had often found 'forbidden'—certainly lacking in their printed readers and text-books—courtship, love, marriage, pregnancy, and so forth. They were deeply interested in such matters, quite properly, as they are already engaged in sexual adventures themselves.

(2) The exercise proved to them that they could invent imaginative fiction, and that they could find a common interest in such work—and a common benefit. They understood when I told them that it helped them understand life by contemplating it in phantasy in this way.

(3) Everyone took part, and even the most hesitant readers could read out their own contributing paragraph, and thus feel part of the enterprise. This helped their reading forward, as they now wanted to read their contribution well, and so made greater effort.

(4) We could discuss spelling, grammar and punctuation in relation to the common need to produce a story 'out there' in the public world, as a published piece, which we could read and read again. And they could see from my version how 'proper' punctuation and layout should look.

(5) In discussing the story and link passages we found ourselves inevitably discussing human nature, motives and the reality of life (would Rex really say 'I hate kids?' Do parents give children away? How long does a pregnancy last?). Thus the story proved a truly literary experience of a kind these children find it hard to get from books. This work brought them closer to reality, and showed them how imaginative work was a means to understand real life.

(6) In such a co-operative effort the cruelty of competitive feeling is at a minimum. Every child—it could be shown—was capable of

contributing something to the contemplation of experience in words, whatever his standard of literacy or intelligence. The story enabled me to establish as a fact among them the equality of all in terms of needs of the sensibility, by example.

(7) The story provided a reasonably early achievement—something done, successfully, and which could be held in the hand, read over, tape recorded and read aloud to them, full of interest to them, at their level. (Other forms read the story, too, with interest.)

(8) Their own illustrations (see Michael Holmes' Rex below) to *The Blind Date* show how the story goes with their search for understanding of the processes of growth affecting them. Rex is themselves as men, tough, sophisticated. Daphne's Audrey (p. 173) was a dolly. But for others Rex and Audrey are their adult selves.

This exercise will suggest many others. And in my course books *I've Got to Use Words* I try to provide for hundreds of free exercises of this kind in essential literacy. As appears here, one is with such children interested in *what each exercise does for each of them*, rather than in 'teaching a subject'.

And once one successful first piece of composition has been done the ice is broken—the teacher has something to discuss in terms of what he wanted, and the pupils have a model. The pleasure they gain is enough indication of the value and point of such work.

Fig. 15

228

6

EQUIPMENT AND SYLLABUS

It remains for me here to give a small chapter of practical notes on lessons I have found useful, on books and equipment. The essence of work with 'low-stream' children is that it can only be done efficiently by a teacher who understands what he is doing, and can be opportunist and spontaneous, devising his tactics as he goes along. For this reason my book is an attempt to give us a glimpse into the nature of the dimension and the purpose of the task rather than a practical manual. Yet I know that a teacher also needs a book to which he can go, on a dull November day, when he has a slight cold, has had a row with his wife, and faces a timetable which says:

1	2	3	4	5	6	7
4B	3C	2B	2C	4B	1C	4D

He needs to be able to look up a list of possible exercises which he can put into use at once, to defend against chaos and despair. So here I am repeating some of the lists I gave in *English for Maturity*, selected and revised for the 'low-stream' dimension. These may be used with the course books *When I Was Young and Able*, and should provide enough material for the normal requirements of a teacher's 'low-stream' work.

EQUIPMENT

First of all let me outline what I feel to be the minimum equipment for a 'backward' class.

A low-stream class requires access to the following equipment for English work:

*Tape recorder and tapes (a Ferrograph if possible)
*Typewriters and duplicating machine
Puppet theatre and glove puppets
*Set of drama rostra (e.g. as made by the En Tout Cas Company)
Percussion instruments
Television set
16 mm film projector

229

Loud hailer or amplifier
Mobile floodlights and spots for drama work
Simple sets of switches and lights for setting up 'broadcasting studios'
Materials for simple drama sets
*Record player and gramophone records of classical music, folksongs, jazz
  and opera etc.
Radio set

The low-stream classes also will benefit perhaps more than others from such school activities as small-holdings and gardens, livestock keeping, boat construction, camping projects and so forth. And from the workshops, pottery and art rooms: a claim to their fair share of these must be fostered.

But I give the above list to establish a special claim from the low-stream children on those practical aids which help their work especially—for one thing because they are not easily capable of abstracting and formal exercises without rounded satisfaction. For instance, an 'A' stream can enjoy exercises in speech training, simply making sounds with their mouths, following formal exercises, abstractly devised, at their desks. A 'C' stream will find this tiresome—but will co-operate much more eagerly, to gain the same benefit, if they are made to set up and work with a tape recorder in a mock 'broadcasting studio', interviewing one another about some subject which interests them. The element of 'let's pretend' may seem infantile to the teacher, and he will, of course, resist allowing the organisation to become an end in itself. Such measures may help, however, to keep him to the dimension of the low-stream child, and to avoid being too abstract.

There is a *primary* need for such equipment for low-stream classes. Too often the children who yield fewer 'results' are given only second place in its use. If a school has only one tape recorder the likelihood is that priority in its use will go to the 'upper' classes because they will use it 'intelligently' and leave it tidier afterwards. But the presence of a splendid piece of expensive equipment is an additional incentive for low-stream children, and a school which really tries to cope with its less fortunate children, I suggest, will try to purchase some of the above equipment for the *sole* use of its 'lower' streams. Those items marked with an asterisk it would seem to me might well be in constant use with low-stream classes in a four-stream entry secondary modern school, and would seem to me essential equipment for any 'remedial' depart ment covering a group of low-stream classes. Where the Authority cannot provide the funds, perhaps a special appeal could be made to local businessmen, rich people, clubs, Parent-Teacher Associations and Old Pupils, for funds to equip low-stream classes with these useful instruments. At Bassingbourn Village College the widower of a woman teacher of backward classes who died while teaching at the college, a Mrs. Hilda Brown, gave the school a set of drama rostra as a memorial to her. I found it a moving memorial to the kindness of a devoted young woman, not only because she had been a friend of my student days. It conveyed a public tribute to humane effort. Much more could be done by such legacies and endowments for secondary modern schools, if the need was made known, and the prestige of the work raised in the public mind.

The other equipment may be shared with the rest of the school, but a member of staff should be appointed to make a special claim for the needs of 'backward' children. He should also concern himself to see that the needs of the reluctant reader are met in the school library, and establish a claim there, so that these children may experience the prestige, value and excitement of books. This means selection and guidance for them, a difficult task. Too many 'library' periods are spent in aimless flicking over encyclopaedias. These children should be encouraged to look at picture books—of reproductions of paintings and sculpture (not excepting the nudes), architecture, geography, biology and botany, popular science, and the rest. Whatever their limitations they will never be impressed or stimulated unless the books are there: I have even found educated and enlightened school governors uncertain about the 'waste' of providing a £3,000 library for a secondary modern school. One has only to spend an exciting half-hour with a boy who has suddenly discovered the fascination there may be in, say, a lavish picture book of Pompeii, to feel all that kind of expenditure justified. In this book I quote two girls' imaginative reactions to reproductions of paintings, each of which justifies alone the cost of the books.

Library work should be supervised, not to censor, but to lead on. There are times when censorship is necessary. At the height of her grief and maltreatment Rose Jameson brought me a crude and sensational story by Neil Bell about a maniac who slept with a girl and then tied her up and beat her to death. (Our Library was shared with adults as a County Branch Library.) This was the worst possible thing for her at this moment and I had the book removed. But in any school library I stocked I would buy several copies of every well-produced book for the young on sex, for instance, and leave them on the shelves: here certainly is one stimulus for literacy.*

THE LOW-STREAM CLASSROOM

It seems to me probably better for 'backward' children to have their own special room and to spend much of their time with one sympathetic teacher who is also their 'form' master or mistress. This assists their stability: there is little point for them in following the restless procedure of moving every half-hour or so from one expert in his subject to the next (a process I would condemn in the secondary modern school anyway). They need, as my book suggests, sympathetic attention to their individual needs from one 'loving' adult, rather than the contact with a variety of minds needed by grammar-school children.

The 'backward' classroom should bear every possible sign of being a gay and happy place: a good teacher will soon have it decorated with the products of the children's own creativity. Headmasters may be assured that to put low-stream children in the worst accommodation will reinforce their feelings of rejection and make it that much harder to do anything for them. It will also drive out staff who are willing to take on the very important service of dealing with these children.

The classroom should contain the following special equipment, to be at hand in the process of spontaneous pursuit of creative opportunities:

A dressing-up box and theatrical make-up
A sink, mirrors and towels etc.
Simple drama rostra
Electric light sockets and switches for projectors and tape recorders
Easels and painting equipment: colour block palettes, brushes, waterpots, supplies of large sheets of paper, scissors, glue, guillotine, coloured paper, cardboard, etc.
Wall boards for the display of paintings, poems, etc.
Special display bookcases and a class library
Picture frames with removable backs to show paintings and other work
Folders and loose paper for 'readers' made by the class, and for duplicated class magazines
Typewriter and duplicator, if possible, stapling machine etc.

Teachers of other subjects may be able to suggest other items, such as news maps, 'museum' cases for displaying items of historic or

---

* The Librarian may like to consider these: *The Facts of Life*, Edna St. Vincent Millay; *Boy Meets Girl*, Edna St. Vincent Millay; *He and She*, Kenneth C. Barnes; *It's Time You Knew*, Gladys Denny Shultz; *Letters to Jane*, Gladys Denny Shultz; *Learning to Love*, Kenneth C. Barnes.

geographical interest, or pieces of pottery or needlework made by pupils themselves. The whole layout of the room should help invite creative activity, and help build up pride among the children in their achievements by displaying them.

Books for the special form library may be chosen from *The Reluctant Reader* (The Library Association, Chaucer House, Malet Place, London); or from National Book League Pamphlets 6 and 7, *The Teacher and the Backward Reader* and *Encouragement to Read* (NBL, 7 Albemarle Street, Piccadilly, London, W.1). The National Book League circulates a special exhibition of these books for reluctant readers, in boxes, of which I give an analysis in Appendix 3.

A class library, however, need not be confined to the 'thin books' of the class reader kind. 'Backward' children will respond enthusiastically to being given 'thick' and handsome books in which they can read some items. Such books are the anthologies by de la Mare, *Tom Tiddler's Ground* and *Come Hither*; the Opies' *Lore and Language of School Children*; and some prose and verse anthologies such as those by James Reeves and the present writer. Some of these 'proper books' should be available on the classroom shelves, with such books as shortened versions of *Huckleberry Finn*, *Oliver Twist*, and some of the excellent readers such as the 'Heinemann Windmill Series'. The teacher can pick from the lists in *English for Maturity*.

A SYLLABUS FOR LOW STREAMS

With this equipment the work with backward classes may be broken up, as I suggest in *English for Maturity*, in rough order of priorities, recognising that all the work will with these classes be roughly doing the same thing for the child, that no project is likely to last for much longer than 20 minutes to half an hour, and that there is little likelihood of any sequence. We may plan the work roughly so:

IMAGINATIVE AND LITERARY WORK

(1) *Poetry*

(*a*) Read poems to the class.

(*b*) Pupils to choose poems from anthologies and write them in their books or read them aloud.

(*c*) Pupils to read poems for amusement only.

(*d*) Pupils to learn simple poems by heart (e.g. from the Opies' books).

(*e*) Pupils to paint pictures of poems.

(*f*) Pupils to use a poem read by the teacher as a starting point for a story, or a poem of their own.

(*g*) Lend pupils poetry books to take home.

(*h*) Use the library to find out about individual poets and their lives (e.g. Robert Graves, including readings from *Goodbye To All That*).

(*i*) Learn or listen to folksongs and folk tales.

(*j*) Read to pupils verse plays, e.g. fragments of Shakespeare or such a play as *Death in the Tree* from *Thieves and Angels*.

(*k*) Pupils to answer simple written questions on poems, e.g. *Bells for John Whiteside's Daughter* by John Crowe Ransom.

(*l*) Read passages from the Bible as poetry and fiction.

(*m*) Discuss some hymns, e.g. *Christ took the bread and brake it, He who would valiant be*.

(2) *Imaginative Composition*

(*a*) Oral composition to various stimuli:

    (i) A picture.

    (ii) Recordings of noises (groans, smashing plates etc.).

    (iii) Family attitudes test pictures (from various psychological tests).

    (iv) Music (percussion effects from *Young Person's Guide to the Orchestra* or electronic music. A very full list is given in *The Secret Places*.)

    (v) Evocative objects—dead weasel, basket of fruit, large fish, a skull, a go-kart, an African drum.

(*b*) Oral composition:

    (i) Telling a story round the class, an episode each.

    (ii) Each pupil to tell a complete anecdote.

    (iii) Interviews in an imaginary situation invented by the teacher, e.g. a detective questioning a smuggler.

    (iv) Conversations in an imagined situation: e.g. between a son, his mother and his girl friend's father.

    (v) Free drama, in groups.

(*c*) Written composition:

    (i) As above, 'free writing' or 'intensive writing' to stimuli of various kinds. Pupils told to write whatever comes into their imaginations: not necessarily a story, or a scene—but free association, often nothing to do with the stimulus at all. Poems and passages may be used as stimuli—not for models so much as to start off a train of emotive association.

    (ii) Writing poems to a model or stimulus as above.

    (iii) Writing stories, serially continued lesson to lesson.

(iv) Writing on near-fictional or on emotive subjects such as:
My family;
Should a wife obey?;
What I like about school;
My best friend;
What I shall do when I leave school.
(The teacher should not insist that each child follows the subject exactly, or at all.)

(v) Planning synopses for charade-like dramas, the dialogue to be spontaneous invention.

(vi) Planning 'broadcasts' by preparing questions for interviews, discussions, talks and quizzes, in writing. These to be rehearsed and then recorded on tape. Transcripts can then be duplicated for reading practice.

(vii) Writing up a visit or a walk in the countryside or town or a visit.

The course books *I've Got to Use Words* provide many such exercises at all levels in imaginative written composition.

(3) *Reading and Prose Fiction*

With 'backward' children, I think we may accept that their major literary experiences will be of two kinds:

(a) the experience of their own imaginative creation, and that of their classmates;

(b) the experience of poems, stories and episodes read to them by their teachers.

Their own technical capacities to read are limited, and so it is difficult for them to achieve satisfaction from the printed page. On the other hand, merely to acquire the technical capacity the children need to have material in their readers which is of primary interest to them, to hold their attention, and give such satisfaction as they can gain from words.

I give below an analysis of books for 'backward children' (Appendix 3, p. 273): most are not close to the major interests of these children, or their inward needs. Few are art and so can provide no deep yield of illumination or relief.

I suggest in *I've Got to Use Words* that many of the poems and passages should be read to the children who follow their own copies. I hope also to produce a collection of children's writing (*The Stripling Pen*) which can also be used in this way, with or without the intention to provoke further writing.

But there is a much simpler solution to the problem of reading at this level which I would like to recommend here. The solution is to give the children *their own creative word art*, in a properly set-out form, as *readers*. Because they work directly from the unconscious, as artists, on matter central to their interests, they develop thereby wit, panache, a capacity to stir the feelings and find beauty and patterns in experience—so these pieces of their own work are much more valuable to them than the work of text-book writers. The vocabulary is theirs, and the imaginative process aids the 'distancing' of experience as 'placed' art. To these pieces of self-made literary experience the teacher can add, of course, those poems and passages from books by finer minds, to extend perspectives, and add variety and range.

If, however, children are given 'readers' made by putting their own work, handsomely duplicated, into stiff cover folders, the teacher will find he has gained their interest and co-operation at once.

Why should this be so? I was brought by accident the other day to see clearly an aspect of children's capacities I had not consciously realised before. Several members of the staff were ill, and a party had gone to hear carols in a Chapel. The rest had to be occupied: could I find a film? All I could find were two amateur films, one of a primary school camp made by our village school, and another of my village by a distinguished resident. Both were silent films—would the first three years really endure this unsophisticated entertainment? *In fact they were delighted by it, and paid it more concentrated attention than they had ever paid to any professional, commercial or documentary film.* With the camp film, particularly, they were silent and keenly responsive. We had no occasion to wonder why—they were most alert and silent when other children were on the screen, children like themselves, simply going about their school and village life. They made the happiest noises when they saw a little boy of six picking his nose, or a baby girl of three bursting into tears, or a long shot of Mum paddling with a great belly over the pool, or an aunt tucking her frock down hastily as the wind and camera caught her in the surf. But particularly they watched avidly children *learning anything by doing it*—making a fire, or a bed, or engaged in social behaviour of any kind, from fighting to flirting.

Children are most interested in other children: and next in how adults behave, and 'what grown-up life will be like'. Thus they concentrate energetically on the activity of other children who are learning to grow up. These are not very original observations: but do we sufficiently apply them to our English work? I think not. We have missed a great mainspring of energy in our work in literacy. To test this I have tried using the duplicated writings of 3 C as readers with 4 B, and various other such change-rounds between classes of child-produced reading matter. It always worked—there was always the naturally engaged concentrated silence, and acute critical interest. They could listen to tape-recordings of the work of children in other classes for long periods. Other teachers have confirmed this impression, and the procedure led to remarkable advances in reading capacity. It was as though we had failed to make our reading matter until then anything that captured the child's natural capacity for efforts which yield satisfaction.

This is the reason why I consider children's course books and reading material should include a good deal of other children's work—stories and poems written by children of their own age, to be used as the starting point for imaginative composition of their own. Less intelligent children are somewhat cut off from the simplest literary experiences— but to them the experience of other children's imaginative creations *is* a valuable literary experience. The child's unforced work inevitably contains unconscious mythological modes, patterns and themes which belong to the child's processes of self-realisation—they spring from the being, untrammelled and unmanipulated, more easily perhaps, than from the less 'academic' child. As I point out elsewhere, children I have taught still find it exciting to discuss eighteen months later the stories they and their classmates wrote in the past—because these for them were a deep literary experience.

The intelligent child is open to more influences—some of the writing by brighter children in Boris Ford's *Young Writers, Young Readers* shows a wide range of influences being absorbed and used for their own pur- poses by sophisticated children. More useful for our purposes are the poems and passages in *An Experiment in Education,* by S. M. Marshall, (Cambridge), while *Let the Children Write* by E. M. Langdon (Longmans) contains some splendid work by children, done with a teacher who on her own realised that the 'real work' towards literacy was a direct imaginative composition.

Mrs. Langdon's pupils' poems can be read to backward children to great advantage. The teacher will do well to seek 'reader' stories, and poems which match in with the pattern of interests as revealed in chil- dren's own work. I have sought in *Visions of Life* and *I've Got to Use Words* to effect this matching by selecting word art which matches the child's deeper interests. In the latter, a 'course book' I include a few pieces of children's own imaginative writings to help reading and to stimulate further writing which the extracts should do because of their 'unconscious' content.

Secondly I propose that, while the teacher may be helped by printed books, his greatest success with less intelligent children will come by the publication of their own written material *among themselves as reading public.* Nothing helps these children towards confidence more than being asked to read aloud their own piece of writing after it has been edited and made 'typographically correct', without having its rhythm, or essential character, including some felicitous oddities, removed (see Judith Ward's remark 'at my disaster' which I have been careful to preserve, p. 161). They can read it easily because *they themselves* wrote it; it looks like proper printed writing; it is there, undeniably, a piece of concrete, satisfying, achieved black and white, which can be repeated and repeated. And it goes with a stage in their development, is *behind* them—as an author's books are *behind* him in his development: it is an *œuvre*, 'memorable speech' at best. They can gain confidence, with this familiar writing, and in this state of confidence establish their acquaintance with the proper look of words and writing.

Thus, I suggest, a great help in the development towards literacy of 'backward' children depends upon reproduction machines, and perhaps secretarial assistants other than the teacher to work them—though the teacher must do the editing. This means, of course, small classes, and special allowances for duplicating work for backward forms. The children can help with duplicating and stapling. One consolation for education authorities is perhaps that the *bulk* will never be much with backward children. It gives tremendous lift to the self-confidence of a 'C' stream to receive their own form magazine—amusing at their own level, local, full of recognised feeling and self-revelation, and, if possible, illustrated. If they use it as a reading book, this can be a great movement towards real purchase and grasp on language. And, if one thinks about it, it is only at their level, a taste of how we, writers and readers, feel about books and literacy. Of course, there are other forms of 'publication' including tape recordings, play performances, construction projects, readings, wall magazines, concerts of song. *But twenty pounds a year spent on duplicating—even professional duplicating—for lower streams in a school would seem to me to be a most valuable expenditure.* Perhaps, even, some enterprising body could set up a practice of receiving children's exercise books with selected pieces of work marked in coloured crayon, editing them, typing them out in a book-face type on stencils, and printing and stapling booklets and magazines. This service to lower streams is one which Institutes of Education, even, might usefully perform. Certainly it would seem to me to have many exciting applications, to the encouragement of literacy among the less intelligent.

Use of children's work in this way can bring surprising advances in reading capacity. To enrich the effects of reading the teacher should frequently read to backward children in a semi-dramatic clear, lively way, while they follow the texts. In this way one can build up a degree of literary experience. For this work, and for the form-room library, the following books may be considered. I don't think that a 'C' or 'D' stream class can study a book week after week, because they have neither the stamina nor the capacity to concentrate. They can answer questions orally or in writing on incidents in a story, such as the questions I give on 'incidents' in *Huckleberry Finn* in *English for Maturity*.

But while serial readings will be found valuable it is better to find and give small literary experiences from short stories, episodes or poems read to the class, rather than labour through a long book.

BOOKS FOR LITERARY WORK

Lewis Carroll	*Alice in Wonderland,* *Alice Through the Looking Glass.*
Charles Dickens	*Oliver Twist.*★
Rex Warner	*Men and Gods* (some incidents).
Mark Twain	*Tom Sawyer,* *Huckleberry Finn,* *Pudd'nhead Wilson.*★
George Orwell	*Animal Farm.*
Maxim Gorky	*My Childhood.*★
T. F. Powys	*Short Stories*, e.g. *The Devil, Captain Patch.*

Short stories by James Joyce, D. H. Lawrence, Ernest Hemingway, E. M. Forster, Joseph Conrad and Scott Fitzgerald as collected in *People and Diamonds*, edited by the present author, and also extracts from *Visions of Life*, a prose anthology compiled by the same. The problem of longer books for the less able reader is not easy to solve. Some schools use Puffin Books (e.g. *The Family From One End Street*). Oxford University Press is producing some new stories, specially written to be adolescent in appeal and not babyish or patronising (e.g. *Jimmy Lane and His Boat*, by Frederick Grice, Windrush Books). There is much work to be done here.

★ Abridged versions in Broadstream Books, C.U.P., 7s. 6d. each.

The form library should also contain a more general selection of fiction such as is given in *English for Maturity*, p. 196—books such as *Tschiffely's Ride*, Twain's *Roughing It*, *The Secret Garden*, *Emil and the Detectives*. Incidents read from these may prompt a child to strive to attempt the whole book. Certainly 'proper' books of fiction must be present and available in the low-stream classroom.

I say nothing about the teaching of reading to those who come from the primary school unable to read. I have never worked at this level and have nothing useful to say about it, except that, again, it makes necessary the reduction of classes to small enough proportions for the teacher to hear each child read to him during a reading period, and also to arrange the work in reading so that children can help one another. The most successful means to foster reading I found was to let children help one another in pairs. Sometimes I would put a good reader to help a bad one, or divide them into pairs of roughly equal capacity. Both methods prevent the face-grinding and anxious disparagement one used to get with 'reading round the class'. The teacher can then go from one pair to another to hear each read. If children are reading their own and one another's work, of course, they have an additional incentive. Such work presupposes a good supply of useful books at the proper level of interest and attainment.

PRACTICAL ENGLISH

Here a reader who has the book may turn to chapter 8 of *English for Maturity*, pp. 127 ff.

But perhaps it is worth giving again some points of particular relevance to work with low-stream children.

First, with these children it is most important that everything said in school by teacher or pupil should *be clear and well spoken*. This takes much time with these children, but it is worth it. A carefully pursued conversation with a child alone, in or out of hours, helps the child both with his self-respect and his capacity for expression.

Secondly, very careful attention should be paid to English in their own lessons by the specialist teachers of these children, not least in the practical subjects. Here the English teacher can usefully co-operate. For instance, in a craft lesson the stages in a piece of constructive work could be put on to tape. The children will probably write too slowly to get even notes down on paper in a craft lesson. So the craft teacher can either present a tape of the processes to the English teacher, or invite him to come in and tape-record the stages of work by oral conference. Then the tape may be used for an English lesson, writing up the project or experiment. Similarly, the English teacher could take an English lesson on the pages of a biology or housecraft text-book, as *a reading lesson*, before the children go to biology or housecraft.

Thirdly, with these children, because they respond more adequately to whole situations rather than abstractions, co-operation is very important on imaginative projects. The English teacher can get the children to paint a picture of a poem, but it helps if a whole art period is given to it as well, in the art room. Similarly, the physical training teacher could get the children to dance a story, the music teacher get them to compose percussive music and sound effects. Each act of co-operation reinforces the children's sense of their constructive capacities, especially when one teacher reinforces the creative impulse generated by another.

Fourthly, exercises which are communal, exhibitionistic, lively, and competitive are much liked by 'backward' children. They like oral exercises such as the following:

(*a*) Children are divided into two teams. Members of team 'A' have to try to guess the name of an object as it is being drawn on the board by one of their own team. This pupil who is drawing the object follows instructions from a member of team 'B'. This pupil is blindfolded, and must tell the other what to draw, without mentioning give-away words such as 'spout' or 'pedal'.

(*b*) Members of each team come up to draw a subject for a one-minute talk from a hat. Points are awarded to teams.

(*c*) A team of three 'employers' interview a series of 'candidates' for a job. The class selects the best candidate.

(*d*) The class prepare questions to ask a visitor from the outside world—e.g. a miner, a post office worker, a lathe operator—about life in the mine or factory.

(*e*) A group of children are told to hold a conversation round a table about a topic drawn from a hat (these topics are written on pieces of paper by pupils and collected in. The teacher censors, otherwise shy girls are suddenly asked to discuss 'birth control' or 'rape' by anxious or rude small boys.). These can be tape-recorded, criticised by the class, and then played back.

(*f*) 3–10-minute talks, subjects prepared beforehand, with class criticism.

These oral exercises are very difficult to conduct in an orderly way with children so restless, so little in control of their faculties, and so little able to concentrate. The teacher should be prepared to give up after 10 minutes if things don't go well. He may, on the other hand, find that a game of oral English may go on for an hour or more quite happily. (What happens often simply depends on the psychic weather!)

This brings us to a few straightforward drills and exercises, which we can impose as severe disciplines on the flow of expression created by all the above work.

(1) Answer actual advertisements in the press by writing letters of application. (Follow by mock interviews.)

(2) Write letters asking for information, from travel agencies, youth employment office, etc.

(3) Study consumer research pamphlets (*Which?* magazine) and conduct simple studies of purchased products. Write up the results. Use the pamphlets as readers, and subjects such as hire purchase as exercises in comprehension and composition (*What Is Hire Purchase?* or, later, *What are the Dangers of Hire Purchase?*).

(4) Study advertisements and their claims.

(5) Study newspapers and ask children to give orally or in writing an account of the day's main news from each. Compare newspapers simply from the point of view of the news they consider valuable.

(6) Practise writing an order for a suite of furniture, a set of garden tools, a set of tools for carpentry or to maintain a motor cycle or go-kart.

(7) Have mock telephone conversations of various kinds:
   (a) breaking off an engagement;
   (b) telling the coalman his delivery was underweight;
   (c) asking for a day off because your wife is ill;
   (d) giving the location of a fire or accident.

(8) Write a description of a class-mate for the police. Tape-record these and play back, for the class to guess the identities. (This can be a great success.)

(9) Write reviews of films seen, television programmes, or books read.

(10) Give an account of an accident or some other striking experience you have had (e.g. an operation, an escape from a bull, an incident on holiday).

(11) Write a personal letter to a friend about your holiday, or what you did over the weekend, about your school, or what you do after school.

(12) Practise filling in common forms—for driving licences, passports, medical cards, etc.

(13) Write essays on *My Life when I leave School, People White and Coloured, Keeping Pets, Motor cycle or Car?, The House I would like to live in, Make-up, The husband (wife) I would like.*

(14) Have spelling bees, tests, and other word games.

(15) Have lessons on the following elementary points of grammar and punctuation again, and again, and again.

(a) Where to put a full stop. (*Not*, be it noted, 'how to write a sentence' or, 'what a sentence *is*'. Any child's work will yield a paragraph containing many splendid sentences, even if it contains not one stop. The class can try to put stops in unpunctuated passages chosen from pupils' work and then the teacher can once more stress the usefulness of this punctuation mark.)

(b) How to use inverted commas and how to write direct speech, as above.

(c) The apostrophe.

(d) The proper way to make verbs agree with their subjects—*I was, you were*, and so rather than *I were, you was*. Again this must be taught with low-stream children by taking errors from children's writing or speech and correcting these.

I doubt whether there is much point in teaching further points of grammar to these children at all. (I have put a few *punctuation* exercises in *I've Got to Use Words*.) It is far more important that they should write in bulk, flowingly, excitedly and movingly rather than 'correctly'. 'Correct' English is in any case the invention of academics and scholars, and we seek to impose it on the pupil. Any language is developed intuitively and unconsciously by popular use: Chaucer, Langland, Dekker, Nashe, Bunyan and Clare came before the grammarians. Fluent literacy is a very different matter from 'correct English' —for all of us it is at times a matter of life and death, from reading a notice saying 'Danger, radioactivity' to seeking ways by verbal exchange out of a threatened breakdown of our marriage, or even to secure a sense of significance in life.

Fluent literacy comes from the free imaginative work as suggested in this book—a stern, life-promoting, vigorous discipline. To this practical exercises are useful ancillaries, but they are not the major means to literacy. Once this is appreciated we may throw away the text-books and begin.

PART III

APPENDICES

DRAMATIC WORK WITH
BACKWARD CHILDREN

by Geoffrey Hawkes

We assume the children in 3 A are 'better' than those in 3 C: what light does it cast on our assumptions that 3 C are better at free drama than 3 A? Drama in the 'A' form is becoming self-conscious by the third year; the boys stand about in little knots and in the preparation time there's a lot of talk and laughter which is only a cover for their unwillingness, really, to take part: the girls still play convincingly enough, but you know as you watch that they're always aware there's an audience; there's never that absorption, that possession by the experience that takes you by the heart with its truth, such as you found in their first and second years.

But with 3 C, even in the third year, it is the same as it always was: the boys in charge, the girls very much back numbers. The girls so often seem content to make a play and set it out on paper, without ever feeling the need to act it out. Before the division of 'A' and 'B' streams from 'C', in the first year, the girls had the leadership they needed to take the floor. Now they are passive and even refuse to take part. But the 3 C boys—active, assertive, loudly talking—show not a trace of the embarrassment of their 'A'-stream cousins: there is the same quickening of the atmosphere when they are hatching their plays as there was two years ago. Perhaps introspection and self-analysis come with intelligence; perhaps the more intelligent consider more carefully their impact on others. But there it is: the floodtide of puberty washes each. And yet while the intelligent child, like the poet at the sea's edge, regards it all with a detached wonder, the other, less intelligent, swims in it, scarcely knowing he is immerse.

'C'-stream drama always was as good as that of the 'A' forms: but by the third year it is better. There is no reason why it should not be, if we reflect. The teacher tends to fall into assumptions that because a child is not able to deal very well with the academic situation he is likely to be at something of a loss all along the line. But this is simply not true. Compassion or scorn are as quick in one as with the other, the capacity for good or evil is the same; they love and hate with the same intensity. In fact, the emotions cannot be graded, perhaps because they are older by a million years than the intellect. In this we may mean, when we say all men are born equal, that the love in them, for instance, is the birthright of each. And in such work as drama children would probably benefit most if they were not streamed.

One of the loves of all children, anywhere, is this activity we call drama. It has a central function in their lives, for through it they experience insights into the joys and problems of growth and change. Young children become parents of babies in their play, reaching forward into the dark future. Or they die or suffer loss, in imaginative dramatic fantasy. These young men and women of the third year, acting out adjustments in their groups, experience beforehand the demands that will be made on them as adult creatures in society. Their own dramatic play in traditional games and childhood fantasy play—and school drama—mean a lot to children. Drama has a very special place in the affection of 'C'-stream—'backward'—children in school, for in this realm no one is their peer. So I have found the drama period jealously guarded, and if it is missed through timetable adjustments it has to be made up. A teacher sometimes feels he would willingly miss it, for it is never an easy lesson to take. But the children like it for its vitality and its truth.

The normal lesson begins with some mime. Rose Bruford has some excellent suggestions to make in *Teaching Mime* (Faber) and if these can be related to the main stream of the drama so much the better. The children sit in their chairs, at their desks, facing forward. In this position they are able to concentrate on developing proper movements of their hands and fingers, and a proper positioning of the head. At a suggestion from the teacher they pick up needles and examine them before sewing up a tear, or taking a thorn from a finger. I call to mind, as I am writing this, many lovely moments with these children at their mime. Once when they opened boxes to find birds with injured wings, the care and tenderness with which they spread out the broken pinion while holding the bird in the three-finger grip they'd been taught showed their quick capacity for love of something in trouble. All except James Carr that is, who with a quick deft movement wrung a neck—but he bears a curious grudge against all creation. This kind of work is done in absolute silence, the teacher commenting briefly but without mentioning individual names. Hands and wrists are wonderfully expressive, and quantities of strength or tenderness or precision can be sought for and found in rapid sequences. The pupils in 3 C, as is usual with many less able children in my experience, have, on the whole, little ability to persist in any one operation for long. Thus rapid changes of subject will help train them in a variety of absorbing modes of dramatic expression. These children should always be asked to portray something definite, in human terms rather than abstract ones. Thus they should never be asked to show 'greed' for example, but rather a miser counting copper: not mere 'cruelty', but the cruel strength of a witch imprisoning a bird. In this way the boys and girls of this group have been led to react imaginatively to texture and line by handling ponies, silk or stone blocks. Often, too, they have been asked to work in pairs to a common end. By this work an unspoken sensitivity of each other's intentions draws individuals together as a magnet creates order in scattered steel filings. Indeed, one of the reasons why a teacher does well to give a good deal of time to drama with school children (and by drama I mean creative mime and speech) is that such valuable social benefits quickly come from its use. With an admission class, it brings the children together more quickly and happily than anything else can do, and this is very useful in such a group which is likely to include children poorly adjusted to the school situation. It provides a positive integrating force that has to be seen to be believed. Boys and girls used to regular drama tend to be more open with each other and with the teacher, and more considerate. There are, of course, exceptions. Virginia White was one, a girl who from infant school had never spoken either to any other child or teacher. Her capacity for speech and personal exchange remained apparently unaffected by the hundred or so hours of drama we did together. She remained obdurate and inscrutable outside the ring of flickering faces. There have been moments when I'd thought she'd give. I've seen moments when the other girls have clapped a flowered hat on her head and poured her tea, on some make-believe picnic, or tried to get her out of a burning room, when I'd thought she was going to take part, but at the last moment she always refused and so we failed with her.* But with the others the force of social exchange in drama has proved dynamic. It does not, I think,

* Virginia White was, in fact, an educationally subnormal near-Mongol child who was allowed to enter the school for compassionate reasons, the presence and kindness of other children helping her to be reasonably stable. She is unlikely to live beyond adolescence: of course, I have given her a false name here.—D. H.

readjust children permanently who are out of sorts with the world for one reason or another, but it helps.

From sitting at desks the children move off round the classroom, perhaps just a walk to begin with. Our children do not walk well. They walk confidently enough, but many have a kind of bear-like gait. To try to counteract this the walk is commented on: here good examples are useful. Then they are quickly introduced to imaginative obstacles such as marshy ground or fallen tree trunks, so that a balanced movement is encouraged. They then move, assuming different character roles. They are 'given' wooden legs or move like thieves through a moonlit bushy garden. The walkabout is usually done in silence just as the mime at the desks was. I sometimes find this difficult to ensure with 'C'-stream children, they talk so readily as soon as they move away from their desks. But there's no doubt that specific movement tends to deteriorate with excessive talking. However, group work with completely free speech follows next and with it the excitement mounts. Silent mime, of course, is useful for achieving absolute control of a class, and order is very necessary to a successful drama lesson. Giving these boys a 'completely free hand' would be asking for disaster, even when they've had a good deal of experience in drama. The silent disciplined work is essential, but after a time it feels incomplete. Real drama is born through the spoken word and this follows when the children form themselves acting units of 2, 3, 4 or 5. More than five proves rather unwieldy.

The children are expected in their group work to sit down first in orderly quiet and to talk quietly about the play they are to prepare. Sometimes they do just this, but more often they sit on desks or window-sills and arrange things at the tops of their voices. There seems no real cure for this, the excitement at this stage being genuine. And then they dress up from the junk box. In this work 'C'-stream children are always given a definite theme to work to. And so, for that matter, are 'A'-stream children, usually. But 'A'-stream children with their wider reading habits have a somewhat greater diversity of situation to call on, and so have rather more ideas to work out. Within the theme, however, both are free to improvise as they will. One week it might be 'trouble with parents', another 'the old people's outing'. Natural leaders crop out as soon as preliminary class discussion of the theme has finished, for each group is free to organise its own particular interpretation of the given idea. Kenneth Prime in 3 C is one. He's the boy who is always drawing tragedy in one form or another: he can only just read and write three- and four-letter words, but he arranges group drama more quickly and more effectively than any 'A' boy I've yet taught, and the others accept what he tells them. In one of his recent art lessons Kenneth was asked to draw and paint his newly arrived little brother: he drew him all right, but put a burst hot water pipe just over the baby's head. When he first came to us he was unwashed and untidy, but towards the end of the first year he began arriving as spruce and alert as the best. Of course many factors may have contributed to the change, but I'm sure school cultural work, of which drama is a part, was one of them. (See work by Kenneth Prime discussed, above, p. 137.)

When ideas have been hammered out the children come up and say they're ready, and when this has been checked they are allowed to get themselves dressed from the boxes. These contain hats, sticks, strips of coloured stuff, handbags and other bric-à-brac, and in addition to these there are a number of simple coloured cloaks which simply envelop their everyday garments. To see them dressing up is always a great experience, and the 'C'-class boys (not, I think, the girls) have a greater flair than the 'A'-stream children in their ability to improvise costume. Sometimes, too, they are allowed make-up, nothing elaborate, a bit of red and black, or green, just enough to suggest a character. Too much make-up, like too much costume, hinders the drama. With too much costume their natural movement is impeded and with too much make-up the actions are thrown somewhat out of gear, so that instead of the known faces of friends appearing to them, mobile masks appear. A box of safety-pins is useful in helping with costume, and it will be found useful to have tapes sewn on to the odd pieces of material. Kenneth improvised a wonderful Moorish costume the other day with the remains of a silk top hat, a piece of flame-coloured silk, a long flowered shirt which he somehow tied at the ankles, a lost property scarf and an umbrella: a kind of Moorish Robinson Crusoe in fact. The top hats were given us at the break-up of an old family house, together with a chauffeur's uniform and sticks; anything and everything is grist to the drama mill, but the hats were something special, there was a kind of poetry about them that the boys and girls loved. Tall, black, and shining, they have defied the bright twentieth-century sunshine on the roof playground and conjured up Mayhew's London, or with the green top-coat have produced a cut-glass accent in a minute where a year of speech drill would have failed.

Just of late this group has been tackling scenes from the classics. The 'A'-stream children of course are ready for the scripted play, and even take to excerpts out of Shakespeare or Eliot. I give them such excerpts where the words are worth the saying. But 'C'-stream children, with their low reading ability, are generally at a loss trying to act with a script in the hand, so they are told the story and have bits of it read to them. Sometimes a few sentences are printed out on card for a boy to include in his part, but more often once they have the story, they improvise. This is how the actors in the Italian *commedia dell' arte* worked. The plays made in this way move far outside the expectations of the original authors; the 'doctor' asks Lady Macbeth 'What's the matter with you, gal?' and Macbeth shoves him off—'You leave her alone, she's not feelin' too good. She'll be all right in a minute', and then adds, 'If you don't shut up that moanin' I'll come over and belt you.' In a similar way I've seen a dozen boys on top of an ark made of desks shouting ripe insults at the man dodging the burning raindrops in Obey's *Noah*, or the knights accusing Archbishop Becket, saying 'We knows you've been over in Paris playin' about with them French gals; disgustin' I call it, a bloke of your age.' Shocking! Until one remembers what a remarkable effort of imagination it is, this extravagance from a 'backward' boy. And this imaginative extravagance makes drama. Occasionally the work goes flat, at least for the adult watching. If it does the teacher must just sit patiently through it and keep faith: he should never break into the play and try to re-arrange and improve: this, I find, does no good. Of course, if a play is to be worked up for a more formal presentation the teacher must intrude as a kind of producer. But in class work he should hold on to his seat, even if the noise is alarmingly loud, or a boy has reached the ceiling. The teacher must act a part himself, and appear calm. Of course, the work needs the sanction of authority. At a primary school I could sometimes detect the image of the headmistress frozen on the other side of the frosted door-glass wondering whether on earth she should go in or not, and usually deciding that she would not—for she was a woman to understand what was being done. She realised that in this extraordinary mêlée individuals may be brought into a corporate body, with a burning out of inward disturbances of hate and fear; and sometimes the shaping of a diamond from a rough stone. Of course this work goes on with a great deal else in English—spelling drills at one extreme, and the reading and writing of poetry at the other, towards literacy. But in freeing children to enter into other possible experience, entering into the lives of others, gaining self-possession in mind and body, and stirring the imagination, drama, as a continuance in disciplined forms of children's natural play, changes children more quickly than any other 'subject'. It can be seen to civilise them. And as David Holbrook shows in this book, it can be one root of imaginative writing. Certainly it is a most successful stimulus and training in imaginative grasp on experience for 'backward' children, and the therapeutic, character building, effects are most apparent with them. With 3 C it is truly the 'ceremony of innocence'.

THE WEAKEST GO TO THE WALL

TEACHERS' ACCOUNTS OF THEIR CONDITIONS OF WORK

Early in 1962 I wrote to the *Guardian* to ask teachers of backward children to write to me, to tell me about the conditions under which they worked. I said I was particularly interested in whether they found these children treated as 'lesser beings'. The editor kindly published my letter, and some 40 letters arrived. Most of them confirmed my impressions of the treatment of backward children as set forth in this book. I was deeply shocked by many of the brutal things said about children in low streams, and to hear of the many sad ways in which they are treated. In this appendix I include quotations from the letters I received under various headings. All the writers have been made anonymous, though names and addresses were supplied. I give at the end a letter from a man who was obviously a most valuable member of the profession, but who was driven out by the unacceptable conditions of his work. This splendid letter, disturbing as it is, may stand as an Epilogue to this book. Unless changes are brought, swiftly and thoroughly, in the content, organisation and atmosphere of the education of the lower half of the secondary school, particularly when the new external examination comes, we shall be establishing a group of resentful and wasted men and women in the community, and continuing to drive out of teaching the very people who could offer them sympathy and understanding, and help them develop into adults who could contribute their potentialities and good human qualities to the social good.

The correspondents had much to say about the attitudes of teachers and headmasters to children in the lower streams of secondary modern schools, and even primary schools.

I have noticed that many of these teachers tend to regard C children not perhaps as 'Lesser beings', but as difficult, uninteresting, and unteachable. I think they believe that any success I have had is due to my being middle-aged, married, and a mother, and wonder how I have the patience to cope with the work . . .   T.

Too often, in all types of school, the less able classes are wholly dependent on the goodwill and efficiency of their own individual teachers, and very little interest is taken in them by the head, who has his eye on examination passes. . .

S.

The children need more personal and friendly contact with the staff. The C and D streams need more basic teaching from class teachers and less specialised teaching. It is ridiculous that a child with a reading age of 8 or 9 should be expected to read, write and remember difficult new words in science lessons when it has difficulty with words like 'house'. Because there is little understanding of the slower children by ill-informed members of staff many emotional troubles develop.

M.

I have the most profound respect for these young people and the deepest contempt for the superficial pedantry of their headmaster, whose sole concern is the G.C.E. passes, and who lumps together all 'non-G.C.E's' as second-class citizens worthy only for people like myself to keep quiet.

H.

I only had a year's teaching experience when I started this work, and the first three months were frankly terrifying! Headmasters are not interested in this part of the school's work, now that the emphasis is on the acquiring of G.C.E. certificates. It is therefore difficult or impossible to persuade him to spend money on books or equipment for these children. Some heads, with the best will in the world, find it difficult to keep up with the established outlay, and assure you that little can be done.

S

An inspector said 'if they can't read when they come to you at the secondary school they never will' (I have, of course, taught many non-readers to read).

W.

A headmaster stated on behalf of a transferred child, 'He knows nothing, wants to know nothing, and probably never will.'

From what I have seen so far (I came over from primary school work) the attitude to slow learners is simply to 'keep them occupied'. It doesn't seem to matter whether what they do is valueless and monotonous. 'Discipline', too, is far more important than sympathetic understanding and help, for this may be noisy and disturb the studies of the potential G.C.E. and R.S.A. candidates! So the rest of the school has to plod along in the wake of the academic boys— examinations every six months included . . . some headmasters lack the courage to admit that less-than-average pupils must not be expected to do the same work as their 'brighter' schoolfellows. Part of the trouble is doubtless the tradition of examination, fear of what 'the office' and the inspectors may think, and so on.

B.

Two years ago I left a small Northern Grammar School, with a cosy sixth form and many very amiable children to teach in a Secondary Modern which it was hoped to develop as a Comprehensive School (I'm 2nd in the Dept.). In fact, we have no 11 + passes (not that that means very much) but a great diversity of talents and abilities and a tremendous opportunity for comprehensive education as the children come nearly all from a big L.C.C. estate and are socially completely integrated (no 'us' or 'them' between their parents). That they remain so in spite of all efforts to batter them into submission to an entirely unimaginative ideal of education (in spite of the fact that we have 'House Tutors' and that sort of thing) is a tribute to their own basic humanity. I suppose you will be familiar by now with this complaint of mine, as you will probably have heard it from several sources in other schools. It is that the 'naughty' and the 'lazy' are put 'down' from one stream to another, instead of being treated sympathetically and firmly while being asked to do work which intellectually stretches them to the fullest extent. 'Putting down' is a common G.S. solution, but won't do in this kind of school as it gives no one a fair chance, least of all those in need of remedial teaching, who become equated with the anti-social elements in the school. Isn't it infuriating to see emotionally disturbed children trampled on in this way?

Not content with this, the H.M. has this term created a 4 Special, a group containing all the 'trouble makers' in the 4th year, bawled at them in his usual fashion, and left them to others to 'nail down'. There are many stories I could and will tell you about this class, which contains children from last year's 2nd, 3rd, 4th, 5th, 6th, 7th, 8th and 9th streams. (Don't think I accept streaming uncritically, but the 4th year is no place to try innovations of this kind with such children, and they themselves have been told why they're there and which is, in fact, extremely difficult to 'keep down'.) What strikes me about them though, is the tremendous thrusting energy, much greater than mine, which they display when their attention is really caught up in something which is 'on their list'—sex and teenage life out of school and 'interest stories'. This territory, 'ours', it is not work to explore; but poetry (even where it obviously strikes home), and any kind of writing is 'theirs' and academic, and they seem to feel subconsciously that *this is work* and I should make them do it! The distinction here between life and school is classically sharp.

My last story is about the library, which I have had charge of this term. The Library Supervisor came last Friday. She is charming and accommodating but with a mind of her own, and when I was at last allowed to see her I put the case as forcibly as I could that the library must cater for the children in the school, that they must be led on from simple stories and magazines, etc., etc. I *think* she appreciated my point of view, and said that out of £370 perhaps £150 might be spent on academic works (the head wants *the whole lot* used for 6th-form books and suchlike). I was called in this morning, and this conversation took place:

H.M.   Miss X tells me you want to buy Sec. Mod. books, that you think the
       library's too academic. £1,500's been spent on Sec. Mod. children
       and no more is being spent.
ME: (Gasps and 'ohs'.)
H.M.   We have to think of when we have a 6th form* and if we don't get
       the books in advance etc., etc.
ME: I think I'll have second thoughts about looking after the library then.
Needless to say, I am leaving the school in July and I hope to find my way
into a school where there is work with children of all abilities, run by
enlightened people.   K.B.

        * Next year we may have a sixth with 3 in it. The other 1,197 in the school?

Perhaps the most disturbing indication from the letters received was
that the moral implication of some things said to the children, besides
having a negative effect on their self-possession, seemed to be at odds
with common decency.

It is terrible the way these children are discussed by heads in their presence,
and by teachers too—they use words like 'ineducable' and so on—on the
assumption that the children are too moronic to grasp the implications I
suppose . . .
   I have heard prefects in a primary school being adjured by the head from
the platform in assembly to 'tell on your best friend if it is in the interests
of the school that you should do so'.
   Could this be a true interpretation of the Christian doctrine which they
have been subjected to five minutes earlier? I wonder!   G.

Many teachers spoke of the need they felt to counteract disparagement:

I have often felt sure that I have been privileged to hand out the first bit of
praise they have ever received in their 11 years on earth! I have proved to
them for the first time ever that they *can do something* and I have watched a
non-existent confidence take root and flourish.   W.

But nearly every teacher confirmed that 'backward' children are simply
not treated as equals with other chilren:

There is a great disparity when it comes to school outings. Frequently the
A and B streams are taken to various local affairs but the C streams are not
thought worthy to be considered.   C.

Sometimes the Head of my last school would ask a child from A or B class to
read the first verse of the hymn at Assembly but never would he ask a backward child who had made great strides and was able to cope with the verse in

question—even from memory. You have no idea how backward children feel this slight. *E.G.*

It is true that schools still exist where the less able are neglected, but the general position is much improved over ten years ago. Without doubt the chief factor in influencing neglect of the less-able is pre-occupation with examinations and the reflected glory that good examination results bring to the school. Any child who is unlikely to produce good examination results is 'not being a credit to the school'. It follows that the best material and the most useful staff will be channelled to the examination stream. In many schools this stream forms but a small percentage of the whole school and one is left with the dismal picture of a small, highly favoured and equipped group as the one bright spot in a wilderness of frustration. The great pity of it is that in the few schools known to me where this position exists the heads are so much like ostriches. The only teaching they do is restricted to the elite and they have come to believe that the whole school looks like this group. They are turning out lay-abouts, ne'er-do-wells and dregs on the community at the rate of ten for every academic success, as measured by five 'O' levels. *R.C.A.*

At any large school there may be 15%–30% turn round of staff each year. This is bad for the school as a whole but it does affect the lower streams more proportionately, since it is the teachers who deal with these streams who move around more: the old vicious circle, is it not? The principle seems to be that, if we grant that children, *qua* children, are worthy of the same attention, then those engaged on external exam-work are worthy of more regard because in this respect the two kinds are not equal. *P.*

The regular and better teachers are often kept with the 'A' and 'B' streams because these children bring 'results'. The lower streams have temporary teachers, or new and inexperienced teachers:

As a casual labourer in the field (I was a supply teacher unable to take a permanent job) I found that I was always given the lowest stream. One class I took in late February had had six teachers since January. When I had been there a week a girl came to me and said, 'Miss, do you think you might be staying with us? Are we all that awful?' I managed to stay with them for the rest of the year, fortunately. As a supply teacher my duty was merely to replace temporarily sick teachers. I should never have been given the responsibility of a class like that. Since then I have seen posts with retarded classes advertised, with the lure of extra money, so that possibly the position is changing, but not, I fear, in all schools . . . *S.*

The youngest and consequently most inexperienced members of staff are diverted to the younger and more backward classes so that the work of the brighter children is not interrupted while the teacher is learning to teach . . .

S.

Ten years ago, it was common to find the backward class as far removed from the head's room as possible, with the throw-out equipment from other classes and taught by (*a*) the newest member of the staff, too green to protest or (*b*) the unfortunate one whose turn to do the dirty work had just come up on the rota, or (*c*) the person who had been silly enough to fall out with the head last term.

Today, there is a more subtle approach. The head sets out to show the world that he is interested in the whole school and 'wastes' one of his permitted allowances to recruit a teacher to act as Head of Department for what is known as (*a*) the remedial department, (*b*) the lower streams, (*c*) the removed classes, (*d*) the special department, (*e*) the recovery groups, etc. The Head then delegates his responsibilities and can never be accused of neglect. That this move is so often merely a 'face-saver' is obvious from the following remarks, all made during the past twelve months:

(*a*) 'I've wasted a good P.S.R. on my dimwits, but it keeps them quiet'
(Headmaster).

(*b*) 'What is your precise job, Mr. X?'
'I'm Head of Department for Backward Children.'
'But your salary, quoted on your application form . . .'
'Well, I'm called Head of Dept. but I only get a graded salary.'
'Only Scale 1?'
'Yes'.
(Applicant for admission to Supplementary Course)

(*c*) 'Have you any control over your timetable?'
'No. It is worked out at a meeting of the Heads of Departments.'
'But you are a Head of Department.'
'Yes, but I'm not called to these meetings.'
(Head of Department for 'remedial' work in a large school)

(*d*) 'What control have you over requisitions?'
'I am given an annual sum for the department to spend at my discretion.'
'How much last year?'
'Ten pounds.'
(Man responsible for four backward classes in medium-sized school)

This type of head delegates his responsibilities and then makes it impossible for the delegated power to be carried out. If a Head of Department is to do his job properly he must have:

(*a*) considerable freedom within the time-table;
(*b*) power to devise his own schemes of work—or general principles by

259

which he intends to work, as a set scheme of work implies lack of freedom to work opportunistically;

(c) power to equip his department with such material as he needs and a fair share of the capitation allowance of the school.

Some heads have no idea at all of how to delegate responsibility properly.
R.C.A.

Methods of teaching backward children came in for strong criticism:

They (teachers) often have no idea where to start and tend to spend too much time on formal spelling and language exercises from text-books. *T.*

Secondary modern trained teachers are not familiar with the basic methods required in the teaching of reading and have no idea where to begin. *M.*

The timetable is too rigid, classes change too frequently from room to room and consequently as much as half-an-hour may be wasted each day. *M.*

There are too few opportunities for the children to talk either to each other or to the teachers where a very firm discipline is imposed. Speech is a very neglected form of communication in the secondary modern school and as the ability to speak reasonably well comes before reading or writing I feel that this is very important. *M.*

A slow boy of 14 . . . had been given two compositions at school—'Show how you think the Monarchy is incompetent in England', and 'The country-side in winter' . . . he was from a poor house near the Docks in Salford . . .
H.

I had a girl in my class who had some wonderful exercise books. The Headmaster showed them to me with great pride and they were beautiful, but I discovered her I.Q. was 58. The work in her book did not correspond with the work she did for me. It took me quite a while to find *that she could copy beautifully but had no idea what it was all about.* She could not write the simplest sentence off her own bat, and I discovered she could read nothing, not even 'it' and 'even'. Too much emphasis by Heads for *tidy* books—as soon as backward children begin to learn they themselves will see the difference between clean and dirty work. *E.G.*

For backward children the pace and dimension are different: but in some schools the timetable is too 'sacrosanct' to allow for this:

As a primary school teacher I had always been accustomed to having my own class for nearly every lesson, so that I had time to help individuals or groups while the rest of the class were employed on other work. I believe this kind of organisation is still essential for slow learners in the secondary modern schools, at least during the first two years. In practice I find that the timetable is sacrosanct and that despite its futility, so far as the less-than-average boys are concerned, 'specialisation' must be the key-note. Accordingly they never spend more than an hour a day with any teacher and traipse from one end of the school to the other in order to receive the 'Benefit' of the system! Although lipservice is paid to the need for special treatment for these boys, in practice they are treated as the 'lesser creatures' you mention . . . the timetable, I am told, cannot be changed.

I was asked to stay longer, but in view of the fact that the rigid timetable could not be altered and that the D children must be taught in batches of forty, regimented like soldiers, I decided to look elsewhere.　　　　*M.*

No doubt some of the difficulties of backward children in reading and writing may be traced to emotional disturbances just at the time when they were learning the shape of words. Some may be due to too large classes, so that they were neglected, and fell behind at the time when children normally learn the basic elements of literacy. But it seems hard to find acceptable that children above the educationally subnormal intelligence quotient of 70 should not know their alphabet by the time they reach the secondary school. The rejection of 'failures' obviously begins well before the 11-plus examination:

Would you credit it that it is possible for children to come to the secondary school not knowing their alphabet? There are dozens of such children. I have just been handed three thirteen-year-olds who cannot get from A to Z and cannot recognise letters . . .　　　　*G.*

Slower readers from the primary schools, who, because of their low I.Q.'s, were unable to begin word building until the age of nine or ten years make little or no progress in the secondary modern school. . . . Many children cannot read adequately, therefore cannot spell, therefore cannot write. . . . There is no provision to pass on detailed information from the primary to the secondary school about the exact stage in reading that the children have reached yet this is very important.　　　　*M.*

I am convinced that the biggest stumbling block for most backward children is the inability to read. Because classes of six- and seven-year-old children are too large, because of the stress in primary schools of the 11-plus examination, and because we have not enough remedial teachers, too many children enter senior schools unable to read. Obviously they can make no sort of progress.　　　　*S.*

The effects of being rejected continue after secondary education. Some of the same ('B' stream) children now appear at centres of further education. In 'Liberal study' work in technical colleges, teachers find many problems similar to those of teaching backward children: indeed, as one teacher said, 'the ex-secondary schoolboy becomes the part-time day release student and so you will perhaps agree that our problems are sometimes the same'. He goes on:

> When I came into the work I was warned that I should have to lower my sights, but I never realised how much they have to be depressed (and me with them) . . . How can I hope to discuss the 'affluent society' with young apprentices who, in many cases, don't know what 'society' means? . . . one has to start with the fundamentals of English . . . there is something very wrong with the way in which these young people have been educated. . . . Any attempt to discuss current affairs, the bomb, housing, music, colour bar, and to draw out comments in class or in writing is weary work and the students find reading aloud most difficult, almost none of them read anything at all, and the idea of borrowing books is foreign to them.   *H.*

I have given my opinion earlier that a 'proportion of children in low streams are mentally ill', it seems the problem of detecting and treating mental illness is a familiar one to the teachers of backward children:

> Many of the children in the C and D streams have some form of mental or emotional difficulty. Teachers are not familiar enough with the children they teach to discover all these cases and are often unwilling to consult the educational psychiatrists, the psychologists and the school medical service when they do suspect that the children are in difficulties.   *M.*

Records are sometimes inadequately kept, and are unhelpful:

> I have been appalled at the difficulty of discovering anything about the child's previous school history, home background, health, etc. We have the record cards passed on to us from the primary schools, but although I have examined every one, they have yielded only a few clues to the problems of individual children. The most remarkable case concerned a fourteen-year-old boy who exhibited symptoms of what I considered mental sickness. His school records revealed nothing but a long history of low attainment and non-co-operation. Upon referring the matter to the Child Guidance Clinic it transpired that he had a long case-history, beginning with a suspected brain injury *at the age of two*. Nothing was known of this in his present school, which he had been attending for three and a half years!   *B.*

Some teachers suspected that often 'backwardness' was caused by other undetected physical defects:

> There may be undetected physical reasons for the children's backwardness.

The overburdened school health service and the teachers of large classes in primary schools may have failed to spot deafness or visual deficiency.   *M.*

Yet these teachers who work successfully with backward children often speak of the pleasantness of their personalities:

So often the children in a low-stream are far more attractive in personality than, for example, the prissy little prefects. . . .   *G.*

Teachers confirmed that the 'backward child' requires love:

Maladjustment shows in the child's inability to concentrate for any length of time. To help children like these, one must have time to give them individual attention, in many cases to give them a 'love' which they do not experience at home. We need to have small classes to do this. No human being can do this for thirty-odd children.   *S*

The nature of backwardness itself was analysed by some teachers, and those with experience speak of other potentialities which sympathy can bring out in these children.

In my Open Air School for 140 Delicate children, three main causes of backwardness are recognised:

1. Loss of schooling;
2. Low intelligence;
3. Emotional disturbance or maladjustment.

All these three can be, and often are, combined. . . . We recognise also that a low intelligence quotient does not always indicate low mental ability but rather a brain which does not fit into standard patterns. . . . I suggest there are some children with a reasonable verbal factor but an otherwise low intelligence who are as capable of appreciating and producing literature as their cleverer fellows.   *S.*

I feel sure that any success is due as much to the fact that these children have had sympathetic friendly treatment from someone who is really interested in them, as to any particular method. Only with a small group could this be achieved.   *S.*

Teachers had the following suggestions about books required for backward children:

What I do find goes very well is any story dealing with deprived children, such as children who are picked up in the ruins of Naples as orphans of the war and after various harsh treatments find someone in England to care for them . . . *Oliver Twist* they love.   *G.*

There is an inadequate supply of graded books for slower readers containing interesting material in an attractive form. *M.*

Publishers do not produce suitable books and hopefully offer junior school books (children in secondary modern schools are not interested in 'Aunty Jane's' exploits, or Milly and Mathilda's trips round the countryside). *S.*

An orthopaedic worker in hospital found that many secondary children could not read, and had seldom been given any remedial aid:

If there had been any attempt it had been in the first year of the secondary modern school with graded readers suitable for infants. This reduced the child to self-consciousness and he was frightened other people in the class would find out what book he was reading. Reading books written especially for older backward readers seem non-existent in the majority of schools my pupils attended. *H.*

I have discussed elsewhere (p. 238) the possibilities opened by giving the children loose-leaf work-folders in which their own work, correctly written or typed and duplicated to look typographically exact, was collected for use as readers. Other teachers have had success with this method:

Books of suitable length and vocabulary were non-existent until the first requisition arrived. At this time, and often afterwards, individual and group folders were the answer. The girls suggested topics, wrote in rough, and read back to me, often correcting their own mistakes. The work was rewritten, put in the folder, read to me and corrected where necessary. At a later date individual work was read by a child to the rest of the group. *C.*

Of course, some reports indicated that good work was being done here and there for backward children:

My own school is very small and the headmaster knows every child individually and does his best for it. The backward classes are as small as he can conveniently make them. Our problem is that the English we try to teach is a foreign language in this part of London. . . . *S.*

In Special Schools the less able child is only regarded as less able in some respects and is never treated as a lesser creature. On the contrary a disproportionate amount of time is spent on this child at the expense of the brighter child in our type of school. *S.S.*

Here at any rate they are certainly not regarded as 'lesser creatures'. Their problems are discussed as fully as any of their more able companions. I am given most sympathetic consideration when I ask for any special books or material, or permission to take them on special outings. I think I am right in saying the girls feel it is rather different in the forms U 4 and S 4 for which I am personally responsible, but not in any way inferior. I think the formation of a class club, which no other form has, and on which other forms look rather enviously, has helped to give them quite a fillip. This club meets for an hour every Wednesday morning . . . for talks, debates and symposiums . . . the procedure is entirely in their hands—talks by outside visitors—they had a week at camp on Morecambe Bay, trips round the lakes, club parties . . . these experiences have drawn these children out and made them more articulate. . . .

I have now established myself with all children in the school as a teacher who allows them to make their own choice of occupation from materials available in the room. They, in their turn, through the drawings, sculpture, crafts, express their thoughts, needs, wishes and fantasies. My task is to encourage diaries, news books, poems, stories. I try to get them to talk on paper: they have pen pals; make books on their hobbies, pigeons, bird spotting, etc. Children who read are helped to make notes—summarise stories, read and criticise. Work in school is continued at home—all tasks are finished and marked. Children have individual folders: there is also a class folder containing unfinished work. Records of work can be shown on charts. Daily notes taken of each child's work. Children show interest, first through making their own books, looking for material for class newspaper. *Their work is often typed by pupils taking typing in the 4th and 5th year.* History and geography models are made from clay, waste material and *papier maché.*   M.R.

Another teacher sends an account of an exchange of tapes between a ' C' class and children at a school for the blind, which suggests many such possibilities:

At our request County Hall put us in touch with a school for blind and partially blind children for the purpose of making contact between my class and a group of girls and boys of similar age in their school through a tape 'letter' or 'magazine'. My children made their first tape in the spring term. It consisted of personal introductions, news about themselves, their hobbies and pets, some short messages of friendship, two 'pop' songs sung by one of the girls, some choral speaking and the singing of an Austrian folk song.

The following term a group of the blind children recorded a most impressive tape for us, consisting of replies, reports on school activities, some piano and guitar pieces and singing, an excerpt from a play they had performed.

Now we are preparing our second tape, in which we shall be including some different items, such as, for instance, two scenes of dramatic reading from *Tom Sawyer*, the book we are doing in literature. We chose the engagement scene between Tom and Becky and the graveyard scene. Again we shall have some poetry, this time chosen by some girls who want to say it individually. There will be two American folk songs, school and home news and of course thanks for the tape received, messages of appreciation and replies.

We are also trying to arrange a date for inviting the group over for a short afternoon's entertainment and tea, for which my children will bake and make sandwiches, decorate the room, etc.

My 'C' class have adopted their new friends with an almost passionate possessiveness, which was evidenced by a spontaneous reaction when I told them that we were going to invite their group for an afternoon—'Well the others' (i.e. the rest of the school) 'mustn't see them', meaning that this time *they* were being 'special'. In fact they have gained a sense of importance. They also become very interested in the practical problems of the blind and marvel at the many things which these children can do.   *E.S.*

But finally, here is a letter which seems to me to sum up the problem as a public and human question. Here is a man who has tried to give service to the less able child, but who has in the end become frustrated and driven out of teaching. Many will follow him unless the nature of the problem is seen more clearly, the content of the work changed, conditions improved, and teachers given prestige and authority for this work.

I gave up teaching a year ago and returned to my former profession, commercial art. The principal reason was that I found increasingly unacceptable the situation in which the less able children in schools are, to use your own words, treated as '"lesser creatures" who deserve less attention from our society'. I am, of course, open to the criticism that anyone who feels as I did should stay and fight. However, I am like most other people in that I engage in fights only when there's some prospect of winning, and in this case I saw none. It appeared to me that the trend was intensifying, partly because of the national concern with finding and training the best of brains for the modern age and partly as a result of the secondary modern schools' anxiety to gain status through examination results. From both sources the result was a large residue of children who, unable to compete, were regarded in practically every school I knew as rejects.

I became a teacher in 1949 through the post-war Emergency Training Scheme. Before this, and before becoming an artist, I had—and I mention this because it bears on my attitudes towards backward children—spent several years in all kinds of occupations: I was at various times a clerk, a factory hand, a lorry-driver, a small-time professional boxer, a builder's labourer, a farm worker, a navvy, a shop assistant and one or two other things. My first teaching appointment after my year's training was at a large, well-appointed secondary modern school built just before the war. The school had at that time three streams of children: as its numbers grew in the 'fifties they were increased to five.

Initially, I was told that as a specialist teacher I was not expected to produce results from C classes, and it was plain that they were seen generally as an inconvenience in the school. At that time the school was slightly embarrassed for accommodation by the loan—legacy of the war—of four rooms to an infants' school. In consequence, two small dining rooms (not equipped for classroom use) had to be used, and these were the permanent homes of C classes. It was accepted that they had not only the poorest accommodation and equipment, but also the poorest teachers; on one hand there was strong competition among the staff to obtain the best classes, and on the other the Head's policy was to allocate students, part-time teachers and people of doubtful ability to the bottom streams. 'She can do least harm there', was a phrase I heard from him—and from other head teachers—afterwards.

My special interest in backward children arose when, with the growth of the school as the 'bulge' came in, special problems were created by mischievous and delinquent children in the lower streams. I was asked several times to take these children in to overcome difficulties which might have been created if they remained in classes where they belonged under the streaming system: 'I can't leave him with Miss X,' the head or his deputy would say, 'because he'll play her up dreadfully: will you have him with your children?' In quite a short time I had classes made up almost entirely of Teddy-boys, delinquents, bad girls, truants, and all kinds of adolescent anarchists.

I got on extremely well with these children because, I imagine, I had lived and worked with roughnecks, near-criminals, and all kinds of nice, ill-educated people. I have always felt aware of the thinness of the veil between respectability and its opposites, though this sentiment did not go down well on the one or two occasions I expressed it to teaching colleagues. (If I may digress, one of the most wonderful salutary experiences of my life was at about eighteen, in my boxing days. I had always assumed that people recognised my grammar-school background wherever I was, until one day in the dressing-room of an East End boxing arena an old man told me about the prowess and rewards of a young fighter he knew—and added: 'And he's only an effing yobbo like you.' Something like that ought to happen to every prospective teacher.)

Looking back on this period with the difficult elements of the lower streams in that school, it is hard to know whether rage or laughter is indicated by the astonishing things I recall. We had a New Head, a brisk bureaucratic type, who arranged a ritualized examination of the whole school in all subjects every term: three days in which the atmosphere and trappings were those of a grammar school's matriculation week—strange rooms, invigilators in shifts, foolscap papers, duplicated exam papers arranged and worded to have the ring of scholarship. The children in the bottom streams couldn't read the questions, and used to sit staring out of windows for three days. Some of them had quite passable general knowledge, and I suggested to the Head that they might be able to answer some questions if the tests were given orally to them. He rose from his chair and looked at me as if I were insane. 'Good heavens,' he said, 'but that would give them *an unfair advantage!*'

Some of the things were not comical from any point of view, however. The Head would buy no equipment for the backward children. 'I apply business principles,' he was fond of saying. 'I put in money where there is likely to be a return, and there is no return from these children.' When I asked for some special consideration for a boy, he said: 'Some people are born good, some are born bad. These children won't learn and won't behave because they were born bad. It's as simple as that.' Nor was he the only head teacher from whom I heard this sentiment. The Head of the next secondary modern school, a mile or so away, used regularly to announce that he gave children one year to 'make good'—i.e., produce results. 'After that,' he would say, 'the weakest must go to the wall.'

The truly appalling thing was that the children knew all of this. They knew they were unwanted and despised, they knew they had the fag-ends of facilities and the worst teachers. They had been in bottom classes from their infant-school days, and by thirteen or fourteen they were fully aware of the position. My conclusion, in fact, was that a good deal of intractability and delinquency of adolescents was being promoted not by un-Christian homes and working mothers (great themes in prize-day speeches these) but in the schools themselves.

I left that school after seven years, and was transferred temporarily to a junior school in another part of the town. I said I should like to take a C class, and remained there teaching these children until last year. Here I saw the situation at another stage, and I was even more appalled. The neighbourhood was a poorer one than at the other school, and there was a higher proportion of children from unprivileged homes. The Head was a kindly little man who never punished children or spoke harshly to them. Nevertheless, he was willing to provide absolutely nothing for the bottom streams. The school was overcrowded, and three classes had to use a couple of classrooms in the infants' school and a sports pavilion along the road. I was stationed with my C-children permanently in the infants' school, where the head-mistress was actively hostile to their presence; she was friendly to me but vindictive to the children—would stop them in the corridors, for example, to tell them they were 'a blot on the landscape and a nuisance to everyone'.

I took these children, four different C classes in four years, with literally no equipment. The only books we had (true, there were piles of them) were gifts from the infants' headmistress of condemned readers. I kept one or two when I left as strange souvenirs: they had pictures of boys in Norfolk suits, little girls in Victorian dresses, antediluvian trams and open-top buses. We had a box of pens thrown-out when the other classes were supplied with new ones—every one chewed, splintered and corroded.

In the four years, none of these C classes was allowed music, drama, physical education or any of the socio-educational titbits such as dancing. The school hall and the other facilities for them were fully booked by other classes and, as the Head said, 'someone simply had to be left out'. In the four years, the Head only ever set foot in my classroom once—and that was when the infants' headmistress reported to him that she had seen me smoking in class. There were weekly changes with other classes for religious instruction and the girls' needlework, but for much of the time these never took place. Taking the C children was not popular, and as often as not I received notes at the last moment to say Miss Y was giving an I.Q. test, or 'finishing some work', so please would I keep my children today.

One continual problem was the chronic absenteeism of several of the C children. My classes numbered about thirty, and there was always a nucleus of seven or eight who, with their parents' connivance, stayed away much as they liked. Quite often we would see them from the window, shopping for their mothers or playing in the street. The Head never pursued this—I suspect because he would just as soon have had the less attractive children not there anyway—and I was never able to arouse the attendance officer's interest, probably because the majority of the children concerned were from problem families and the investigation would have meant trouble and inconvenience. Thus, there were some children who never learned, simply because they were not there with any regularity. Incidentally, I often wonder how widespread this kind of absenteeism is. Working at home now, I am always seeing children in the streets who obviously should be at school, and on my trips into town a couple of times a week I see groups of boys riding up and down on the trains and playing on the stations.

There are very limited 'special school' facilities in my town for educationally sub-normal children. I always had a few children who were on the waiting lists for places, but never knew any of them actually to get one; however, two or three times I had children from the special school whose parents wished not to have the stigma of 'going to the barmy school'. It was very difficult to get a child on the waiting list. Application had to be made to the town's educational psychologist, who would visit the school some time later—usually without notice, so that there was a strong chance of the child's being absent. After she had tested him a report came to the school, and one had to try to make out a case for special treatment.

The classes were, of course, much too large. I had a number of children who simply needed individual attention. At the time when I left the school a young woman had a C class of about 45 strong at the bottom of the school. I approached the Head to ask if something could not be done about this. He said he would not be pressed into panic measures, and after investigation, criticized the teacher because she was devoting her time—or trying to—to individual cases. 'Of course she can't cope,' he said to me. 'She could manage adequately if she taught them as a class, instead of messing about with one child at a time.'

I suppose what finally gave me the sensation of knocking at a brick wall was the school's inspection. The Head hinted to me beforehand that teachers were not well thought of who let their headmasters down by telling tales to the inspectors. I told the inspectors nothing—and, of course, they found out the position in a day. They interviewed the Head, they went through the books and the registers, and one particularly nosey woman asked the children all about me when I was not there. At the end of the inspection I had a long talk with the inspector who had spent most time with me, and asked her what was to be done for the less able children. Her replies conveyed to me that to start dealing with the problem would involve acknowledging first that the problem was there, and this she thought undesirable. So all that emerged was a report praising my sympathy for the C children, and passing on to other matters.

When I left the school the C classes were still without equipment or books, still stationed in a resentful infants' school, and still barred from the various activities on the fringe of the curriculum. The huge C class at the bottom was beginning to move up, and after I left I heard that some of its representatives had had a glorious 'smash-up' in the school's new wash-rooms and toilets. I don't blame them. I'd have smashed the windows too.

So far as I can summarize my experiences, I would say the following. The less able children have, it seems to me, become increasingly disabled in both junior and secondary schools by the competitiveness of present-day education. Schools have to make the most of finite resources, and the natural tendency is the one expressed by my former Head, to use the money and materials in directions where 'results' are anticipated. I have no doubt also that the rise in working-class living standards in the last fifteen years has played a part in the rejection of 'inferior' children by teachers. The children in the higher classes are generally nicely-dressed and appealing, the C children the scruffy and unattractive ones. When I was a junior-school boy in this sort of district a nicely-dressed child was a rarity; now there is a clear division and I suppose teachers would be more than human if they did not respond to it.

I have never known a child for whom something might not have been done. I don't mean that I think teachers could achieve transformations of C children if only they had better facilities and were helped by more sympathetic attitudes. Obviously all kinds of things and all kinds of people are involved. I think, however, that below-average children need only more careful attention for their difficulties to be overcome, and that a great deal could be done for those who are genuinely handicapped in some way. I would reckon that a third (perhaps more) of the backward children I have known have had psychological defects of one kind or another. I could give many, many examples of what I mean here. One boy, for instance, with whom I had success was something of a terror in the junior school: he used to have tremendous tantrums, would fling himself on the floor and scream and so on. He had no father, and his mother had a brain injury and was a pitiful figure. All he needed, as far as I discovered, was friendship and praise. I used to praise him until he purred: his tantrums ended, he worked assiduously and his whole personality began to glow. The sad thing here was that my fears for the consequence of his changing schools at eleven-plus were realised; within a year I was being asked if I could help because he had become difficult again.

Though divisions and segregations have to be made for practical purposes, I have concluded that the streaming system is anti-social. The marking-off of children as inferior begins in most infants' schools and creates from the start an attitude to and a circumstance round them. However, it is not my purpose in this letter (you have not requested that anyone should do so) to say what I think should and should not be done. I should like to add one other thing, in case my experience is thought exceptional. Not long ago the newly-appointed Head of the local special school told me he had called a meeting with a view of forming an association of teachers of backward children in the area. He had been astounded by teachers who recounted at this meeting that they worked in schools whose heads had said 'I will not spend school money on backward children.'

The writer ends with a postscript which sums up the whole argument of my book: but it is a sad thought to end with, that a man who understands so well should no longer feel able to carry on his valuable work with these children.

P.S. One observation which I should have made is that the subjects—music, drama &c.,—my C children never had are ones with special importance to them. I had many reasons for thinking that perhaps the biggest factor in backwardness was a kind of emotional starvation.

Can our society afford to discourage such talent? The children under discussion, after all, as I have pointed out before, make up three-eighths of our whole population. Are 20,000,000 English people 'duds'? They belong educationally to the rejected 'C' and 'D' streams, for whom, under the present system, and with the present attitudes, school is too often the experience of frustration, boredom, the antagonism of 'educated' people, and irrelevant routines. The low streams are breeding grounds for unhappiness, instability, despair and delinquency. Much wonderful work is being done: but a few simple reforms, not costly, combined with a considerable change in fundamental attitudes, could give these millions of human beings a new release of potentiality, and a joyful sense of belonging in the community, on equal terms with those who have been fortunate in being born with quicker gifts of mind. That there should be rejected low-stream children at all, is in itself a comment on the deficiencies of other qualities in the more intellectual sections of the community, who develop the patterns of our education. And it is a mark of deep inadequacies in contemporary England, in our concepts of what civilisation is, in our attitudes to human beings, and our national capacity to live well and fully.

BOOKS FOR LOWER STREAMS
OF THE SECONDARY SCHOOL

NOTES ON A NATIONAL BOOK LEAGUE EXHIBITION

I am very grateful to the National Book League for the loan of their exhibition THE TEACHER AND THE BACKWARD READER for the month of August 1962, to enable me to study the books available for English work with 'backward' children. The Exhibition includes most of the books on pp. 21–37 of the Library Association pamphlet *The Reluctant Reader* (February 1962, from The Library Association, County Libraries Section, Chaucer House, Malet Place, London, W.C.1). The Exhibition was selected by Mr. S. S. Segal, Chairman of the Guild of Teachers of Backward Children. It aims to help the teacher of backward pupils in secondary schools. Some suitable books were not available for the Exhibition or were out of print when the Exhibition was made. But there is no doubt that it represents as complete a collection as possible of books available for the teacher's work with 'C' and 'D' streams in the secondary school.

The Exhibition is stimulating and provoking, and teachers should certainly try to arrange for it to be available for them to see at their local institute or through their local education authority. The charge for hiring the Exhibition is £2 15s. 0d. (£2 to members). Notes are being collected by the League from teachers, and the Exhibition will later be revised.

As a headmaster recently said to me, one can always distinguish the books belonging to the low streams. One can, of course, tell a low stream itself—it is less tidy, and less attractive than an upper stream, in appearance and manner. This difference is reinforced by the equipment supplied to the low stream: and books are no exception. The piles of books belonging to the 'C' and 'D' streams will be older and more battered, thinner, uglier, and printed on a lower grade paper. Their content will be vulgar, thin, and unprepossessing. From the low stream piles we may take in a whiff of the ancient Board School, even of Victorian England, and the contempt for the factory hand of industrial hard times. The content of most low stream books will be brutally related to dustbins, public transport, drains, water-supply, to facts, and the virtues of docility.

Even this excellent Exhibition is a sad revelation of the lack of adequate material, and of the lack of enterprise and devotion given to the needs of those children who generation by generation grow up into three of every eight English people.

Of three large hampers of books only a few volumes relate to the inward phantasy needs of these children. Not one relates to the deep preoccupations of the young adolescent from 13 to 15, with emotional difficulties of adolescence, the pangs of entering adulthood, the problems of personal relationship and social pattern—except perhaps the somewhat coarse-handed attempts of E. W. Hildick, to represent the 'sec. mod.' child's world. And of dozens and dozens of books for classroom use there was only one adequately produced reading book which I myself would even consider using in the classroom.

From this Exhibition I have made below a selection of those books which I consider to be the best—those which could be used successfully in the kind of work towards literacy such as I outline in this book. I have only selected those books which I would want to use in school conditions. The selection has been rigorous, because I have tried to measure the content of these books—their substantial appeal—against the appeal of children's own imaginative work reproduced as readers, and the appeal of their own pulp-reading and comic matter. In the short amount of reading time at our disposal I feel it is important that the content should satisfy my demands for rich imaginative substance, both to nourish the imaginative powers, and to provide a culture of words to take the place of the empty verbal culture of pulp books, rock'n'roll songs, and film dialogue. Of course there is a difference between what one endorses in the classroom, and what one leaves on shelves in a school or class library. But this Exhibition reveals the prevalent weakness of separating 'reading' from other English work, from the content of reading matter, from creative English and library entertainment.

I give a selection of books for the teacher, and a selection of general titles, mostly non-fiction, for purchase for school or class libraries. A class of backward children with free and frequent access to the best of these library books would be in no sense underprivileged for *non-fictional* reading matter. British book production for children is of a very high standard of printing and design. But this Exhibition serves only to emphasise the wide difference between expensive books produced on non-fictional subjects, expensive books of fiction produced for younger and brighter middle-class children (conspicuous here by their absence), and the dreary and mean rubbish produced for classroom use with 'the dregs'.

The examination of hundreds of school books produced for less able children is a depressing experience. Many of them are so meanly produced that they can only be rejected out of hand. To touch them contaminates with the stale airs of rejection. They are thin, the cloth covers are ragged at the edges, and tawdry in colour. The paper is cheap and poor, the type bluntly ungracious, the layout degrading, and the portrayal of human life within offensively low. Many are no better than comic papers, or the hideously printed game and puzzle books sold in small paper shops in the suburbs. The nature of these productions is to be grimly functional—no one could ever suppose they were intended to delight or entertain, though their titles frequently speak of 'pleasure' or even 'joy'. It is baffling to attempt to suppose where the publishers were able to find artists bad enough to commit the execrable drawings, since any school art class could produce drawings twenty times as good. With the poverty and inefficiency of their lamentable production goes a tone of fourth-rate moralising and mundane exhortation—most are heavily didactic, even in their choice of human stories—which are usually about such figures as Grace Darling, Captain Cook, and other Victorian favourites. There are some morally encouraging modern additions, e.g. 'Shot by the Japanese'. The crude and false supposition is here exemplified, that an ill-told and ill-printed story about heroic docility or patriotic integrity will generate courage, purposiveness and sound character in 'the dregs'.

Hardly one book, apart from the non-fiction books, takes into account the reality of the child's need for phantasy and imagination, such as Dickens championed a century ago in *Hard Times*. Where production is a little better, as with the Ladybird Books by Wills and Hepworth of Loughborough, the texts, particularly the religious texts, are banal ('Pharaoh was really worried'), and the drawings belong to the era of Victorian oleograph sentimentality, especially in the portrayal of Christ and Biblical figures. (Compare, say, a possible edition of extracts from the Authorised Version, with illustrations by Eric Gill and Marc Chagall.)

The bulk of classroom text-books are grotesquely Philistine, and far below the level of printing and production of the popular press and advertising. They are therefore archaic and ineffectual, since they lose the battle of eye appeal and emotional sympathy before they are picked up. Attempts to put this situation right by imitating the magazine or newspaper in format seem to me to sell the creative possibilities of teaching down the river.

The re-telling of 'the world's great stories' in various forms in books for less able children destroys most of the point of the epithet 'great'. In mangled, re-told, or decimated illustrated form these have none of the qualities of the original, and have thus lost any reason to be preferred to new stories by modern writers, however far short of classics these may be. *David Copperfield, Treasure Island, Lorna Doone* reappear in various forms at what must be about one thousandth of the original length, and containing barely one word written by the original author. Only Daniel Defoe's piece of sturdy journalism *Robinson Crusoe* survives this treatment (Pictorial Classics, Oxford University Press, 2s. 6d.). Of *Gulliver's Travels* only a lamely bizarre tale remains, containing less of Swift than Hollywood, while such a book as *Coral Island* becomes merely bloodthirsty and sadistic, without even Ballantyne's wordy ebullience to disguise it.

The fiction section, then, is barren of art, and though it contains some quite good reading books specially written for schools (e.g. the *Active Readers* [Ginn] and the *Wide Horizon Reading Scheme* [Heinemann]), the section is uninspiring, and far from being related to the needs and experience of the older 'backward' pupil.

The non-fiction section, on the other hand, is full of beautiful and striking books, some written by leading authorities and scientists, such as Sir Julian Huxley.

So we have an overall picture, once more, of what our industrial-commercial civilisation considers valuable. Or, if you like, another demonstration of its essential inefficiency. Children need to explore their inner experience through phantasy: this faculty is not nourished. Instead, their attention is sent outwards, towards things that 'go', and the material universe which undoubtedly exists, but answers no metaphysical questions. There are dozens of lavishly produced books on scientific and technical subjects, from stars to the wonders of engineering. There are lovely books on the modern crypto-metaphysical pursuits—archaeology, dinosaurs, the origin of life. But these seldom go beyond asking 'How?' to ask 'Why?', even when considering such problems as language and 'the growth of civilisation'. They assume that we move 'from drumbeat to tickertape': they assume Progress, and express none of the doubts backward children must inevitably feel about the 'march of man'.

Problems of the significance of human life are left to a few unscientific, unlovely, sentimental religious books, of Bible stories and so forth. Two or three books on sex attempt unsteadily to straddle the gap between biology and the world of values and the life of emotions. In the quest for a sense of significance through love a young person will find a psychologist advising him to masturbate on his wedding night.

In the educational books this exhibition exhibits the failure of educational theories about reading directed by psychometric psychology to be anything but beside the human point. The classroom books for teaching English are without exception based on principles that fail to engage the mainspring of the child's interest—which is in the way words open up experience, and give power over it. *I would not want to use, and cannot recommend, one English practice book from this exhibition.* All the text-books, word-games, schemes and exercises, seem to me to be too mechanical, based, if anything, on psychological theories and factifications, rather than on insight into the mental, emotional and psychic needs of the child, or a recognition that teaching is an art. (By contrast some of the science books, such as the Rathbone series (Adprint) provide admirably for the child's sense of enquiry, delight and wonder in experience, while Helen Borten's books *Do You Hear What I Hear?* and *Do You See What I See?* (Abelard-Schumann) seem to me profoundly imaginative and close to the true scientific spirit.)

There are some books here I would use *faute de mieux*, but there are too few books like *Madeline*, a well-produced, imaginative, engaging book for 12-year-olds. There were none for children 13–15 who belong to this sophisticated decade. From this selection of books 'backward' children might be supposed to be heartless, sexless, without the experiences of human ambition and aspiration, and unacquainted with suffering.

The Exhibition does not contain one book of poetry, song, drama or folklore (e.g. children's traditional games). This marks its gravest deficiency. As I hope I have shown in this book, 'backward' children have more than a fair share of sorrow and many aspirations. A chief means to understanding life, gaining self-respect, and unleashing their potentialities, is by poetic phantasy. An education which fails to develop the poetic function in them will fail to bring them towards literacy or articulateness.

The Exhibition is a microcosm of our whole education. Where it fails is in providing nourishment, here in terms of printed matter, for the rich civilising processes of the imaginative word. Elsewhere such a lack can perhaps be disguised by intellectual substitutes, as by material giving non-fictional information. At this level, however, the anaemia cannot be disguised, and the inefficiency of our neglect of the poetic function is sadly exposed.

BOOKS FOR THE TEACHER

The Causes and Treatment of Backwardness, Sir Cyril Burt (U.L.P., 8s. 6d.)
The Backward Child, Sir Cyril Burt (U.L.P., 35s.)
Backwardness in the Backward Subjects, Fred. J. Schonell (Oliver and Boyd, 25s.)
The Psychology and Teaching of Reading, Fred. J. Schonell (Oliver and Boyd, 15s.)
The Everlasting Childhood, R. P. Menday and John Wiles (Gollancz, 16s.)
Backwardness in Reading, John Duncan (Harrap, 6s.)
Survey of Books for Backward Readers (U.L.P., 4s. 6d.)

Addenda (not in the Exhibition)
An Experiment in Education, Sybil Marshall (Cambridge, 25s.)
Let the Children Write, Margaret Langdon (Longmans, 8s. 6d.)
Our Adult Society and Its Roots in Infancy, Melanie Klein (Tavistock Press, 3s. 6d.)
Coming Into Their Own, M. L. Hourd and G. E. Cooper (Heinemann, 21s.)
Four to Fourteen, Kathleen Lines (Cambridge)
The Unreluctant Years, Lillian N. Smith (American Library Association, Chicago, 1953, 36s.)
The Origins of Love and Hate, Ian D. Suttie (Penguin Books, 3s. 6d.)
Healing the Sick Mind, H. Guntrip, (Unwin Books, 7s. 6d.)
From Paediatrics to Psychoanalysis, D. W. Winnicott (Tavistock)
The Child and the Outside World, D. W. Winnicott (Tavistock)
The Child and the Family, D.W. Winnicott (Tavistock; also in Penguin Books)
Feeling and Perception in Young Children, Len Chaloner (Tavistock, 12s. 6d.)
Envy and Gratitude, Melanie Klein (Tavistock)
The Undiscovered Self, C. G. Jung (Routledge)
English in Education, ed. Brian Jackson and Denys Thompson (Chatto and Windus)
Some Emotional Aspects of Learning, Marjorie C. Hourd (Heinemann)

The Secret Places, David Holbrook (Methuen, 1964)
Unwillingly to School, Jack N. Kahn and Jean. P. Nurstein, (Pergamon Press, 15s.)
The Excitement of Writing, ed. F. Clegg, (Chatto and Windus)
 (see also the Bibliography in *English for Maturity*)

BOOKS FOR USE AS READERS IN CLASS

First Year
 Dolphin Books (U.L.P., 2s. 3d., 3s. etc.)
Other Years
 None suitable.
 Perhaps *Pitman's Ships Series* (Picture Reference Books: 2s. 6d.)

COURSE BOOKS FOR CLASSROOM USE

None suitable

Addenda

I've Got to Use Words. A course book in four volumes for imaginative work in English for low stream children, by the present author. (Cambridge University Press)
Reflections. An English course for students aged 14-18. (Oxford University Press)

ANTHOLOGIES FOR CLASSROOM USE

None available in the Exhibition

Addenda

The Key of the Kingdom, Denys Thompson and Raymond O'Malley (Chatto and Windus, 5s. 9d. each)
Heinemann Poetry Books, I–IV, James Reeves

Anthologies by the present author

Iron, Honey, Gold (C.U.P., four volumes, 7s., 7s. 6d., 8s., 9s.)
People and Diamonds (C.U.P., 7s. each volume)
Thieves and Angels (C.U.P., 7s. 6d.)
Visions of Life, four volumes (C.U.P. 6s. each)
Children's Games (Gordon Fraser, 8s. 6d.)

BOOKS FOR A CLASS OR SCHOOL LIBRARY
FOR LESS ABLE CHILDREN

Fiction

'The Wide Horizon Reading Scheme'
'The Active Readers'
In appearance these were unattractive, and on the whole seemed rather dull. There are books in the Heinemann 'New Windmill' Series edited by Ann and Ian Serraillier which are more attractive, e.g. *The Wheel on the School, The Call of the Wild, Men and Gods, Shane, The Cave, The Railway Children, Tom Sawyer, Huckleberry Finn,* and *Little Women.*

'The World's Great Stories' (Oxford University Press)
  Robinson Crusoe, Daniel Defoe
  King Arthur
  Aladdin and Ali Baba
Chanticleer and the Fox (*The Nun's Priest's Tale* re-told) Barbara Cooney
  (Constable, 12*s*. 6*d*.)
The Christmas Rocket, Annie Molloy (Constable, 12*s*. 6*d*.)
The Three Happy Lions (Bodley Head, 8*s*. 6*d*.)
The Story of Ferdinand, Munro Leaf (Hamish Hamilton, 7*s*. 6*d*.)
Madeline, Ludwig Bemelmans (André Deutsch, 15*s*.)

Further Fiction and Poetry (not in the exhibition)
Tom Tiddler's Ground, De la Mare (Bodley Head, 25*s*.)
The Poet's Tongue, two volumes (Bell, 8*s*. 6*d*. each vol.)
Come Hither, De la Mare (Bodley Head, 30*s*.)
The Lore and Language of Schoolchildren, I. and P. Opie (O.U.P., 30*s*.)
The Secret Garden, Frances Hodgson Burnett (Puffin Story Books, 3*s*. 6*d*.)
The Family From One End Street, Eve Garnett (Puffin Story Books, 3*s*. 6*d*.)
The Wheel on the School, Meindert De Jong (Lutterworth, 12*s*. 6*d*.)
The Windrush Books (Oxford University Press)

Non-fiction
'The Junior True Books' (Muller, 8*s*. 6*d*. each)
  Your Body and You
  Tools for Building
  Book of Seasons
  Toys at Work
  Animals of the Sea and Shore
  More Science Experiments
  Plants we Know
  Deserts
  Rocks and Minerals
  Dinosaurs
  Cloth
  Honeybees
  The Air Around Us
  Pets
  Cowboys
  Indians
  Tropical Fishes
  African Animals
  Jungles

Black's 'Junior Reference Books' (9s. 6d. each)
  The Story of Aircraft
  Deep Sea Fishing
  Coal Mining
'Science Picture Books' (Brockhampton, 10s. 6d.)
  Push Pull Lift
  Let's Find Out
  How Big is Big? (a most imaginative book)
Do You Hear What I hear?, Helen Borten (Abelard-Schumann, 12s. 6d.)
Do You See What I See?, Helen Borten (Abelard-Schumann, 12s. 6d.)
                    (both highly recommended)
'Rathbone Books' (Adprint, 21s. each)
  Puzzle of the Past
  The Story of Evolution
  Feast and Famine
  Man Must Move
  The Story of Prehistoric Animals
  The Adventure of Engineering
  From Magic to Medicine
  The Story of Music
  The Story of Dance
  The Story of Theatre
  Adventure of the Sea
  Man Must Measure
  Men, Missiles and Machines
  Adventure of the Air
'Picture Biographies' (Nelson, 12s. 6d.)
  Joseph Lister
  Mary Queen of Scots
  Man of Justice
  Alfred the Great
  Explorer Lost
  Edmund Kean
'Study Books' (Bodley Head, 8s. 6d.)
  The Study Book of Lamps and Candles
  The Study Book of Printing
  The Study Book of The Land
  The Study Book of Food
  The Study Book of Oil
  The Study Book of Coal
  The Study Book of Power
  The Study Book of Water Supply

The Study Book of Time and Clocks
The Study Book of Farming
'Open Your Eyes to Nature' (Chatto and Windus, 10s. 6d.)
Come and See
Living Things
Nature Around You
Out of Doors
'Open Your Eyes to History' (Chatto and Windus, 10s. 6d.)
Man's Forward March
Family Tree
Looking at the Past
'Play Ideas Books' (Chatto and Windus, 8s. 6d.)
Plants that Heal
The Plants we Eat
Things to do with Seeds
Things to do with Plants
Things to do with Trees
'The World of Nature' (Oliver and Boyd, 7s. 6d.)
A Bud is Born
From Caterpillar to Butterfly
Opening Buds
From Flower to Seed
The Hidden Life of Flowers
The Wonders of Life, 1 & 2 (Blackie, 9s. 6d. each)
You Yourself (Blackie, 6s.)
Ladybird Nature Books (Blackie, 2s. 6d. each)
British Birds, 1, 2 & 3
Puffin Picture Books, 2s. 6d. each
Fish and Fishing
Postage Stamps
Pond Life
The Human Body
Village and Town
The Story of a Thread of Cotton
About Railways
About a Motor Car
Living Pictures
Better Handwriting
Gregory (Hamish Hamilton, 12s. 6d.)
The Magic Stones, Alain (Faber, 10s. 6d.)
Rooftop World (Faber, 8s. 6d.)
Life and Living, 1, 2 & 3 (Longmans, 4s. 3d.)

Home Farm, Parts I and II (Chatto and Windus, 3s.)
The Times Book of Zoo Animals
Children of the Fishing Boats (Hutchinson, 8s. 6d.)
Children of the Hidden Valley (Hutchinson, 8s. 6d.)
A Picture Dictionary of Living Things (Cassell, 12s. 6d.)
Peter and Pamela Grow Up, Darwen Findlayson (7s. 6d.)
Looking at the World Today (Black, 8s. 6d.)
Mountains and Valleys: The World in Pictures (Adprint, 4s. 6d.)
Looking at Scotland, John Wright (Black, 8s. 6d.)
How They Were Built: Bridges, Roads (O.U.P., 10s. 6d. each)
(It is impossible to praise these scientific and technical
books for children too highly.)

Teachers should remember that the above (perhaps £50 worth*) is but a small selection from a selection. There are many school books for these children below the standard of the National Book League Exhibition, and there are also many fine and beautiful books for children not given in the non-fiction section. But the chief problem for teacher and publisher is the lack of books which are imaginative, simple and beautifully produced, which yet relate to the emotional needs, and need to understand life, of the young adolescent of 12–16. These, in the throes of modern urban life, remain starved in the midst of its grotesque Barmecide popular culture, and the task of bringing them a nourishing culture of the word has hardly yet been taken up.

* Prices are correct at the time of going to press, but are subject to increase.

INDEX

INDEX

death, children's contemplation of, 52, 78, 95, 106, 115–16, 117 ff., 125, 129, 133, 154–5, 222
Death in the Tree, 203, 234
Defoe, Daniel, 276
Degas, 21
Delacroix, Eugene, 21
de la Mare, Walter, 149, 233
Dekker, Thomas, 208, 243
delinquency, 6, 13, 23, 138, 258, 272
depressive attitudes of children, 10, 15, 20, 23, 116
destructive attitudes of children, 195
Devil, The, 239
Dickens and Crime, 29 n.
Dickens and Education, 29 n.
Dickens, Charles, 12, 15, 29–30, 190, 239, 275, 276
Dickinson, Emily, 20
discipline in classroom practice, 28–9, 38, 196, 207, 255
drama, 19, 55, 58, 84, 87, 216, 218, 229, 234, 241, 247 ff.
dreams, interpretation of, 44–5

Eccles, Sir David, 15
Education Act of 1944, 4
education
  aims in, 4 ff., 14, 15 ff., 41–2, 192
  subjects in, 8 ff.
Education and the Working Class, 13
educational psychology, 12, 16, 22, 277
Effects of Intemperance, The, 86
eleven-plus examination, 33
Eliot, George, 21, 59, 125
Eliot, T. S., vi, 252
Emil and the Detectives, 240
emotion, fear of, 150
emotional conflict in the teacher, 25, 205; *see also* teachers, attitudes to backward children
emotions of adolescents, 59, 97, 178, 247–8, 271
Empson, W., 123
encouragement, need for, 206 ff.
English for Maturity, 4, 8, 9, 192, 193, 209, 229, 233, 240
enjoyment of work, 199
environment, 39; *see also* society
envy in children, 38, 39, 118–19, 120, 123
Envy and Gratitude, 122

equipment for low-stream class, 229 ff.
examinations, 3–14 *passim*, 34, 66, 84, 92, 145, 164, 179, 207, 255
  G.C.E., 4, 13, 33, 34, 255
  C.S.E., 5, 13
  eleven-plus, 33
Experiment in Education, An, 30, 199 n, 237
exchanges between schools, 265

failure, feelings of, 18, 20, 44, 195, 196, 208, 272
family, child and, 82, 97, 106, 111, 117, 125, 143, 151, 203–4, 221
Family From One-End Street, 239
father, child and, 151, 194, 207, 227; *see also* Oedipus conflict
'father figure', teacher as, 183
film, 58, 85, 104, 120, 220, 236, 242
Finnegan's Wake, 208
fluency achieved by children, 187; *see also* literacy
Ford, Boris, 237
Forster, E. M., 239
Freud, Sigmund, 30, 39, 76
Frost, Robert, 203
frustration and feelings of futility in low-stream children, 5 ff.

G.C.E., 4, 13, 33, 34, 255
Gill, Eric, 275
Goodbye to All That, 234
good, child's quest for, 86, 151 ff., 195, 199, 207–8
Gorki, Maxim, 239
grammar in low-stream reading, 227, 243
grammar school, 4, 9, 11, 13, 15, 34, 41
Graves, Robert, 234
Grice, Frederick, 239
grief in children, 117 ff., 122, 133
Grimm, Jakob and Wilhelm, 132
Guardian, The, 11, 135, 183, 254
guilt in children, 38, 69, 72
Gulliver's Travels, 276

Hamlet, 76
Hard Times, 275
hatred, 23, 95, 123
Hawkes, Geoffrey, 55, 138, 218, 247 ff.
Heinemann Windmill Books, 233

287

INDEX

INDEX